THE SINGERS OF LAMENTATIONS

BIBLICAL INTERPRETATION SERIES

VOLUME 60

THE SINGERS OF LAMENTATIONS

Cities under Siege, from Ur to Jerusalem to Sarajevo...

BY

NANCY C. LEE

BRILL
LEIDEN · BOSTON · KÖLN
2002

This book is printed on acid-free paper.

Library of Congress Cataloging-in-Publication Data

Lee, Nancy C.
The singers of Lamentations : cities under siege, from Ur to Jerusalem to Sarajevo / Nancy C. Lee.
p. cm. — (Biblical interpretation series, ISSN 0928-0731 ; v. 60)
Includes bibliographical references and index.
ISBN 9004123121 (alk. paper)
1. Bible.O.T. Lamentations—Criticism, interpretation, etc. 2. Laments. I. Title. II. Series

BS1535.2 .L44 2002
224'.306—dc21 2002018330

Die Deutsche Bibliothek – CIP-Einheitsaufnahme

Lee, Nancy C.:
The Singers of Lamentations : Cities under Siege, from Ur to Jerusalem to Sarajevo... / by Nancy C. Lee. – Leiden ; Boston ; Köln : Brill, 2002
(Biblical interpretation series ; Vol. 60)
ISBN 90-04-12312-1

ISSN 0928-0731
ISBN 90 04 12312 1

PRINTED IN THE NETHERLANDS

For

Hedwig Jahnow
Women in Black
friends in my adopted homeland
Charles and Melrose Lee

after the wars are all fought . . .
after the politicians have accomplished their work,
after the noble sufferer, the other, the neighbor, the old,
the child, the soldier, the mother languish . . . so long,
finally shall come the poet, woman without name,
true daughters sons of God shall rise, singing us on.

CONTENTS

ACKNOWLEDGMENTS

The process of researching and writing on biblical texts is more than a journey of the mind—it is a journey of one's entire self. Yet, little did I know when I embarked upon analysis of the book of Lamentations, with its account of ancient Jerusalem's destruction, that it would take me to stand before the charred and desolate ruins of villages, cities, and anguished human lives. For when I began the dissertation upon which this work is based, the war in Bosnia was in full force, the war in Croatia still smoldering, and the war in Serbia over Kosovo yet to unfold. The poetic images in Lamentations held too much in common with these contemporary wars and their human suffering to neglect comparative research between these contexts and a humanitarian response.

Thus through a Fulbright fellowship I traveled to this region (and lived in Osijek, Croatia) in the year just after the Bosnian war ended (1996) to investigate something of the role of *lament* in poetry and liturgy. I traveled throughout Croatia and Bosnia (it was nearly impossible to travel to Serbia at that time), listening to accounts of what had happened and collecting lament poetry. In the spirit of the Fulbright ideal, I went as much to learn from these folks and their life-wrenching experiences, and what light they might shed on Lamentations, as to share what I knew. To this end I thank the Fulbright committees in the U.S. and Croatia, advisors Andrew Small, Saša Brlek, Loredana Maravić, ambassador Peter Galbraith.

In my biblical literature classes at the Josip Strossmayer University in Osijek, Croatia, most of my students had survived the war in that town under siege for eight months; a number of them were refugees who had lost their homes in the destruction of nearby villages. On that first day of class in the fall of 1996, two students in different classes distinctly remembered the day during the war when the lament of Psalm 27 was read during Mass: "though an army encamp against me, my heart shall not fear; though war arise against me, yet I will be confident. . . ." The Evangelical Seminary also in Osijek was shelled, went into exile during part of the war, though some remained behind, and after the war ended continued to receive bomb threats. In such an environment the school stood unswayed as a remarkable community of acceptance of Croat, Serb, and Bosniak students alike, in addition to many internationals.

My experiences overseas continue to inform my scholarship. I was overwhelmed by the extraordinary hospitality, selflessness, and faith of people from every cultural background and religious heritage in the old Yugoslavia. Ecumenical cooperation among people of faith there, both before, during, and after the war, was greater than anything I've seen in the U.S. The list is long of those who demonstrated such hospitality, interest in my work, assistance in locating lament poetry, and vulnerably shared their very difficult stories of recent years. I am grateful for their patience for any errors, blindspots, or offenses in this work by an outsider (yet another one!), yet sympathetic.

In Osijek, Croatia, my special thanks to my hosts Marta and Višnja Pavičić and to Višnja for her assistance as a professional translator; Fulbright advisor Elvira Petrović at the Pedagoški Fakultet, Strossmayer University, colleagues and my students there, especially Lidija Matorić; thanks to Drs. Davor Peterlin, Peter Kuzmić, Damir Spoljarić, Antal Balog, Miroslav Volf, Corneliu Constantineanu, Brett McMichael, Steve and Michelle Kurtz, Maryl and Daniel Darko, staff and students at the Evangelical Seminary; Revs. Toma and Ksenija Magda and family and the Osijek Baptist Church; Liam Collins, Fulbright fellow Mary Kay Gilliland and Jim Sinex; Ivica Koprivnjak with Roman Catholic MIR; Dr. Darko Fischer, president of the Jewish Association in Osijek; Ef. Enes Poljić, imam of the Mosque; Sandra and Marija Vučković and her parents in Antunovac Tjenski.

In Vukovar, special thanks to Marija Koprivnjak; and to the people in the Gašince refugee camp in 1997.

In Zagreb, Croatia, great thanks to researchers at the Institute for Ethnography and Folklore Research: especially Tanja Perić-Polonijo, Grozdana Marošević, Simona Delić, Antonija Kiš, and Seka for help with library resources; very special thanks to Boris Peterlin at the ecumenical Christian Information Service; the NONA women's refugee center, Đurđa Miklaužić, Nataša Novačić, Ana Kvesić; to Željko Mraz, general secretary of the Baptist Union of Croatia; Nela Williams.

In Dubrovnik, thanks to Dr. Ivana Burđelez at the International Center of Croatian Universities; Don Ivo Bjelokosić at St. Vlaha Catholic Church, Bishop Želimir Puljić; Fr. Pijo Pejić of the Franciscan monastery; Jani Hansel of Deša refugee service; Ef. Salkan Herić at the Mosque.

In Sarajevo, Bosnia, tremendous thanks to Ivo Marković, the Franciscan monastery, and members of his interreligious choir, Pontanima; special thanks to Moric Alahambri, president of the Jewish Association, for sharing his stories with me.

In Tuzla, profound thanks for their hospitality, friendship in faith, and help with my research projects to Vesna and Duško Kolak, Anđelko and Anđelina Savić, the Tuzla Baptist Church, and students Leila and Željko Puja; thanks to Father Stefan at the Serbian Orthodox Monastery at Papraća, Bosnia, for their hospitality and help.

In Konjic, thanks to Adis.

For permission to quote their poetry, thanks to Borislav Arapović, Kruna First-Medić, Marija Koprivnjak, Biljana Obradović, Ferida Duraković, Abdulah Sidran, Ljubica Ostojić, Dara Sekulić and to all the poets cited herein for their inspiring voices. Thanks to Michelle Levy for connecting me with Biljana. Finally, for their close friendship and inspiring example of long and selfless work in the former Yugoslavia, I am grateful to Amy Gopp and Brett McMichael.

My profound thanks go to my mentors; now I see they are "oral poets" each: to Dr. Thomas Downing for his remarkable sermons in Chapel Hill that never avoided the dark side of faith or the griefs of the human condition; to Dr. Elmo Scoggin who taught me not only the basic mechanics of Hebrew, but the poetic spirit of the language and its multifaceted richness; and especially to Dr. Walter Brueggemann whose guidance of my master's thesis on Jeremiah greatly influenced my interest in prophets and lament. I am grateful for his early reading of this work. Thanks to Dr. Mishael Caspi for his early encouragement, whose work in oral traditions and poetic spirit profoundly influenced my method.

My profound thanks go to my doctoral advisor, Dr. William P. Brown, at Union Theological Seminary in Virginia (now Union-PSCE). His scholarly expertise and rigor, openness, humane guidance, and encouragement of my odd plan to combine scholarly analysis of an ancient text with study of a contemporary context all made for a dissertation process I believe could not have been matched for me elsewhere. I am extremely grateful to my committee members, Sibley Towner and S. Dean McBride, Jr., for all their immeasurable expertise and help along the way; to Sib, Carson Brisson, and Brenda Barrows for the treasures of poetry communion; and to Linda Quinn for helpful library resources. My thanks to Isam Ballenger for his early help and contacts, to supportive faculty at Union-PSCE, the late Ken Goodpasture, Donald Dawe, and Stan Skreslet who demonstrate commitments to international exchange and scholarship that helped lead me out of the U.S. and limited frames of reference; Doug Ottati for the continuing relevance of Niebuhrian realism.

I thank colleagues in the SBL Composition of Jeremiah group, and in the Lamentations in Ancient and Contemporary Contexts consultation. Special thanks to the following scholars for conversation and feedback on this work: Tod Linafelt, Walter Brueggemann, Kathleen O'Connor, Susan Niditch, Erhard Gerstenberger, Carleen Mandolfo, Danna Nolan Fewell, and Adele Berlin.

Finally, a heartfelt thanks to two people from Bosnia-Herzegovina whose vision has greatly inspired me—Ivo Marković of Sarajevo, director of the Eye to Eye interreligious service and Pontanima choir, and Borislav Arapović, extraordinary poet and bible translations scholar. For the opportunity of working together on different projects, I am deeply grateful. Special thanks to Mattie Kuiper at Brill for her helpful guidance, and to editors David E. Orton and Rolf Rendtorff.

Last but not least I thank dear friends' support in this effort—Hal, JoAnne, Kurt, Johann, Sylvia and Ted, Cindy, Tom and Sue, Linda, Jean(s) and Genie, Marilyn and Margaret, Elizabeth, Lidija M., Paul V., Les M., Sharon and Wayne, Sabi, Mujo, Alma, and Selma Edrenić, Paul P., and especially Brian. Endless gratitude to my family for their untiring presence and support. And to God I'm grateful for all this and more, but especially for giving us lament, to mourn for what we once gave thanks.

Nancy C. Lee Elmhurst College, Chicago

ABBREVIATIONS

AB	Anchor Bible Commentary
ABD	Anchor Bible Dictionary
ANET	J. B. Pritchard, ed., *Ancient Near Eastern Texts Relating to the Old Testament*, 3d ed.
ARA	*Annual Review of Anthropology*
ASJ	*Acta Sumerologica*
BI	*Biblical Interpretation*
BSac	*Bibliotheca Sacra*
CBQ	*Catholic Biblical Quarterly*
DJD	Discoveries in the Judaean Desert
DSS	Dead Sea Scrolls
EJ	*Encyclopaedia Judaica*
GKC	*Gesenius' Hebrew Grammar*, ed. E. Kautzsch, rev. and transl. A. E. Cowley, 2d English ed. (Oxford, 1910)
HTR	*Harvard Theological Review*
HB	Hebrew Bible (following BHS)
IB	Interpreters Bible Commentary
ITC	International Theological Commentary
JAAR	*Journal of the American Academy of Religion*
JAOS	*Journal of the American Oriental Society*
JB	The Jerusalem Bible
JBL	*Journal of Biblical Literature*
JCS	*Journal of Cuneiform Studies*
JFR	*Journal of Folklore Research*
JR	*Journal of Religion*
JSOT	*Journal for the Study of the Old Testament*
JSOTS	Journal for the Study of the Old Testament Supplement Series
KTU	Die keilalphabetischen Texte aus Ugarit (AOAT 24/1–1976) ed. M. Dietrich *et al.*
LU	*Lamentation over the Destruction of Ur*, S. Kramer edition
LXX	Septuagint (Göttingen)
MT	Masoretic Text
OTL	Old Testament Library
RGG	*Die Religion in Geschichte und Gegenwart*
SBLDS	Society of Biblical Literature Dissertation Series
ZAW	*Zeitschrift für die alttestamentliche Wissenschaft*
4QLam[a]	Lamentations fragment from Qumran Cave 4

Devastation of war along a street in Vukovar (N. Lee, 2000)

CHAPTER ONE

INTRODUCTION

This city was catching up with us, clasping us
in its arms and around our necks; we watched it from above—
caesars of the moment, breathing in its own breath:
human bodies, divine blossoms . . . stillness of a Japanese cherry . . .
those that were dear to us and nested in our bosoms . . .

Ferida Duraković, "Morning Glory, Sarajevo"[1]

In the old town of Vukovar
there was a sweet smell of limetrees
the sun floated along the Danube and
the river carried people through their lives.

In the beautiful town of Vukovar
doves once flew,
there once stood
the old tower of a proud church . . .

A black cloud hung
over the ancient town of Vukovar
beautiful lime-trees fell
"tambura"[2] were silenced.

Now the ghastly ruins stand.
And the white doves fly far away
and tell the sad tale:
"Oh world that was Vukovar. . . ."

Slavica Crnjac (1995), "Vukovar"[3]

[1] In *Contemporary Poetry of Bosnia and Herzegovina*, ed. and transl., Mario Suško (Sarajevo: International Peace Center, 1993), 173.
[2] Traditional musical instrument.
[3] Transl., Dalia Kuća, in *Pismo iz rasapa* (Writing from Turmoil), ed., Đurđa

. . . .
In the City, those still living
  reject the consolation of history
  where everything gets repeated.
The City watches sadly
  the freshly drawn omens of destiny:
  unplanned new graveyards
  wherever the beast had trod,
  having come from its infernal darkness.
The City full of hollow silence:
  with just the church bells shivering
  and the wounded minarets
  speaking quietly with the heaven,
  pianos in the shattered chambers.
And the wind howls among the trees,
  inside the broken statues,
  inside the cracked, gray tombstones.
What is the City trying to hear? . . .
Spirit, appear! . . .
What is the destiny of the wounded City?
Those who listen can still hear its pulse,
the strong, seething life in its ancient roots . . .

Ljubica Ostojić (Sarajevo, 1995),
"Record of the City in Blank Verse"[4]

Since time immemorial, poets and singers have personified the cities, lands, and communities they inhabit, from ancient Ur to Sarajevo. With affection and pathos, they identify with its persona, rich symbol of the fullness of life that once was, as Ljubica Ostojić of Sarajevo writes,

> Every night I have a dream that I re-build and heal the wounds of the destroyed cities. And then, they are the same again, as at the times before the infernal powers and human madness and misery came. They are familiar and eternal. But the city in which I lived this hell, sticks to my own being. And our pain and deterioration became the same. Will our wounds and ruins ever heal into scars? . . . God almighty alone knows that. These are the poem-charms. They might be helpful, should life return into the numb and helpless words. Should they become the lasting words.[5]

Miklauzić (Zagreb: Multimedijski ženski centar, NONA, 1995), 16; published on the NONA webpage, www.videodocument.org/nona/WriTur.htm.

[4] Selection from "Record of the City in Blank Verse," transl. by Zulejha Riđanović, in *Sahat kula* (Sarajevo: Međunarodni centar za mir, 1995), 77–92.

[5] Ibid., 79.

Singers from the ancient city of Jerusalem, poets of the biblical book of Lamentations witness to their city's invasion, destruction, and suffering in the sixth century BCE.[6] As lament literature, the book has not attracted nearly as much scholarly attention as most other biblical books. And yet, given the great destructions in Europe and the world in the 20th century which continue into the present, and given the slow disintegration of 'community' in the West, the unrelenting relevance of this poetry cries out to be heard and understood.[7]

Thesis: Oral Poetic and Socio-rhetorical Methodologies

Scholars have employed various interpretive methods with the book of Lamentations. For most of the modern period, historical/literary concern about the written authorship of Lamentations held sway, particularly the refutation of Jeremianic authorship.[8] Form criticism made a greater contribution to the interpretive analysis of Lamentations by its identification of two key genres in the book—the communal dirge and the lament (prayer). The present study will build

[6] If occasionally herein the term "singer" is used interchangeably with "poet", it is with an understanding that ancient or traditional oral poets who composed (and this includes prophetic figures) usually performed (sang or chanted) their poetic songs. Such a composing/singing process in predominately oral cultures need not require literary writing.

[7] However, interest has been finally steadily growing in the 1990s. See bibliography and Claus Westermann, *Die Klagelieder: Forschungsgeschichte und Auslegung* (1990), English transl., *Lamentatiaons: Issues and Interpretation* (1994); Iain Provan, *Lamentations*, New Century Bible (1991); Paul Wayne Ferris, Jr., *The Genre of Communal Lament in the Bible and the Ancient Near East* (1992); F. W. Dobbs-Allsopp, *Weep, O Daughter of Zion: A Study of the City-Lament Genre in the Hebrew Bible* (1993); Patricia Tull, *Remember the Former Things: The Recollections of Previous Texts in Second Isaiah*, SBLDS 161 (1997); Johan Renkema, *Lamentations*. Historical Commentary of the Old Testament (1998); Robin Salters, *ICC Commentary*; Tod Linafelt, *Surviving Lamentations: Catastrophe, Lament, and Protest in the Afterlife of a Biblical Book* (2000); forthcoming, Erhard Gerstenberger's new FOTL on Psalms and Lamentations, and numerous commentaries forthcoming (by F. W. Dobbs-Allsopp, Adele Berlin, Kathleen O'Connor, Wilma Bailey, and others).

[8] See the summary on the authorship debate in Iain Provan, *Lamentations* (Grand Rapids: HarperCollins, 1991), 7–19. The question has occupied scholars for at least the last 300 years. D. Hillers noted that in 1712, H. von der Hardt proposed that the five chapters were written by Daniel, Shadrach, Meshach, Abednego, and King Jehoiachin, respectively!; *Lamentations*, OTL, rev. ed. (New York: Doubleday, 1992), 11. Rejection of Jeremianic 'authorship' of Lamentations has been the longheld consensus among modern scholars, with a few exceptions, though the ancient versions and sources unanimously ascribed Lamentations to Jeremiah (LXX, Vulgate, Targum, Syriac, Babylonian Talmud [*B. Bat.* 15a], and rabbinic writings; Provan, *Lamentations*, 7.

on the findings of form criticism, yet propose that a more comprehensive approach is needed to understand the complex poetry/songs of Lamentations.

Such a comprehensive approach, in my view, is best attained by integrating methods. What primary methods might prove fruitful given the nature of the poetry of Lamentations? First, I will use an 'oral poetic' method (from folklore and anthropology) as employed extensively, surprisingly, by only a few biblical scholars and teachers in the last 100 years,[9] especially H. Gunkel, H. Jahnow, the Scandinavian School, Robert C. Culley,[10] Mishael Caspi[11] and Susan Niditch.[12] The field of folklore, and oral poetic analyses across cul-

[9] Certainly form criticism and rhetorical criticism, which continue to offer insight, have been carrying on fruitful, biblical poetic analyses for decades (see below), focusing on the text, yet perhaps without sufficient underpinning of an understanding of the dynamics of oral poetic performance and context in traditional cultures. For a historical overview of the use of oral traditional methodology by biblical scholars, see bibliography and Robert C. Culley, "Oral Tradition and Biblical Studies" (1986); Patricia Kirkpatrick, *The Old Testament and Folklore Study* (1988). For an English overview of the work of the Scandinavian school, see D. H. Knight, *Rediscovering the Traditions of Israel* (1973), esp. H. S. Nyberg, *Studien zum Hoseabuche* (1935), H. Birkeland, *Zum hebräischen Traditionswesen: Die Komposition der prophetischen Bhcher des Alten Testaments* (1938), and Eduard Nielsen, *Oral Tradition* (1954). See also H. L. Ginsberg, "The Rebellion and Death of Ba'lu" (1936). Note the treatments by W. F. Albright, "Some Oriental Glosses on the Homeric Problem" (1950); Stanley Gevirtz, *Patterns in the Early Poetry of Israel* (1963); Frank Moore Cross, *Canaanite Myth and Hebrew Epic* (1973); "Prose and Poetry in the Mythic and Epic Texts from Ugarit" (1974); and later, "Toward a History of Hebrew Prosody" (1998); William Whallon, *Formula, Character, and Context: Studies in Homeric, Old English, and Old Testament Poetry* (1969); William Urbrock, "Oral Antecedents to Job: A Survey of Formulas and Formulaic Systems" (1976); Robert E. Coote, "The Application of the Oral Theory to Biblical Hebrew Literature" (1976); David Noel Freedman, *Pottery, Poetry, and Prophecy: Studies in Early Hebrew Poetry* (1980) and *Divine Commitment and Human Obligation* (1997); Yehoshua Gitay, "Deutero-Isaiah: Oral or Written?" (1980); Werner Kelber, *The Oral and Written Gospel* (1983; rev. ed., 1997); Martin Jaffee, "The Hebrew Scriptures" (1998).

[10] Robert C. Culley has been foremost in utilizing an oral poetic approach in published works: "An Approach to the Problem of Oral Tradition" (1963); *Oral Formulaic Language in the Psalms* (1967); "Oral Tradition and Historicity" (1972); "Oral Tradition and the OT: Some Recent Discussion" (1976); "Exploring New Directions" (1984); "Orality and Writtenness in the Prophetic Texts" (2000); "The Confessions of Jeremiah and Traditional Discourse" (2000).

[11] Mishael Caspi has furthered a scholarly focus on oral traditional methodology as co-chair of the NAPH group at the SBL. His fieldwork especially relevant to the present study is in oral poetic lament traditions in Yemen, Palestine, and Lithuania; M. Caspi and Julia Ann Blessing, *Weavers of the Songs: The Oral Poetry of Arab Women in Israel and the West Bank* (Washington, D.C.: ThreeContinents Press, 1991); orig. publ. by M. Caspi as "'My Brother, Vein of My Heart:' Arab Laments for the Dead in Israel," *Folklore* 98 (1987): 28–40.

[12] Susan Niditch, especially, has been advocating folklore methodologies: *Folklore and the Hebrew Bible* (1993); and idem, *Oral World and Written Word: Ancient Israelite Literature* (1996); see previously, "Composition of Isaiah 1" (1980).

tures, is indebted foremost to performers of oral epic poetry in former Yugoslavia in the first half of the 20th century, and their early researchers Matija Murko, Milman Parry, Albert B. Lord, and others.[13] Their seminal research in epic poetry spawned decades of development of an "oral-formulaic" theory of poetic composition/performance which allowed for poetic analyses truer to the dynamics of traditional contexts than afforded by literary criticism alone. Scholars have used the method to analyse not only actual traditional song performances but also to interpret "oral-derived" written poetic texts.[14] Scholars who have followed the Parry/Lord method and some who critique and modify it continue to recognize that *repetition* of formula and themes (though not verbatim) is a main feature of oral poetry.[15] As will be seen, such repetition is a feature pervasive in biblical Lamentations.

The oral genres of *dirges* and *laments* have not received as much scholarly attention, though they are pervasive across cultures and

[13] See the various treatments of this work in John Miles Foley, esp. *Oral-Formulaic Theory and Research: An Introduction and Annotated Bibliography* (New York: Garland, 1985), Introduction in *Comparative Research on Oral Traditions: A Memorial for Milman Parry*, ed. J. M. Foley (Columbus, Oh.: Slavica, 1987), 15–27; and *The Theory of Oral Composition: History and Methodology* (Bloomington: Indiana Univ. Press, 1988).

[14] J. M. Foley's term for works that "reveal oral traditional features but have reached us only in written form"; *Immanent Art*, 15; Parry's original incentive to research the performance of Yugoslavian oral epic poetry had been to shed light on the classic "Homeric problem" of 'composition' of the Iliad and the Odyssey, now regarded by many as a kind of oral-derived text. The field of folklore was for a time overly preoccupied with whether written texts were originally oral or written (and this was reflected in some biblical studies), but this determination is no longer seen as important or necessary. Niditch suggests analyzing biblical texts in terms of their "traditional" characteristics, since traditional cultures generally utilize an oral style which is often inscribed in its written works as well. She suggests the distinction between oral and written composition in the Hebrew Bible has been overstated; *Folklore*, 6–9; *Oral World*, 1–7. Of more complexity and ongoing exploration are the nature of "transitional texts" that are further removed from oral poetic cultural context, and literary texts that minimally reflect remnants of oral culture. See the efforts to define what comprises "traditional" by Dan Ben-Amos, "The Seven Strands of Tradition: Varieties in Its Meaning in American Folklore Studies," *Journal of Folklore Research* 21 (1984): 97–131; Richard Handler and Jocelyn Linnekan, "Tradition, Genuine or Spurious?" *Journal of American Folklore* 97 (1984): 273–90; Ruth Finnegan, "Tradition, but What Tradition, and For Whom?" *Oral Tradition* 6/1 (1991): 104–24.

[15] See J. M. Foley's discussion of the "mechanism versus aesthetics" debate, *Immanent Art*, 3; Niditch, *Oral World*, 9–11; Caspi and Blessing found that the women of their study used formulas not as Parry's verbatim repetitions, but as "principles of formal arrangement," and were more interested in the "rhythmic value of the song" (*Weavers of the Songs*, 7, 12).

through history.[16] Psalms of lament (prayer songs) received more attention by biblical scholars in the last half of the 20th c. after Gunkel set the stage.[17] But the seminal work by a biblical scholar describing cross-cultural uses of dirge (funeral lament song) in relation to Lamentations was by Hedwig Jahnow in *Das hebräische Leichenlied im Rahmen der Völkerdichtung* (The Hebrew Funeral Song in the Context of Folk Poetry, 1923).[18] Unfortunately, her work has also been neglected.[19] It is an ironic and profound tragedy that this scholar who drew important attention to dirges and laments prior to WWII was

[16] Dirges and laments are for the most part chanted or sung by women across traditional cultures; besides the usual biblical references, Ezek 32:16 is suggestive: "This is a lamentation [קִינָה, dirge]: it shall be chanted. The women of the nations shall chant it"; cf. the Irish term, to "keen" or wail for the dead. See Marta Weigle's comment, "Until recently, it has been difficult to analyze and appreciate women's expressive forms simply because those forms were not considered except when related to the female domestic sphere and work, reproductive life cycle, or child rearing (de Caro ix–xiv) . . . Both the ethnographic and the historical records long remained basically androcentric; women's expression, oral or otherwise, was not considered a worthy focus for and measure of the creative, aesthetic uses of language in a full range of social situations and cultural contexts"; "Women's Expressive Forms," in *Teaching Oral Traditions*, ed. J. M. Foley (New York: MLA, 1998), 298–99. For a brief treatment of terminology of dirges/laments in classical Greek tradition, see "dirge", "lament" and "elegy" in *The New Princeton Encyclopedia of Poetry and Poetics*, ed. A. Preminger and T. Brogan (Princeton: Princeton Univ. Press, 1993). See Euripides' play, *Suppliant Women*, transl. R. Warren and S. Scully (New York: Oxford Univ. Press, 1995).

[17] Esp. in the published works of Claus Westermann, Walter Brueggemann, Erhard Gerstenberger, and Samuel Balentine.

[18] BZAW 36 (Giessen: Alfred Töpelmann, 1923). See below. While as will be seen Westermann disagrees with Jahnow on genre(s) in Lamentations, his following critique is highly suggestive, especially given that many scholars have regarded the poems as originating not too long after the destruction of Jerusalem in 587 BCE:

> It is difficult to understand how, in the wake of Gunkel, Jahnow, and the Scandinavian school, . . . almost none of the interpreters of Lamentations has taken seriously the notion that these laments might actually have been spoken by the shocked survivors as they mourned the catastrophe of 587 BCE (*Lamentations*, 61–62).

Likewise, many scholars suggest the acrostic structure likely attests to later "editing", though why this must be the case is seldom argued. Acrostics in the Bible are always found in poetic texts. I shall make a proposal about the acrostic code below; cf. David Noel Freedman, "Acrostics and Metrics in Hebrew Poetry," *HTR* 65 (1972): 367–92, and more recently, idem, "Acrostic Poems in the Hebrew Bible: Alphabetic and Otherwise," in *Divine Commitment and Human Obligation* (Grand Rapids: Wm. B. Eerdmans, 1997), 183–204.

[19] See the anthology by German women scholars honoring her, including Jahnow's early article "Die Frau im Alten Testament"; Hedwig Jahnow u.a., *Feministische Hermeneutik und Erstes Testament* (Bonn: VG Bild-Kunst, 1994); see Westermann's tribute in his commentary, *Lamentations*, 8.

deported in 1942 (at age 63) to Theresienstadt where she died a year and a half later.[20]

The present study will, in part, build on Jahnow's work, but will critically analyze the book of Lamentations using an oral poetic methodology that goes beyond identifying genres and their elements to an interpretive analysis of *how* the individual poets in this oral-derived text produce meaning as part of (and at times in defiance of) their larger tradition. The analysis will be concerned not only with the standard forms, patterns, and formulas utilized by poets of Hebrew traditions. It will also explore how each poet casts traditional forms in his or her unique style (or better, "individual" style)[21] in response to a given context.[22] An oral poetic method considers the artistry of poets, both those well-known—such as Homer, Hosea, Hesiod, and the lesser known, like al-Khansa, the Bedouin poetess of the Sulaim tribe, known for her compositions of lamentations prior to the Islamic period.[23]

In the words of Niditch,

> The goal is to understand the composers, participants in lengthy literary traditions, and the ways they infuse ancient traditions with their own individual artistry, adapting them to their own times and to the concerns of their audiences.... Context also has to do with respect for creators of pieces of folklore, people who are set in culture, time, and place, with attention to their own voices, styles, and skills.... Concern with the historical setting of the created composition rather than with historicity leads to biblical scholarship that is, in fact, very

[20] Ibid.

[21] S. Niditch, *Oral World*, 11. As folklorists dealing with oral poetry would attest (as well as postmodern literary critics), any claims to literary 'uniqueness' are technically impossible, since every poet draws upon prior speech and traditions. For this reason, I will prefer the term "individual style" over "unique" where it is possible to discern a particular poet's characteristic style. In "Form Criticism and Beyond," James Muilenburg had stressed the need to consider, beyond the typical forms, "the individual, personal, and unique features of the particular pericope"; in *Hearing and Speaking the Word*, 31–33. For a thorough overview of biblical rhetorical criticism, see Phyllis Trible, *Rhetorical Criticism: Context, Method, and the Book of Jonah* (Minneapolis: Fortress Press, 1994).

[22] For recent summaries of definitions of oral theory see Rosemary Lévy Zumwalt, "A Historical Glossary of Critical Approaches," 75–94, and Mark C. Amodio, "Contemporary Critical Approaches and Studies in Oral Tradition," 95–105, in *Teaching Oral Tradition*, ed. John M. Foley.

[23] M. Caspi and J. Blessing, *Weavers of the Songs*, 3. On the renown of individual poets in different cultures, see R. Finnegan, *Oral Poetry*, 170, 210. One thinks also of Walt Whitman's famous dirges for Abraham Lincoln, "When Lilacs Last in the Dooryard Bloom'd" and "O Captain! My Captain!"

> interested in 'history'. Such an approach treats biblical literature as coming from real people. . . . It encourages us to to search for these real people and their worlds rather than to check the accuracy of their information . . . It is, then, an approach that steers a course between biblical scholarship as a means of historical reconstruction and . . . as a wholly reader-responsed variety of literary criticism.[24]

This additional but important element—the *individual* style in the works of a particular poet—is the missing link, methodologically, in appraising a relationship of the poetry of the prophet Jeremiah to that in Lamentations. That appraisal is only a consequence of using an oral poetic method, and was not the primary aim of this study. (Of course such an exploration is tentative as it is limited by the quantity of texts preserved that are demonstrably composed by an individual poet.) Such an approach reveals, in my view, that Jeremiah is not "the" poet of Lamentations either, but is likely *one poetic singer among others* featured there, not its single literary 'author'.

In the spirit of oral poetic method, but especially out of concern for those many suffering in the recent wars in 'former Yugoslavia', this study will also undertake two new *comparative* tasks. First, it will draw as much as possible on research of dirge/lament songs orally performed among South Slavs, moreso in the past, as a potential heuristic window on the "oral-derived" text of biblical Lamentations.[25] Second, it will present for a wider audience some of the literary lament poems by native authors I collected while traveling through the region for a year (1996/97) and later, poems written from the context of the recent wars, siege of cities and villages, and suffering of individuals of diverse ethnic background.[26] Obviously, something of the impact and understanding of the poetry in its native language is lost in the English translation for outside readers/hearers. Compa-

[24] *Folklore*, 12, 25, 27; *Oral World*, 2.

[25] For newer contextual approaches in biblical scholarship and interpretation, see *Reading from This Place: Social Location and Biblical Interpretation in Global Perspective*, ed. Fernando F. Segovia and Mary Ann Tolbert (Minneapolis: Fortress Press, 1995).

[26] Obviously, this collection cannot be complete, though I aim to make it moreso. Unfortunately, little of the large amount of poetry produced has been translated for a world audience, even now after 10 years. Much of the material herein is from Bosnia and Croatia, but some account will be given as well to poetic expressions of suffering of Serbian people who had little to do with the horrific policies of some of their leaders. I am aware that terminology for ethnic designation is problematic—the war produced simplistic 'us-them' divisions and labeling people, perpetuated by the international media, when in fact distinctions were much more blurred among South Slavic peoples themselves, due to living together in communities and not always noticing or caring about such differences.

risons will be made between biblical Lamentations (and other ancient texts) and this contextual written poetry with an ear for any 'traditional' oral poetic elements still reflected therein (both locally and universally-defined), such as the personification of cities under siege.[27] Thus in a dialectic conversation, poetic traditions might mutually inform and inspire one another, not only about formulaic expressions and artistry of meaning, but also especially about justice, and *surviving*, and silence, and expressing grief, and preventing future contexts of suffering, death, and destruction.[28]

And herein is the relevance of integrating a socio-rhetorical method, along the lines of Walter Brueggemann's work, which has focused on the constructive and destructive power of rhetoric, both social and biblical, especially *lament* forms.[29] From a U.S. cultural perspective, Brueggemann suggests in his article, "The Costly Loss of Lament," that there has been a neglect by scholars of this genre prevalent in biblical discourse, and this has adversely impacted theological, liturgical, and social contexts.[30]

> We have yet to ask what it means to have this form available in the social construction of reality. What difference does it make to have faith that permits and requires this form of prayer? . . . [Without it] a theological monopoly is re-enforced, docility and submissiveness are engendered, and the outcome in terms of social practice is to re-enforce the political-economic . . . status quo. . . . In regularly using the lament form, Israel kept the justice question visible and legitimate.[31]

[27] These latter tasks of research of the region are undertaken here as my own beginning, with more research to follow.

[28] On the importance of this theme, see Tod Linafelt, *Surviving Lamentations*.

[29] Its world-constituting (and deconstituting) social force. On Brueggemann's essential methodology, see *Israel's Praise: Doxology Against Idolatry and Ideology* (Philadelphia: Fortress Press, 1988), 1–28. Ruth Finnegan touches on this dimension in *Oral Poetry*, 274: "Poets and performers of lament songs or praise poems create and re-order the situation through their poetic expression . . . create and recreate the world." Such a move toward addressing the social power of rhetoric and poetic tradition is compatible with "functional" approaches in folklore that recognize the roles of particular genres in shaping society. Thus, for example, Dan Ben-Amos notes that B. Malinowski's approach views folklore genres as "a contributing factor to the maintenance and continuity of social groups," or can be, in the view of E. Leach and R. Firth, "a manipulative and divisive rather than a cohesive and integrative force." Ben-Amos suggests that genres may function "in individual attempts to cope with conflicting forces"; Introduction, *Folklore* Genres (Austin: Univ. of Texas Press, 1976), 23–24.

[30] Brueggemann would be the first to admit that lament, of course, has not been neglected by African-American traditions. For the power and wide-ranging influence of lament and the spirituals, see Wilma Ann Bailey's "The Sorrow Songs: Laments From Ancient Israel and the African-American Diaspora" (forthcoming in *Semeia*).

[31] "The Costly Loss of Lament," *JSOT* 36 (1986): 59–63. A striking example of the use of lament for social impact (drawing on the dirge/mourning motif) can be

The biblical forms of lament were concerned in part to critique social injustice within the Israelites' own social and theological community, giving the people a voice (thus laments functioned similarly to the prophetic tradition).[32] A contemporary "loss of lament" from this perspective might prove disastrous. Just so, according to Samuel Balentine, who in his 1994 book *Prayer in the Hebrew Bible*,[33] moved beyond the ancient text to make a stunning observation based on his research of pre-WWII religious contexts in Europe. He broadly suggested that the lament traditions of the Hebrew Bible were severely neglected by Christian biblical scholars, theologians, and churches in their liturgies in western Europe, Germany, and the U.S. before and during World War II. This neglect of a genre concerned with suffering and social injustice contributed to our general failure to raise protests against the Nazi movement and intervene to prevent the Holocaust/Shoah.[34]

It would be a study in itself to consider how the longstanding, national epic poetry in old Yugoslavia (which in part *lamented* its being dominated by foreign political powers), actually contributed to that country's *resistance* to Hitler through the partisan movement, led primarily by Serbs. In the last decade however, such national epic laments served a different and disastrous end in a "costly *abuse* of

seen in the international women's group, "Women in Black," that began in Israel in protest against government policies, and the group by the same name that has been active in Belgrade in the last decade, also protesting government policies.

[32] In the Bible's prophetic theology, injustice and idolatry resulted in loss of land and exile; see W. Brueggemann, *The Prophetic Imagination* (Philadelphia: Fortress Press, 1978).

[33] S. Balentine, *Prayer in the Hebrew Bible* (Minneapolis: Fortress Press, 1993). Balentine's attention in this work to "prose prayers" (following M. Greenberg and others) which are embedded in biblical *narrative* contexts, unleashed from the institution of the formal cult/liturgies, has something important to say about the role of popular lament in contemporary contexts.

[34] *Prayer in the Hebrew Bible*, 3–12, 245–59, esp. 250. Balentine's incisive analysis offers a critique of some key aspects of the German neo-orthodox tradition, especially its one-sided preoccupation with the "sovereignty" of God and the "praise" Psalm traditions. On the other hand, he says, "The biblical literature portrays lamentation as not only a *post-crisis* reflection but also an *in-crisis* response that speaks to the pain of the moment . . . The golden age of [theological studies of the] Hebrew Bible, however, . . . promote[d] a confessional response marked by an overriding commitment to *theo*logy, not *anthropo*logy, to divine sovereignty that transcends human failure . . . In the wake of . . . unrestrained barbarity, confessional accents on divine dominion in history may seem to have only a 'lacquered depth' . . ."; *Prayer*, 259. Cf. instead Walter Brueggemann's recent *Theology of the Old Testament: Testimony, Dispute, Advocacy* (Minneapolis: Fortress Press, 1997).

lament." As Michael Sells has suggested in *The Bridge Betrayed: Religion and Genocide in Bosnia*, during this time, some leaders' opportunistic political use of some epic poetry traditions contributed to the recent wars among peoples of former Yugoslavia and even genocide (see below).

The two basic approaches outlined above, oral poetic and socio-rhetorical, will combine in this study to produce the *thesis* that in the biblical book of Lamentations, two lead poetic singers are presented in dialogue when the text is analyzed in light of previous poetic traditions (prophetic and psalmic), the context of the sixth century destruction of Jerusalem, and comparisons with South Slavic dirge and lament poems. One of the poets can be identified as a prophet by virtue of his formulaic prophetic rhetoric. He is likely to be identified as Jeremiah by detailed poetic analysis, by virtue of *how* he uses specific genres and poetic techniques, favors terms and imagery to build themes in response to the context, which are evident also in the prophet's poetry in the book of Jeremiah.[35] The other lead poet, appearing second in Lamentations, is a female lament singer. She responds to the prophet's description of the suffering of the personified city ("Daughter Zion" or "Jerusalem"). She is also identified by locating her comparable poetry in the book of Jeremiah, using the same above criteria. She shall be referred to herein as "Jerusalem's poet" as she sings on behalf of the suffering city.[36] Just what these poets are saying about their context—and how they are shaping it through their vulnerable, yet daring voices—is the subject of this study.

Survey of Scholarship: Lamentations; Genres Across Cultures; Lament Elements in South Slavic Poetry

Apart from a few theological studies of the book of Lamentations, 20th century scholarship has been preoccupied with two general

[35] A larger body of Jeremiah's poetic work handed down would provide better evidence to confirm or refute my claim of his poetry in parts of Lamentations. The 'tradition' found in the superscript to Septuagint Lamentations that Jeremiah lamented some or all of the work is discounted as evidence at the outset of this analysis. Evidence for his individual style in Lamentations is sought in the text itself.

[36] While it is not necessary to *identify* the poets in Lamentations, I am suggesting more importantly that the traditional oral poetic context of that time gives

questions: genre and authorship.[37] The title of the book comes from early Jewish traditions' designation of it as קינות, "dirges," also reflected in Septuagint's *Threni*. In the late 1800s, Karl Budde had noted the striking adaptation of the dirge (קינה) by the Hebrew prophets and in Lamentations. Robert Lowth, however, had already seen this in 1787 and regarded it as evidence for maintaining Jeremiah's connection to Lamentations, indeed, that Lamentations contained the most extensive example in the Hebrew Bible of a prophet's use of the dirge for communal purposes.[38] To this matter we shall return.

Serious consideration of the genre(s) of Lamentations received major impetus with the work of Hedwig Jahnow in *Das hebräische Leichenlied im Rahmen der Völkerdichtung* (1923).[39] By a comparative analysis of the dirge (*Totenklage*; or funeral song, *Leichenlied*) across a wide range of world folk literature,[40] both ancient and modern, Jahnow aimed to illumine the Hebrew genre implicit in biblical examples and fragments.[41] She drew on the work of anthropologists and folklorists with examples of dirge songs from ancient Egypt, Assyria, Babylonia, Greece, Rome, Etruria, the Celts, and Germany, as well as from modern cultures still performing dirges in the early 20th century: in Palestine, Africa, Asia, the Americas, Corsica, Sardinia, Greece, Serbia, Bulgaria, and Romania.[42] Scholars continue to study dirges from additional cultures, such as the modern Maori of New

serious warrant to the above approach and shall be most fruitful for the poetry's interpretation.

[37] For an overview of scholarship, see C. Westermann, *Lamentations*, 1–85.

[38] On elegiac poetry in the Hebrew Bible, see Robert Lowth, *Lectures on the Sacred Poetry of the Hebrews*, vol. 2, transl. G. Gregory (London: J. Johnson, 1787), 121–61. Gunkel called Lam 1, 2, and 4 "political funeral songs"; "Klagelieder Jeremiae," *RGG* (Tübingen: T. C. B. Mohr, 1912), 1500.

[39] (The Hebrew Funeral Song in the Context of Folk Poetry) BZAW 36 (Giessen: Alfred Töpelmann, 1923). C. Westermann suggested in 1990 that there had been little serious work done on genre in Lamentations since Jahnow and Gunkel, but rather scholars who dealt with the book focused on conceptual or thematic content; *Lamentations*, 58–61, 73.

[40] Jahnow does not distinguish between dirge and funeral song, but uses the terms interchangeably, as well as "Leichenklage" (funeral complaint); Jahnow, *Hebräische Leichenlied*, 2, 8.

[41] As in 2 Sam 1:19f; 3:33f; I Kgs 13:20; Jer 22:18; 34:5. Jahnow noted that examples of the funeral song also appear in the Apocrypha and in the New Testament; ibid., 2.

[42] Ibid., 3–4.

Zealand,[43] the Akan of Ghana,[44] the Luo of East Africa,[45] and China.[46]

Jahnow's definition of the dirge song included the following motifs[47] shared across cultures:[48] frequently a proclamation of a death, followed by a narration or complaint (*Klage*) describing the death/destruction, often accompanied by weeping;[49] melancholy over the transitoriness of the deceased/destroyed; an accusation (*Anklage*) against the perpetrator, perhaps with a provocative motif, i.e., a call for justice, revenge, or a curse;[50] a call and response performance style that allows for different voices,[51] including perhaps a direct address of the

[43] In B. Mitcalfe, *Poetry of the Maori* (Hamilton & Auckland: Paul's Book Arcade, 1961), 20, cited in R. Finnegan, *Oral Poetry* (Bloomington & Indianapolis: Indiana Univ. Press, 1992), 13.

[44] J. H. K. Nketia, *Funeral Dirges of the Akan People* (Achimota, 1955), 66f, cited in R. Finnegan who notes that these dirges are chanted rather than sung, and sometimes performed by drums; *Oral Poetry*, 55, 118, 120; cf. idem, *Oral Literature in Africa* (Oxford: Clarendon Press, 1970).

[45] H. O. Anyumba, "The Nyatiti Lament Songs," in *East Africa Past and Present* (Paris: Présence Africaine, 1964), 189–90, cited in R. Finnegan, *Oral Poetry*, 58.

[46] Wang in A. Dundes, ed., *The Study of Folklore* (Englewood Cliffs, N.J.: Prentice-Hall, 1965), 311, cited in Finnegan, *Oral Poetry*, 273.

[47] Cf. C. Westermann, *Lamentations*, 7; idem, *Praise and Lament in the Psalms*, 167.

[48] Performance of dirges in South Slavic regions, according to Radmila Pešić (1985), was still found primarily in Montenegro, Herzegovina, Kosovo, Lica, Dalmatian Zagorje, southwestern Serbia, and Macedonia; "tužbalica" in *Rečnik književnih termina*, ed. Dragiša Živković (Beograd: Nolit), 838–39. See below for more detailed treatments.

[49] Jure Kaštelan, in a literary poem from his collection *Pjetao na krovu* (Cock on the Roof; 1950) renders dirge imagery: "My eyes today are as hundreds of springs . . ."; in Ante Kadić, "Postwar Croatian Lyric Poetry" [i.e., post-WWII] *American Slavic and East European Review* 17 (1958): 523.

[50] A curse poem from the context of war in Osijek, Croatia, was published in 1992, in connection with the death of the first child killed there by the eight-month-long Serbian militia siege. In the first lines, the poet clarifies its genre: "not a dirge . . . nor a prayer", but "a curse." She renders the curse as invoked by "woman", by her country personified as "mother", and by the earth, all against soldiers who killed the girl. It was written by the child's teacher, Kruna First-Medić, entitled "For the Girl Ivana Vujić (To Those Who Killed Her from the Barracks [called] 'Milan Stanivuković')," transl. Višnja Pavičić, in *Na Grani od Oblaka* (Osijek: "Tehnokamen,' 1992), 37. The vengeful nature of the poem is connected to outrage over injustice, which contains themes of no burial and no mourning for the perpetrators as even the earth and nature cooperate in rejecting them, yet which accept the girl's body in burial; cf. the same poetic themes found in Jer 14:16; 22:18–19 and elsewhere. The poet asks God to make the perpetrators' own children renounce them. In another poem, "To a Woman (refugee, displaced and any other)," First-Medić laments the life women must lead, beginning "A woman is a lonely island/the saddest between heaven and earth . . ."; transl. Lidija Matorić. At the close of the poem she describes a nun, Blaženka Perković, alone in a cellar defiantly praying in Vinkovci that no more will be killed, but to no avail; ibid., 47.

[51] The dialogical nature of Israelite dirges is also emphasized in *Encyclopaedia*

dead[52] or the dead speaking;[53] brief questions; a summons to mourn; mourning over the incomprehensibility of the event; impact of the death/destruction on the survivors; mention of the manner of death, especially if unexpected or due to some violence; a reconciling motif (a making peace for the survivors with their loss by the fact that the individual's death was brave or noble, the burial honorable, leaving an honorable memory and a good name); praise for the deceased;

Judaica (Jerusalem: Keter, 1971), 485–93. A call and response, dialogical pattern will be discerned in Lamentations below.

[52] The oral poetic motif of addressing the dead can be seen poignantly adapted in literary poems, for example, from Sarajevo, Bosnia: in Dara Sekulić's "Jewish Cemetery":

> Silent you rest/in all languages/Only the birch trembles . . .
> Outliving yourself/you're a sign of life/and nothing touches your sleep. (44)

In "Abdulah Sidran's "Those Traversing: To Sarajevo Sephardim, at the Jewish Cemetery":

> Sleep, you who have crossed the last/
> road of all. Sleep, time will pass on./Sleep. . . . (101)

In Džemaludin Latić's "Your Death":

> My friend, who believed my love had touched its very bottom,/
> the vast valley of my life/which I frequent these days/
> is deserted, hopelessly empty. (167)

Transl. and ed., Mario Suško, in *Contemporary Poetry of Bosnia and Herzegovina* (Sarajevo: International Peace Center, 1993). An extraordinary use of this theme appeared after the death of the poet Milan Milišić in the siege of Dubrovnik, Croatia, in 1991. Abdulah Sidran in Sarajevo wrote a poem in which he addressed a letter to Milišić now gone, "An Epistle to A Friend from Dubrovnik"; see discussion by Marko Vešović in the afterward to *A Blind Man Sings to His City* (Sarajevo: Međunarodni centar za mir, 1997), 151–52; for a collection of poems written about the siege of Dubrovnik, see Božena Korda, ed., *Ranjenom, Dubrovnika: ratna poezija 1991–1992* (Zagreb: Fond za spas Dubrovnika "Sveti Vlaho", no date).

[53] An extraordinary use of this traditional motif in a literary poem is the entire premise of Vesna Parun's "Mati čovjeka" (Mother of Man) from 1947, cited in Ante Kadić, "Postwar Croatian Lyric," 518–19. In it a dead son speaks to his surviving mother, lamenting it would have been better had he not been born to her for all the grief he has brought her, yet he symbolizes not just one man but all humanity:

> Better had you given birth to bleak winter, o mother, than to me./Had you given birth to a bear cub in a lair, a snake in a nest. . . . And if you had given birth to a bird, o mother, you would have been a mother./You would have been happy, you would have warmed the bird in your wings/. . . As it is, you stand alone and alone you share your stillness with the graves; bitter it is a man to be while knife is friend to man.

a contrast motif (comparing "then and now,"); and occasionally a prayer to God.[54]

Jahnow showed that the performance of the dirge is often, though not always, found in close proximity to the burial of the dead and to shared mourning customs across cultures,[55] including Israelite.[56] Numerous cultures share the following customs: the shearing of one's head or hair,[57] tearing one's clothes,[58] wearing sackcloth or other mourning garments,[59] mourning with head and/or feet

[54] Jahnow notes that prayer was expressed along with the dirge in some Christian and Muslim cultures that were investigated; Jahnow, *Hebräische Leichenlied*, 98–101, 171, 178; this is evident in the Hebrew book of Lamentations. In modern Serbia, priests may offer fixed prayers when dirges (*tužbalice*) are performed; Barbara Kerewsky-Halpern, "Text and Context in Serbian Ritual Lament," *Canadian-American Slavic Studies* 15 (1981): 54. Prayer offered during mourning is found in 2 Sam 15:30; Neh 1:4–11; Jonah 3:8 (ordered by the king of Nineveh). In later Judaism certain prayers of worship were omitted for the mourner as inappropriate, by exacerbating the grief or calling for confession of sin (i.e., the Tahanun prayer and Ps 20). Moreover, the traditional Jewish greeting to a mourner is related to the fate of Jerusalem, reflecting biblical Lamentations: "May the Almighty comfort you among the other mourners for Zion and Jerusalem" (*EJ*, 485–93).

[55] Xuan Huong Thi Pham, *Mourning in the Ancient Near East and the Hebrew Bible*, JSOTS 302 (Sheffield: Sheffield Academic Press, 1999). Unfortunately, I have only just obtained this work upon the completion of my own but am gratified to know the author had recognized in Lamentations the reflection of a mourning context with its dialogue of speakers, including the comforter and the mourner; Pham writes from her own context of suffering in Vietnam.

[56] E.g., 2 Sam 3:31–34; Jer 16:4–8. Though biblical periods of mourning (seven days, a month, etc.) vary, Israelite mourning customs have remained fairly constant from the biblical to Talmudic to modern periods; *EJ*, 485–93. Biblical texts that deal with dirges, burial, and/or mourning rites/speech are the following: Gen 23:2; Lev 10:6; 21:1–6, 10–11; Deut 14:1; 2 Sam 1:17–27; 3:31–35; 15:30, 32; I Kgs 13:20; Amos 5:1–3; 16–17; 8:3, 8–10; Jonah 3:6; Isa 1:21–23 (contrast motif, as in Jer 2:21); 22:4–8, 12; 32:9–14; Mic 1:8–16; 3:7; Jer 4:28; 8:18, 21–23; 9:9, 16–21; 14:2–6, 16b, 17–18; 15:5; 16:4–8; 22:10, 18–19; 31:15; 34:5; 41:5; Ezek 2:10; c.f. 5:1; 7:18; 8:14; 19:1–14; 24:15–18f; 26:16–18; 27:1–36; 28:12–19; 32:2–16; Joel 1:5–13; Nah 3:7; Zech 7:3–5; 11:2–3; Ps 35:13–15; Esth 4:3; Job 2:13; Ezra 10:6; Neh 1:4; Ep Jer 1:31–32.

[57] Practiced in ancient Babylonia, and Egypt, modern Zanzibar, Albania and Arabia; Jahnow, *Hebräische Leichenlied*, 5; also in ancient Israel (Deut 21:12 for the captured maiden; Am 8:10; Is 22:12; Mic 1:8–16; Jer 16:6; Ezek 7:18; Job 1:20), but see the prohibition of shearing the hair in Israel in Lev 19:27; 21:5; and Deut 14:1–2. In later Judaism, letting the hair grow became a sign of mourning; *EJ*, 485–93.

[58] In ancient Israel (Gen 37:29, 34; Lev 10:6; Josh 7:6; 2 Sam 3:31; 2 Kgs 19:1 = Isa 37:1; Esth 4:1; Job 1:20; 2:12), ancient Babylonia, and Greece, and in modern times in Arabia, Palestine, and Egypt; Jahnow, *Hebräische Leichenlied*, 5.

[59] In ancient Israel (2 Sam 3:31; 14:2; Am 8:10; Isa 22:12; 32:11; Ezek 7:18, c.f. 27; 26:16; Ps 30:12; 35:13; Lam 2:10; Jonah 3:6 [king of Nineveh]; widow's garments

War-damaged Statue of Mary, Osijek Cemetery (N. Lee, 1996)

bare,[60] throwing dust on the head,[61] the practice of self-injury,[62] rolling or lying on the ground,[63] providing comfort for the bereaved through a feast, bread, or drink,[64] though in Israel *fasting* by the mourner is also widely attested.[65]

Jahnow thus concluded from the performance of the dirge along with other mourning customs across cultures that "the Israelite dirge in its own sphere of customs is heard like the dirge of other ancient and modern peoples." And so with a degree of caution, she suggests "parallels from the funeral poetry of these peoples can be drawn upon in order to fill the gap in our knowledge of the Israelite funeral song."[66] In particular, the modern funeral songs of Arabia, Syria, and Palestine that have sprouted from the same soil as Israel are expected to have the closest affinity to ancient Israelite dirges among the various cultures.[67]

in Gen 38:14, 19; mourning garments also in ancient Babylonia, Arabia, modern Syria, the Sahara; ibid., 5–6; parts of modern Bosnia, Croatia; Tanja Perić-Polonijo, "Oral Poems in the Context of Customs and Rituals," *Institut za etnologiju i folkoristiku* 33/2 (1996): 392, fn. 10; and Serbia; B. Kerewsky-Halpern, "Text and Context," 55. Texts in the Hebrew Bible that depict the donning of festive garments, as for a marriage, etc., also serve a poetic device to symbolize the move out of mourning into a time of rejoicing (e.g., Ps 30:12; Isa 61:10).

[60] In ancient Israel (c.f., Ezek 24:17; Mic 1:8; but cf. 2 Sam 15:30, Jer 14:3–4, Esth 6:12, where the *covering* of the head indicates mourning); *EJ*, 485–93; but the *uncovering* of the head in ancient Rome, modern Syria, Palestine, Bulgaria, and Romania; Jahnow, *Hebräische Leichenlied*, 6.

[61] In ancient Israel (Josh 7:6; 2 Sam 13:19; Jer 6:26; 25:34; Ezek 27:30; Lam 2:10; cf. Ta'an 15b); *EJ*, 485–93; also in ancient Greece (e.g., in the *Iliad*), Egypt, and modern Corsica, Arabia, and the Sahara; Jahnow, *Hebräische Leichenlied*, 6.

[62] Found only occasionally in ancient Israel (Jer 16:6, but see especially the prohibition of self-injury to set Israel apart from the other nations in Lev 19:28; 21:5; and Deut 14:1–2); found in ancient Babylonia, Greece, among modern Arabs in Palestine, Corsica, Albania, Montenegro, and Greece; ibid., 4–5.

[63] In ancient Israel (2 Sam 13:31; Mic 1:10) and later Judaism; *EJ*, 485–93.

[64] In ancient Israel (Jer 16:7–8; Hos 9:4; Ezek 24:17), Egypt, Babylon, Greece, Syria, Arabia, Albania, Italy, among the Huns, Lithuania, and in modern times, in parts of Greece, Albania, Bulgaria, Russia; Jahnow, *Hebräische Leichenlied*, 7; and Serbia; B. Kerewsky-Halpern, "Text and Context," 54.

[65] From ancient to modern times: see 2 Sam 3:35; Ezra 10:6; Esth 4:3; Neh 1:4; Ps 35:13; Jonah 3:7 (of king of Nineveh); c.f. Ta'an. 1:4. Other customs attested in Israel include the covering of the upper lip (Mic 3:7; Ezek 24:17), sitting on the ground, sometimes in ashes (Ezek 26:16, the princes of Tyre; Jonah 3:6, the king of Nineveh; Lam 1:1, the city of Jerusalem; Job 2:8, 13), abstaining from washing (2 Sam 12:20; c.f. Ta'an. 1:6), and beating the breast (Isa 32:12); in later Judaism mourners are not permitted to study the Torah except for mournful passages like Job, Lamentations, parts of Jeremiah, and laws concerning mourning; *EJ*, 485–93.

[66] Jahnow, *Hebräische Leichenlied*, 8.

[67] Ibid. Collections of dirges in Arabia, Syria, and Palestine considered by Jahnow

Jahnow's study also highlighted that in most cultures women played the key social role in performance of dirges.[68] This widely-attested social practice will be suggestive for identifying a female poetic singer in Lamentations. Women mourners are attested in ancient Mesopotamia, Ugarit,[69] ancient Israel,[70] Egypt, Rome, and among ancient and modern Arabs, including Petra, the Sahara, in Judaism, in parts of modern Egypt,[71] Syria, Albania, Corsica, Polynesia, and among Jews in Algeria.[72] Women performing the dirge itself are attested in ancient Greece,[73] Ugarit,[74] Israel,[75] Babylonia, Egypt, Rome, among modern Arabs,[76] as well as in parts of modern Greece,[77] Sierra Leone,[78] Ghana,[79] Montenegro, Bosnia, Croatia, Serbia,[80] and Russia.[81]

Moreover, anthropological and folklore research since the time of Jahnow has continued to compile evidence both for the definition of a stable dirge genre and for cultural and individual variations of it. Ruth Finnegan, in her study *Oral Poetry*, notes that "functionally

included those by G. H. Dalman (*Palästinischer Diwan*), E. Littmann (*Neuarabische Volkpoesie*), and A. Musil (*Arabia Petraea*).

[68] Suggested in biblical texts/contexts (see below); see Ellen Koskoff, ed., *Women and Music in Cross-Cultural Perspective* (Urbana, IL: Univ. of Illinois, 1989).

[69] Paul Wayne Ferris, Jr., *The Genre of Communal Lament in the Bible and the Ancient Near East* (Atlanta: Scholars Press, 1992), 27, 74–75.

[70] Ju 11:37–38; Jer 9:16, 19; Ps 32:11.

[71] P. Ferris, *Genre of Communal Lament*, 78.

[72] H. Jahnow, *Hebräische Leichenlied*, 3, 5–6, 55.

[73] Margaret Alexiou, *The Ritual Lament in Greek Tradition* (Cambridge: Cambridge Univ. Press, 1974).

[74] T. H. Gaster, *Thespis* (N.Y.: Harper, 1950), 369, cited in Ferris, *Genre of Communal Lament*, 75.

[75] Jer 9:16, 19; 2 Chron 35:25. Associated with the performance of dirges and mourning is the *cessation* of joyful music or dancing (Isa 24:8, Jer 31:12; Ps 30:12; Job 30:31; Lam 5:15; Qoh 3:4; cf. Sot. 48a); *EJ*, 485–93.

[76] Jahnow, *Hebräische Leichenlied*, 3, 68.

[77] Susan Auerbach, "From Singing to Lamenting: Women's Musical Role in a Greek Village," in E. Koskoff, ed., *Women and Music*.

[78] R. Finnegan, *Oral Poetry*, 196.

[79] J. Nketia, *Funeral Dirges of the Akan People*, 2f, cited in R. Finnegan, *Oral Poetry*, 196.

[80] V. Karadžić's first volume of collected oral poetry was on women's songs, *Serpske narodne pjesme*, I, 1841; R. Pešić, *Rečnik književnih termina*, ed. D. Živković, 838–39; J. Saulić, "The Oral Women Poets of the Serbs," *Slavonic and East European Review* 42 (1963): 161–83; T. Perić-Polonijo, "Oral Poems," 381–99; B. Kerewsky-Halpern, "Text and Context," 52–60; Mary P. Coote, "Women's Songs in Serbo-Croatian," *Journal of American Folklore* 90 (1977): 331–38; J. M. Foley, *The Singer of Tales in Performance* (Bloomington & Indianapolis: Indiana Univ. Press, 1995), 106.

[81] Patricia Arant, "Aspects of Oral Styles: Russian Traditional Oral Lament," *Canadian-American Slavic Studies* 15 (1981): 42–51; H. and N. Chadwick, *The Growth of Literature*, vol. 2 (Cambridge: Cambridge Univ. Press, 1936), 229–32.

defined poems like love songs, dirges or wedding songs have such a wide incidence that they can be regarded as a near-universal aspect of human culture . . ." Yet she stresses, for example,

> in the *nyatiti* lament-songs of the East African Luo, too, there are different degrees of personal creativity by the singer. . . . Some perform from a relatively fixed repertoire—or from a set of basic structures, which, once learnt, can be modified to suit the circumstances of the funeral to which the singer has been summoned: he adds . . . any knowledge he may possess of the attributes of the deceased. But a gifted Luo singer creates a more individual and developed song, particularly when he is emotionally involved. The song may be so admired that he is asked to sing it again, after the funeral. When he does so, the poem often gains in detachment and depth—being freed from the solemnity of a funeral [it] may rove from the fate of a particular individual to that of other people.[82]

Dirges gathered by Mishael Caspi in the early 1980s, performed by Arab women in Galilee and the Golan Heights, demonstrate many of the same motifs highlighted by Jahnow in the early 1900s.[83] Caspi documented the process by which singers learn their craft and pass it down, noting that several women informants attested to the following custom:

> My grandmother was a eulogizer and my mother learned from her. When my mother was at home alone and remembered a member of her family who had passed away, she sang sorrowfully and mournfully about them. I learned these poems from her, and those who come after me will learn from me.[84]

Caspi also identified motifs in this culture not noted by Jahnow, including a vow to renounce joy and grieve forever, and to redeem the life of the deceased at all costs though the mourner knows this is impossible.

[82] R. Finnegan, *Oral Poetry*, 55, 58, 190, 260; see also idem, *Oral Literature in Africa* (Nairobi: Oxford Univ. Press, 1970). Cf. James A. Notopoulos and his reference to a sizable quantity of formulaic elements in early Greek elegy and in Hesiod's and Homer's works, "Homer, Hesiod and the Achaean Heritage of Oral Poetry," *Hespera* 29 (1960): 181.

[83] I.e., often a complaint/description of the death/disaster; its impact on survivors; praise for the deceased; a dialogue between the deceased and a mourning survivor; sorrow; demand for revenge for wrongdoing (though weakened from earlier periods); sometimes a curse; comfort given to surviving family; weeping; the motif, 'Ah! my brother'; and prayer to God; M. Caspi, "'My Brother, Vein of My Heart'," 28–40, also printed in a larger work that includes Arab women's lullabies and bridal songs; M. Caspi and J. Blessing, *Weavers of the Songs*.

[84] Ibid., 103.

The above findings shall be instructive for a reappraisal of an oral context that shaped biblical Lamentations. The other component in this study, to compare written lament poetry from the recent war context especially in Croatia and Bosnia to biblical Lamentations, will be aided by a basic understanding of the traditional singing of dirges and laments in this region, and to discern whether some traditional poetic elements may still be reflected in literary lament poetry from this region.

First, researchers in South Slavic culture(s) add to the knowledge delineated above. They identify the dirge song in that region as the *tužbalica* (and *naricaljka* refers to other oral lament poems over personal or national misfortune/grief).[85] The tužbalica is regarded as lyric poetry that shares some characteristics with epic poetry. The tužbalica appears as part of traditional, ritual mourning practice upon someone's death.[86] It is improvized (the same verb means "sing" and "compose": "ispjevati"), yet exhibits standard themes, poetic formula, and metrics (usually octosyllabic with tetrasyllabic refrains). Alliteration and assonance are often found in the refrains.[87] T. Perić-Polonijo notes that in Croatian dirges (similar or almost the same as other Slavic dirges), death is *not* named or proclaimed (cf. Jahnow's summary above), but death is often *personified* as a bride to a man who has died and departs, leaving his kinsfolk behind (thus analogies are drawn between funeral and wedding).[88] Stylistic features include hyperbole, similes, and antithesis.[89]

[85] Such a song might also be called *zapijevka/zapevka* (reflecting western/eastern dialects); R. Pešić, *Rečnik književnih termina*, ed. D. Živković, 838–39; T. Perić-Polonijo, "Oral Poems," 396.

[86] Standard features of the tužbalica song include praise/eulogy and remembrance of the deceased, expressions of mourning, a call/summons that the dead one return and thus break free from death, conversation with the dead one as though he or she still lived, belief there is a life after death similar to earthly life, and messages to the deceased from relatives; R. Pešić, *Rečnik književnih termina*, ed. D. Živković, 838–39; see examples in F. Kuhač, *Južno-slovjenske narodne popijevke*, vol. 5, 384–418; B. Kerewsky-Halpern writes that laments for the dead analyzed in Serbia from the 1950s to the 1970s were not primarily eulogies, but were especially characterized by direct conversation with the deceased. Changes in the dirges through these years included a shift away from epic-like narrative to more fragmented narratives interspersed with conversation with the dead and musings by mourners; "Text and Context," 52–60. See also J. Saulić, "The Oral Women Poets of the Serbs," 161–83.

[87] R. Pešić, *Rečnik književnih termina*, ed. D. Živković, 838–39.

[88] For an example of this parallel in a literary poem, see Dara Sekulić of Sarajevo, "The Sun Procession," in *Contemporary Poetry of Bosnia and Herzegovina*, ed. M. Suško, 43.

[89] T. Perić-Polonijo, "Oral Poems," 392–93.

The *tužbalica* is always sung in a sad melody, with wailing, and publicly performed most often by women[90] (often professional mourning singers) who, like the Palestinian women, have also learned the skill from their youth by imitating older women.[91] Women could perform a tužbalica alone, or two alternate singing as one laments and another mourns with her, repeating her words.[92] Also, a group of women may perform a tužbalica in which one singer is the lead and sings a line that is then taken up by each of the others.[93] Or in some areas every singer sings/composes a new line after singing the previous verses—thus a communally composed song. While formulaic features abide in the tužbalica, every performance is a "new" song with improvization and variation, responding to the context and the one who died.[94] This dialogic performance process, also similarly attested in other traditional cultures, is highly suggestive for the songs encoded in chapters 1, 2, and 4 of the book of Lamentations.

Returning to Jahnow's investigation of the dirge in Lamentations, she followed Lowth, Budde, and Gunkel in suggesting that both biblical prophetic rhetoric and Lamentations extraordinarily employ the dirge's customary elements in a "transfered" (*übertragen*) communal sense.[95] In prophetic judgment speeches, the dirge refers not usually to the death of an individual, but to a *personified* totality—the land, city, or kingdom—and to its anticipated *political destruction* (e.g., Am

[90] The singer might be called a *narikača, tužilica*, or *pokajnica*; R. Pešić, *Rečnik književnih termina*, ed. D. Živković, 838–39.

[91] Also Akan girls were expected to learn dirge-singing; R. Finnegan, *Oral Literature in Africa*, 166.

[92] J. M. Foley describes in Orašac, Serbia, "the closest female relative returning to the graveyard at least monthly to re-compose her mourning chant according to the rules of this particular genre"; *Singer of Tales in Performance*, 106.

[93] See "Elegiac Poetry" in R. Finnegan for dirge practices among different ethnic groups in Africa, including groups of women singing (non-dirge) laments (with leader and chorus) among the Limba and the Akan; she notes that in the Akan dirges the words are more important than the music, and the singer has great freedom in composition; *Oral Literature in* Africa, 147–66.

[94] R. Pešić, *Rečnik književnih termina*, ed. D. Živković, 838–39. I am in process of researching more detailed studies (from the late 1980s) on this topic in works of J. Bezić, T. Čubelić, V. Minić, S. Panović, E. Petrović, Š. Plana, R. Radenković, M. Rodić, Đ. Šehu, and N. Vinca.

[95] Jahnow, *Hebräische Leichenlied*, 162. See also H. Gunkel, "The Prophets as Writers and Poets" [orig. publ. 1923], in *Prophecy in Israel*, ed. D. Petersen (Philadelphia: Fortress Press, 1987), 22–73. One of Ruth Finnegan's conclusions about oral literature is that "the same genre can play very different roles in different circumstances, and can be changed *or* developed *or* held static according to the manifold intentions of the people concerned at any one time" (*Oral Poetry*, 260).

5:2: "Fallen no more to rise, Maiden Israel; abandoned upon her soil, no one is lifting her up").[96] Thus the primary function of this "communal dirge" genre[97] in the prophets is to express a national *self-critique* and *warning* that depicts possible, consequential future destruction.

Parts of the book of Lamentations also employ the communal dirge genre, but for a different but related function: to describe and mourn the actual fall of the nation's capital city that has gone forward as predicted.[98] In the book of Jeremiah, the voices of 'D. Zion', YHWH, and Jeremiah all use the communal dirge to depict the present destruction of Jerusalem.[99] Otherwise, this use of a communal dirge to describe immediate destruction is not widespread in the Hebrew Bible, though it is always found in prophetic texts.[100]

Also in South Slavic cultures the traditional dirge historically was adapted for an oral communal dirge (*naricaljka*) for national or community tragedy. These adapted dirge songs exhibit even greater improvisation as, by definition, they are not limited to a ritual context as are dirges for an individual's death.[101] In specific South Slavic regions where many battles and wars were fought, where death was a more frequent occurrence, a type of traditional *war* dirge/lament developed, a genre related to heroic oral epic poetry. Such war dirges by soldiers, performed publicly, had an ideological aim: mourning

[96] NRSV. Jahnow, *Hebräische Leichenlied*, 164.

[97] I refrain from employing the terms "political" or "national" for the *type* of dirge in Lamentations and the prophets, since these adjectives are related more to *how* communal dirges may be employed, for political or national ends, rather than to their subject, *communal* destruction.

[98] In ancient Mesopotamian lamentations over the destruction of cities, the priests sang the communal dirge rather than a prophet, as in the Hebrew tradition. These works are performed by the *gala*-priests using the *emesal* dialect; there is some speculation that they may have been women; Mark E. Cohen, *The Canonical Lamentations of Ancient Mesopotamia* (Potomac, Md.: Capital Decisions Limited, 1988), 13–14. Such works are found on the destruction of Constantinople and cities in Greece; F. W. Dobbs-Allsopp, *Weep, O Daughter of Zion*, 22–23.

[99] As in Jer 2:14–16; 4:19–21, 23–26, 29, 31; 8:21–23; 9:9, 18, 20; 10:19–20, 22; 12:10–12; 13:19; 14:2–6,17–18; 25:34.

[100] Elsewhere it occurs in Isa 1:7–8; Jo 1–2:10, and in Nah 2–3 (regarding Ninevah). Cf. the variant use of communal dirge in an eschatological vision of unfolding destruction in Isa 24:4–12; cf. the similar descriptions of destruction of Jerusalem (possibly in 587), though in a different genre—the communal lament (prayer) psalms, 74:3–9 and 79:1–4; cf. also Ps 44.

[101] T. Perić-Polonijo, "Oral Poems," 391, 396. This may be suggestive for biblical Lamentations as a communal dirge.

the loss of national glory while constructing a national socio-political ideal.[102]

Some literary poems written in the recent wars become a modern type of national or communal dirge/lament that mourns the losses. For example, in his poem "Karlovac za Obranu" Slavko Mihalić (set in the town of Karlovac, Croatia, being bombarded by artillary) carries on a monologue with his father who died a few years earlier and laments to him the current disaster, drawing allusions to other historical battles.[103] Beyond motifs of placing blame, critiquing one's enemies, or sometimes advocating one's nation, such mourning renders with poignant artistry the universal outcry against premature death and loss that oddly enough binds humans together. Bosnian-Croat Borislav Arapović wrote "the last minute of physics: to the high school students who fell defending their homeland":

he stood behind the ruin of a wall
near the end of the morning watch
a freezing gun barrel in his hand
the wind in the nape of his neck
and high-school circles amid his lashes
*
and the lightning struck
his forehead
releasing fingers and circles
scattering formulae from under the helmet
and while tracing the line of his fall
confirmed
the law of gravity

1993 03 12[104]

Serbian poet Milan Mihajlović reflects this lament in this selection from "A Soldier's Shirt":

. . . Trenches protect a man only to cover him,
as the sickle cuts a swath only to spawn,
as the earth gives birth only to bury its dead,
as the Sun will not set only forever shine.

[102] R. Pešić, *Rečnik književnih termina*, ed. D. Živković, 838–39. Any such oral communal dirges from recent context might be instructive.

[103] In *U ovom strašnom Času: Antologia suvremene hrvatske ratne lirike* (In This Terrible Moment: Anthology of Contemporary Croatian War Poetry), eds. Ivo Sanader and Ante Stamać (Zagreb: Školska knjiga, 1994), 61–62. English translation forthcoming from Školska knjiga.

[104] Transl. I. Jerić, in *Between Despair and Lamentation*, 33.

And still the soldier's shirt, stain-filled, unbuttoned,
in the cold and soft trench lies sleeping
with the gun beside it awaiting a new hand
—all this on the verge of a new century . . .

On the Old Square, May 4, 1999[105]

Heroic epic poetry by various South Slavic peoples has had a great deal to do with developing national identity and battling for independence while under the thumb of various imperial powers through the centuries.[106] A sympathetic view of such poetry, and its influence upon later literary poets, is given in G. Champe's overview in *Contemporary Yugoslav Poetry* (ed. V. Mihailovich). She also traces the journey, and dilemma, of literary poets in 20th c. Yugoslavia under pressures by the national socialist state.[107]

[105] Transl. Biljana D. Obradović and John Gery, selection from *Kletva* (Curse), a poetry anthology, reprinted by permission of Association of Writers of Serbia (2001), 201–202; forthcoming in English. In the introduction to this anthology, B. Obradović writes that the earlier edition of the volume contained about 250 authors from 20 countries, including poets in Serbia and abroad and well-known figures such as Gabriel Garcia Marquez and Aleksandar Solzhenitsyn, who wrote out of solidarity with those suffering during the NATO bombing of Serbia. While NATO soldiers were sent to the region, they were protected from having to fight in a ground war (thus no dirges), but were used to operate the technology that could strike from a distance.

[106] For example, according to G. Champe, "Serbian literature, [formerly] written in Old Church Slavic, was independent and fruitful during the early Middle Ages. After the Turks gained a major stronghold in Serbia in 1389, literature, sheltered by a decimated Orthodox Church, took on a popular folkloristic coloration. In the late seventeenth and early eighteenth centuries, Serbian literature underwent a strong influence from Russia [seat of the Orthodox mother church] and became an ornate and rarefied phenomenon, infinitely remote from the spoken language of the people . . . Austrian influence also resulted in estrangement that was actively fostered by the Serbian Orthodox Church . . . Most of the credit for returning the Serbian language to the people is usually given to the philologist Vuk Stefanović Karadžić (1787–1864). It was he who urged the adoption of a single dialect [and written language based on] . . . the folklore of Serbia, Croatia, and all the regions between, of which he was a pioneering collector"; Preface, *Contemporary Yugoslav Poetry* (Iowa City: Iowa Univ. Press, 1977), 13. Karadžić also translated the New Testament into Croatian for the first time, using Luther's version; see N. Lee and B. Arapović, "The Bible in Political Context: New Republics from Old Yugoslavia and Former Soviet Union", *Interpretation* (October, 2001). On a more negative view of Karadžić, see also below. Svetozar Koljević also notes the ambiguous attitude through Slavic history by the Church (Orthodox and Catholic) toward folk songs; e.g., the early Catholic animosity toward folk singing in the Balkans, while nevertheless translating hymns from Latin to the vernacular; "Folk Traditions in Serbo-Croatian Literary Culture," *Oral Tradition* 6/1 (1991): 3.

[107] An esp. important figure was the poet Miroslav Krleža; G. Champe, Preface, *Contemporary Yugoslav Poetry*, 11–41.

While some South Slavic literary poetry bears elements from oral epic,[108] some poets also draw upon traditional oral dirge and lament motifs as noted above (like address of the dead, weeping).[109] Two of the most accomplished poets from the region draw extensively on such motifs, not surprisingly, in light of the past century's wars and suffering in the region. Especially noteworthy is Bosnian poet, Mak Dizdar.[110] In his classic *Kameni spavač* (Stone Sleeper, 1966), he looks for the meaning of inscriptions on *stećci*, ancient tombstones in Bosnia and Herzegovina.[111] Also, Croatian poet, Jure Kaštelan, drew on his experiences in WWII and used elegiac themes in his work,[112] such as "Lament of a Stone," in which a personified stone ironically pleas not with God, but with humans to be removed from all painful human associations:

> Return me to the rock masses, the cliffs, the mountain ranges.
> Return my innocence to the laws of eternity.
> . . . Rulers of the earth, give me peace and sleep.
> Let not your armies clang with their hooves.
> Let not the tears flow.
> Tear me up from the pavement and the streets, from the thresholds of prisons and cathedrals.
> Let tempests and lightning beat upon me. . . .[113]

[108] See a brief discussion of specific poets in Koljević, "Folk Traditions," 3–18; see further examples in V. Mihailovich, ed., *Contemporary Yugoslav Poetry*. Champe notes the prosody of oral poetry can also be detected in literary poems in the original language; also, peculiar beyond the many usual poetic devices are frequent onomatopoeia, and "large families of words may be built on the same root"; Preface, ibid., 34, 38.

[109] E.g., motif of silence of death in Borislav Arapović's "Silence," *Between Despair and Lamentation*, 5; motif of burial occurs in B. Arapović's "On the Chessboard," ibid., 11; C. Vipotnik's "Burial" (127–28); motif of prayer occurs in B. Miljković's "Requiem (VIII)" (156); motif of addressing the dead occurs in D. Maksimović's "The Snow on the Grave" (7), in I. Lalić's "Spring Liturgy for Branko Miljković: 1934–61" (118–22); in D. Horvatić's "The Back of the Devil" (196), in R. Pavlovski's "A Young Man Who Sleeps at Noon" (198–99); the motif of the dead person speaking appears in S. Janevski's "The Poem of a Soldier Six Feet Under the Ground" (29), and I. Lalić's "Voices of the Dead" (113); pages cited are in V. Milhailovich, ed. and transl., *Contemporary Yugoslav Poetry*.

[110] My special thanks to Ivo Marković for sharing Dizdar's work with me.

[111] See esp. the poem "Gorčin", an incription for the soldier; V. Mihailovich, ed. *Contemporary Yugoslav Poetry*, 15. See also L. Simović's "Epitaphs from Karansko Cemetery" and "Epitaph", ibid., 168–70.

[112] See also e.g., "Lullaby of Knives" and "Into Darkness"; ibid., 20–23.

[113] Ante Kadič, "Postwar Croatian Lyric Poetry," *American Slavic and East European Review* 17 (1958): 528.

Literary poets may also reflect other oral traditional stylistic features relevant to the present study, for example according to S. Koljević, "an intimate relationship between nature and personal, or collective, fate").[114] Josip Pupačić expresses this union positively:

and I look at the sea as it foams up to me
and I listen as the sea says good morning
and it listens to me I whisper
o good morning sea I say softly
then again more softly renew my greeting
while the sea listens then laughs
then is silent then laughs then foams. . . .[115]

Sergio Zupičić drew on this theme to express his tragic loss in his poem "Vukovar" (one of the first towns to fall under siege in 1991, and probably the worst devastated). A portion I have roughly translated here; he compares his tears and loss of loved one: "Tomorrow I will no longer have any tears for crying/they will fade like blades of grass. . . ."[116]

Two poets cited above, Borislav Arapović and Biljana Obradović, who sometimes use motifs of death to mourn suffering in the recent wars,[117] whose countries opposed one another, yet show a poignant convergence of pathos in referring to the fate of the "poppy", a wildflower common in the region.[118] B. Arapović was in his native Bosnia during much of the war and wrote "poppies in dalj town" (the name "dalj" is related to "daljni", meaning distant/faraway):

red poppies
white acacia
blue sky

[114] E.g., in Mažuranić, "fine dew, as if heaven were weeping," in *The Death of Smail-aga Čengić* (I. 824); S. Koljević, "Folk Traditions," 7.

[115] A. Kadić, "Postwar Croatian Lyric, 521.

[116] In *U ovom strašnom Času*, eds., I. Sanader and A. Stamać, 123. See also the Bosnian anthology *Nisam mrtav samo sam zemlju zagrlio* (I am not Dead, I only embraced the Earth), eds. Simun Musa and Gojko Susać (Mostar, 1995). I was not able to obtain a copy of this book yet.

[117] See also B. Obradović, "For Your Souls (*The Day of the Dead*)," in *Frozen Embraces* (Center for Emigrants from Serbia, and Cross-Cultural Communications, 2000; 1998), 100.

[118] Interestingly, both of these poets express a kind of 'exile's' lament. The nature of poetry written by people from the region who now live abroad would be a study in itself.

and then they came
and did their deed

so that at dawn
there was no difference
between the squashed petals of poppies
and the splashed petals of blood

1993 03 07[119]

Writing from a location distant from her homeland, Biljana writes in "Blooming in Death":

Large red poppies bloom outside the window
in someone else's garden and I can only watch
not get close enough . . .
They are an illusion that may disappear if I come closer.
All my plants are dying, even the newly planted geraniums
that were ready to bloom, seem to know somehow
life cannot, in the midst of death, sorrow,
despair, but must be a part of mourning.
Amidst prosperity a tiny patch of homelessness,
hunger for hope, a new direction, a way out.
Why have we killed each other, burnt our own homes?
Will we ever again be able to see red poppies in bloom
in our gardens? Be able to have someone else admiring them.[120]

In "Close Pulse" Dara Sekulić of Sarajevo writes,

We're like desolate wood
Tree by tree like dense ribs
linked by deep roots.
When one is felled another's branch snaps.
Falling it leans against its fellow. . . .[121]

Also very common is the oral traditional feature already seen, *personification*. It is often employed by biblical poets (see below in Lamentations). Zlatko Tomičić personifies the earth in "Zemlja":

Now the heavy earth awakes, moves its body from empty sleep.
It hides its face in mists, stretches, but does not rise.
Still it lies and does not breathe,
but deeply, languidly rumbles. . . .[122]

[119] Transl. I. Jerić, in *Between Despair and Lamentation*, 32.
[120] From Biljana Obradović, in *Frozen Embraces*, 106.
[121] In M. Suško, transl. and ed., *Contemporary Poetry of Bosnia*, 45.
[122] A. Kadić, "Postwar Croatian Lyric," 512.

Especially pertinent to the present study, one finds *the city or village personified* by South Slavic poets, ("the dear streets sleep under the snow [and] kiss me with their silence") in Milivoj Slaviček's poem, "The City Loves Me So When It is Deserted and White."[123] Abdulah Sidran of Sarajevo personified the city in "Sarajevo Speaks: I am an Island, in the Heart of the World."[124] Another example of personifying Sarajevo by Sidran can be seen, in the context of recent war, in his poem (cited below) "Planet Sarajevo" in *A Blind Man Sings to His City*. Monasteries "come alive . . . addressed not as a building but as an animate being" in Vasko Popa's *Earth Erect*: "You stride towards your heights/And high love/In the only possible direction" (1972).[125] Also, Cene Vipotnik, imprisoned in WWII, wrote in "Hard Times" that war "left gaping shot wounds" in a nearby wall.[126] Abdulah Sidran wrote a poem in which he describes giving away "the most beautiful books from my family library" to many people during the war as thanks for helping him: "Empty places in the shelves/remember their names/and weep/in the darkness."[127] Note also the contrast motif typical of a dirge.

And death is often personified, and sometimes linked to the fragility of human relationships, as in "Death is Certain" by Ranko Risojević: "Man, don't peek out, don't look through the cracks, she's there, by the well . . . Fascinated, she admires you, while you dominate the stage. . . ."[128] Also in "Death, Dine with Me," the poet Džemaludin Alić says to death sitting across the table, ". . . Find a face,

[123] In V. Mihailovich, ed. and transl., *Contemporary Yugoslav Poetry*, 94.

[124] In M. Suško, transl. and ed., *Contemporary Poetry of Bosnia*, 99.

[125] S. Koljević, "Folk Traditions," 15.

[126] In V. Mihailovich, ed., *Contemporary Yugoslav Poetry*, transl. R. Zrimc, 126. See also other examples in works written before the recent wars, B. Gjuzel's personification of stone in "Homage to Stone," ibid., 209–11, transl., C. Simic. Dubravka Horvatić personifies the future of dead warriors in "The Back of the Devil": "their future has been here for some time . . . it walks the streets, works and sleeps at night . . . it is more learned and shrewder than it could be thought at the youthful time of marching songs"; ibid., transl. V. Mihailovich, 196. Matija Bećković personifies everything a poem might contain in "No One Will Write Poetry Any More," because "The immortal themes will abandon the poems/Unhappy with the way they were understood and versified." "Sea", "sunset", and "sky" will all get up and leave poetry. "So poems will attack poets demanding that they fulfill their promises"; ibid., transl. C. Simic, 207–8.

[127] Transl., Dubravka Dostal, in *The Blind Man Sings to His City*, ed., I. Spahić (Sarajevo: Međunarodni centar za mir, 1997), 29.

[128] In M. Suško, ed. and transl., *Contemporary Poetry of Bosnia*, 93–94.

take up a trade,/rest your industrious hands/that strangled all my beloveds. . . ."[129]

In contrast, Abdulah Sidran wrote "The Woman's Song" (in context of recent war in Sarajevo) in which she speaks of death personified, "a great evil, which walks around, comes into your house, enters your soul . . . the horror that walks." When the woman laments, "shells were falling . . . one even came into our room and he didn't embrace me," the poetry renders a painful yet parallel ambiguity between death personified and her loved one: "had he embraced me just once/for me the war would have been over . . . all I needed was his embrace."[130] Snežana Ivković wrote from the context of the recent war in Serbia, but from her location in North America, "On the Day the Birds of Death Took off for the Thirty-Ninth Time: A Love Letter." She says, ". . . (I avoid putting in the poem anything not yours or mine,/I avoid it so you won't suspect my encounters with Death/on the park path where I walk; sneering at me, unveiled,/Death tells me her vultures have released the sun for us this time). . . ."[131]

These examples of literary lament poetry from the context of the recent wars also reflect something of the continuing living influence of oral traditional elements on South Slavic writers. The selections are not intended to mis-characterize those writers or to overemphasize certain motifs indicative of modern periods, nor to say that the elegiac elements have been dominant.[132] Rather, it is to share something of the beauty and force of these poets' expressions, and to suggest that if a literary culture still bears traditional oral elements in its modern poetry, then even moreso the written poetry emerging within the oral period of a traditional culture like ancient Israel shall likely reflect much of its oral poetry. Thus biblical Lamentations can be more fully interpreted if its oral dimensions encoded in the text are better understood, and recognized as referring to a long, ongoing poetic tradition and participating in a large poetic world. Of course, native South Slavic poets would cast their large world for us far better than I. But in the analysis of Lamentations below, I will quote and compare additional works of South Slavic poets

[129] Ibid., 127–28.
[130] In *The Blind Man Sings to His City*, transl., D. Dostal, 19.
[131] Transl. B. Obradović and J. Gery, in *Kletva* (Curse), 222–23.
[132] Of course the large and complex question of traditional oral influence upon literary poetry in South Slavic cultures is a task for native experts.

who wrote during the recent wars to see what further light they might shed on those ancient poems.

While elements of epic tradition are at work in varying degrees in South Slavic literary poetry, it has also functioned in recent socio-political ideology and war. One is compelled to ask to what extent scholars and social commentators have been sufficiently cognizant of the *socio-political functions* of epic traditions developing in recent context?[133] That nationalistic ideologies of superiority using poetic and/or ethnoreligious mythologies always hold potentially explosive and deadly power should come as no surprise to former imperialist nations and current world powers.[134] Lord Raglan in 1937, suggested that the version of the Serbian epic of the Battle of Kosovo he knew (or heard) seemed to be "politio-religious propaganda."[135] Albert Lord alluded in different writings[136] to the interaction of South Slavic epic poetry and war contexts, and to later politicizing of national epic. For example, in *The Singer of Tales* he writes that in the early 19th c. when epics were being collected and written down, "nationalism was rife and the chauvinism of the day, a chauvinism *not inherent in the tradition itself* but fostered by nationalistic and political forces *outside*

[133] No doubt prophetic voices of lament within former Yugoslavia and among her citizens living abroad raised alarm of impending disaster before the 1990s, but did they have a hearing beyond the region? (The same could be asked for many trouble spots in the world.) When war broke out in Croatia, the international media was slow even to realize or report it. When they did focus attention on Bosnia next, the voices were nearly always those of nationalistic political or military strategists, and slowly moving foreign interveners. Later, the justified premise of preventing Milošević's potential or real action against Muslim Albanians (after his policy of genocide against Bosnian Muslims) was morally compromised, some think, by NATO's bombing Serbia. Outside voices rarely spoke up about the possible injustice of it, or whether it even conformed to "just war" principles.

[134] Whether one observes it in colonizing patterns in the Americas or Europe in the 1930s and 40s and the action that sparked WWI in Sarajevo.

[135] In *The Hero: A Study in Tradition, Myth, and Drama* (New York: Oxford Univ. Press, 1937), 113.

[136] Also in *The Singer of Tales*, 7: "The fever of nationalism in the nineteenth century led to the use of oral epics for nationalistic propaganda . . ."; see also Lord, "The Effect of the Turkish Conquest on Balkan Epic Tradition," in *Aspects of the Balkans: Continuity and Change*, ed. H. Birnbaum and S. Vryonis, Jr. (The Hague: Mouton, 1972), 298–318; "The Nineteenth Century Revival of National Literatures: Karadžić, Njegoš, Radičević, the Illyrians, and Prešeren," in *Multinational Literature of Yugoslavia*, ed., A. B. Lord (New York: St. John's University, 1974), 101–11; "The Battle of Kosovo in Albanian and Serbocroatian Oral Epic Songs," in *Studies on Kosovo*, eds. A. Pipa and S. Repishti (New York: Columbia University Press, 1984), 65–83.

the tradition, was unfortunately mirrored in the songs" (emphasis added).[137] But surely "the tradition's" epic songs before the 19th c. could not be so pure of any trace of cultural, political, or religious chauvinism? On the other hand, constant contemporary references to ancient hatreds among the peoples are unfounded, as the region has also nurtured a longstanding multi-ethnic culture,[138] while major nationalistic conflicts have been primarily located in the 20th century.[139]

Yet, in what strikes one as prophetic in 1986, Michael Nagler, in "On Almost Killing Your Friends: Some Thoughts on Violence in Early Cultures," called scholars to focus not only on abstract theory of oral tradition, but also to

> take its normative debate seriously. We should recall the corrective influence of anthropologists like Malinowsky and Radcliffe-Brown, who pointed out the function of myth in validating social contracts at a time when armchair philologists were speculating about solar mythology or year demons, but we should go further. We should ask ourselves how well did these ideologies about violence or other social issues *work*? . . . To what degree are we ourselves still guided by, perhaps still betrayed by, the same ideologies today? It is a propitious time to take this final step . . . The age of cultural imperialism when the work of "unlettered bards" could not be taken seriously by the learned is well behind us . . . But most importantly, we are in enough trouble to need any and all help in mastering the social problems which we share. . . .[140]

In 1996, after the wars subsided in Croatia and Bosnia, Michael Sells in *The Bridge Betrayed* critiqued the anti-Turkish/anti-Muslim attitudes expressed in Njegoš's *Mountain Wreath* (1847).[141] While some may find reasons to critique Sells' treatment,[142] I cite a passage as

[137] *Singer of Tales*, 136.

[138] See Dzevad Karahasan's poignant description of life in Sarajevo as it was (quoted below); *Sarajevo: Exodus of a City*, transl., S. Drakulić (New York: Kodansha Intercommunal, 1994).

[139] M. Sells, *Bridge Betrayed*, xiv–xv; N. Lee and B. Arapović, "The Bible in Political Context."

[140] In *Comparative Research on Oral Traditions*, ed. J. M. Foley, 452–53.

[141] Sells is a Serbian American professor of religion.

[142] See the review by theologian Miroslav Volf of Croatia who disagrees with Sells' possible implication that the war and genocide in Bosnia were *primarily* "religiously motivated and justified." Volf suggests political, economic, and cultural forces were the primary causes which also used religion as a motivating and legitimizing factor; *Journal of the American Academy of Religion* 67 (1999): 250–53.

it illumines the potential of traditional poetry's socio-political roles resulting in unacceptable horrific ends:

> In 1829, Serbia was granted autonomy from Ottoman rule.... The Kosovo legends became part of the Serbian revolutionary movement.... As early as 1814, Vuk Karadžić had begun to emphasize the importance of the story of Lazar and Kosovo.... The portrayal of Lazar as a Christ figure, Kosovo as a Serb Golgotha, and Muslims as the evil brood of "cursed Hagar" was [sic] to be found in sermons and chronicles.... The key figure in the reconstruction of the Lazar story was... Njegoš... *The Mountain Wreath*... [is] considered by many Serb nationalists to be the central work of all Serbian literature.... [It] portrays and glorifies the Christmas Eve extermination of Slavic Muslims at the hands of Serb warriors....[143] Shortly after the appearance of Njegoš's *Mountain Wreath*, the feast day of St. Lazar... began to take on increased importance. In the 1860s the feast day of Prince Lazar was combined with the feast day of Vid... a pre-Christian Slavic god.... In 1892 Vid's Day appeared for the first time as an official holiday in the church calendar.... It was on Vid's Day in 1914 that Gavrilo Princep, who had memorized Njegoš's *Mountain Wreath*, assassinated Archduke Ferdinand and set off World War I.... On the occasion of the 600th anniversary [Kosovo, 1989] of Lazar's martyrdom, the resurgent Serb nationalists began to harness excitement in order to heighten the symbolism of the event.... A Serb writer exclaimed in 1989, "Is there anything more beautiful, more sincere and more profound than those pictures and verses [of Njegoš] written out from memory, not dictated by learned people or copied out of collected words...."[144]

[143] Koljević tries to give a more nuanced and contextual reading of the composition of *The Mountain Wreath*, suggesting that in his written epic, Njegoš actually recast the character of Bishop Danilo, who in oral epic versions cries, "Let us slaughter Turks in Montenegro!", but who in Njegoš's version is repulsed at the idea, yet is powerless to resist the forces that carry it out. Koljević's implication is that Njegoš's literary epic presents more of the ambiguity of the leader's moral dilemma than the oral versions; Njegoš himself was not only a poet but the prince-bishop of Montenegro; *Folk Traditions*, 7–10.

[144] *Bridge Betrayed*, 37–39, 41–51. Sells suggests that up to the 19th c., the most famous and influential oral epic hero in Serbia was Prince Marko Kraljević, who served as a mediating figure between the Serbian Orthodox and Ottoman Muslims; ibid., 37–38. Sells goes on to say,

> Radovan Karadžić likes to appear in public with a *gusle*, the stick-fiddle used by bards to recite epic poetry.... His soldiers are accompanied by *gusle* players. As the *gusle* player sings, the Serb soldiers pass around an alcoholic drink and make the sign of the cross before drinking. They sing: "Serb brothers, wherever you are, with the help of Almighty God/For the sake of the Cross and the Christian Faith and our imperial fatherland/I call you to join the bat-

How enemies are portrayed in politico-religious traditions evokes a question as to how the poets of biblical Lamentations (and other biblical laments) dealt with this matter in struggling to understand its defeat in war, and the suffering of its people—ancient Israel (see below).

Returning to Lamentations, through the 20th century most scholars who analyzed its genres[145] followed Gunkel[146] and Jahnow, including the former's suggestion that Lam 1, 2, and 4, while essentially communalized dirges, also reflect a mixture of dirge and lament (prayer), and that Lam 3 contains an individual lament, and Lam 5 a communal lament. We may pause here to note that there is a consensus in form critical scholarship (in biblical studies) on the basic difference between these two genres—the dirge and the lament. While both genres deal with the general topic of suffering and loss, the lament prayer (modeled in many psalms) is essentially a *plea* addressed to the deity for intervention for help (thus it is characterized by second person speech). The dirge, on the other hand, *forewarns against* or *commemorates* the fact of a death and/or destruction (and usually employs third person speech).[147]

The scholarly consensus on the genres of Lamentations was challenged by C. Westermann in his 1990 commentary. He diverged sharply from Jahnow's basic conclusion.[148] Westermann suggested that while there are some elements of the dirge in Lam 1, 2, and 4, these are insufficient to label any of the texts as clearly representing

tle of Kosovo." . . . He speaks of the *gusle* epics as being songs of "our people" . . . thus using them to divide Serb from Slavic Muslim. Such a definition of "our people" ignores the fact that the *gusle* epics were a major aspect of folk culture for both Muslim Slavs and Orthodox Serbs, who shared the same epic traditions, conventions, and sensibility. Christoslavism . . . was critical to the genocidal ideology being developed in 1989. . . . In their acts of genocide from 1992 through 1995, Radovan Karadžić and his followers integrated the Kosovo tradition . . . into the daily rituals of ethnoreligious purification (ibid., 50–51).

[145] E.g., W. Rudolph, M. Haller, Eissfeldt, F. Nötscher, N. Gottwald, E. Dhorme, O. Plöger, D. Hillers, H. Boecker; see Westermann summary of scholarship in *Lamentations*.

[146] H. Gunkel and J. Begrich, *Einleitung in die Psalmen: Die Gattungen der religiösen Lyrik Israels* (Göttingen: Vandenhoeck & Ruprecht, 1933), 136, 397–403.

[147] In sum, a lament appeals to the *deity* for an intervening response of help; a prophetic dirge appeals to the *people* for a response, if the destruction has not yet happened.

[148] For Westermann's full argument against Jahnow, see *Lamentations*, 1–11.

the dirge genre. The genre of these chapters and all of the book, Westermann claimed, is the *lament* ("plaintive lament," as prayer) or *Leidklage*,[149] such as are found in the psalms. He suggested these laments do contain some elements of the dirge due to the context of destruction and death.[150] It is important to note that Jahnow did not fail to see that Lam 1, 2, and 4, as communal dirges, also contained elements from the communal lament (prayer) psalms.[151] Westermann, however, wanted to invert Jahnow's conclusion on the primary genre, from dirge to lament.

Westermann's definition of the lament includes the following variable elements: address of the deity, three-fold complaint (to/against the deity, against one's enemies, and about one's suffering), confession of trust in the deity, petition to the deity, assurance of being heard, vow of praise, and praise of the deity. Only the petition and the complaint to/against the deity are always present in a lament, while the other elements may vary.[152] In my view, an analysis of the genre elements in Lam 1 and 2 nevertheless reveals that lament elements, uttered particularly by the voice usually labeled as "D. Zion", do not occur in greater measure than communal dirge elements uttered by the other voice (see discussion below). Thus Westermann's claim, that *the lament* is the primary genre of each chapter and of the entire book of Lamentations, is unconvincing.

Rather than conclude, as both Jahnow and Westermann do, that one genre dominates the other in Lamentations, this study suggests the poets intentionally use both genres in Lamentations. They are held in tension, yet work together for certain purposes, and both

[149] Westermann, ibid., 9. It is the case that the general term in English, 'lament,' is often used indiscriminately and unhelpfully to refer to dirge/mourning speech or to plea prayer speech, and the same problem in meaning may occur with the general German word, 'Klage,' if not clarified, according to Westermann, *Praise and Lament in the Psalms*, 170.

[150] C. Westermann, *Lamentations*, 7–8. E. Cothenet had suggested that Lamentations in general more closely resembles the lament than the dirge genre; "Lamentations" in *Dictionnaire Catholicisme hier, aujourdhui, demain* (1967) 6: 1725–32.

[151] Jahnow, *Hebräische Leichenlied*, 168–69, 174. One might say instead that in Lamentations a singer of communal dirges appears side by side with a singer of laments (prayers). In his ongoing study of meter in Lamentations, David Noel Freedman has reaffirmed Budde's basic recognition of the *qina* (dirge) meter, though with variations, in Lam 1–4; "Acrostic Poems in the Hebrew Bible: Alphabetic and Otherwise," in *Divine Commitment and Human Obligation*, ed. J. Huddlestun (Grand Rapids: Wm. B. Eerdmans, 1997; orig. publ. 1986), 184.

[152] C. Westermann, *Praise and Lament in the Psalms*, 52–81, 165–213.

reflect serious modifications from their occurrence elsewhere in biblical texts due to this context of extreme crisis. In fact, the modifications will help to illumine the originating socio-historical context.[153]

The significances of these genres have not been completely recognized by commentators. For example, there is another attested purpose of the dirge genre across cultures recognized by Jahnow but overlooked by scholars in the last century. That is, the dirge serves a formal social function in a community by raising "*the voice of public justice*" (*die Stimme der öffentlichen Gerechtigkeit*) when the dirge or funeral singer *identifies and accuses the murderer* who caused a death.[154] In this case, as Jahnow explained, the usual "complaint" about death in the dirge moves to "accusation" against the perpetrator:

> When a murder is dealt with, then often the voice of public justice is raised at the bier of the slain in the form of the funeral complaint (*Leichenklage*). Here *the complaint becomes the accusation* (*die Klage zur Anklage*), and often the name of the murderer is intoned by the lips of the funeral singer for the first time.[155]

Jahnow also noted that this voice of justice is implicitly linked to the motif of the "spirit" or "ghost" (*Geist*) of the slain one itself crying out for justice or revenge against the perpetrator[156] (analogous to the

[153] That both these genres serve important purposes in context is also argued by T. Linafelt who suggests that in Lam 1 and 2 "the combination of the genres is not haphazard or confused. Rather it participates in the fundamental dynamic of survival literature . . .: the paradox of life in death and death in life"; *Surviving Lamentations*, 75.

[154] H. Jahnow, *Hebräische Leichenlied*, 88.

[155] Emphasis added. Here is Jahnow's full statement: "Wenn es sich um einen Mord handelt, dann erhebt sich oft an der Bahre des Erschlagenen die Stimme der öffentlichen Gerechtigkeit in der Form der Leichenklage. Hier wird die Klage zur Anklage, und oft ertönt von den Lippen der Leichensängerin zum ersten Mal der name des Mörders" (ibid.).

[156] Jahnow cites the practice in modern-day Corsica of the dirge-singer's displaying a bloody article of clothing from the victim's body as a way to evoke blood vengeance, as well as the attested practice in Corsica in a Christian dirge of an exhortation to forgive the enemy; ibid., 88, 171. Jahnow gives other examples of dirges from modern cultures (including Palestine) in which the accusation against the perpetrator aims to serve public justice; including in Bearn in France, Sardinia, and Corsica, where, for example, one dirge singer complains about the violent actions of the perpetrator, another calls for vengeance in the pursuit and punishment of the perpetrator, and another dirge calls for the perpetrator to remove himself from the community before vengeance is enacted. In Corsica at least, often the complaint over the murdered victim in the dirge even aims to evoke a *confession* from the perpetrator; ibid., 89. Zora Neale Hurston notes a similar belief in the folklore of African-American slaves, that the murderer is harrassed by the spirit of

biblical text of Gen 4:10 wherein the blood of Abel cries out against Cain).[157] S. Kramer had noted the elements of accusation and revenge in an ancient Mesopotamian dirge from Nippur (c. 1700 BCE).[158] In light of these findings, Westermann's attempt to subsume all accusations in Lamentations under the biblical lament prayer genre misses a potentially important part of the wider cultural and socio-rhetorical context.

Instead, the poems of Lamentations that are communal dirges should be seriously considered in light of this popular social use of the dirge.[159] Indeed, the poetic singers' striking adaptation of the accusation of the dirge will be seen below to participate in their indictment of YHWH, who is charged with the deaths of innocent ones and administering punishment that is unjust in its excessiveness. Recognition of this dynamic will help balance a scholarly over-emphasis on the poets' theme in Lamentations of Jerusalem's sin and punishment.[160] And while the lament genre's accusation of one's enemies, including YHWH, is certainly at work in Lamentations as scholars have seen, the dirge genre nevertheles joins forces with it to offer its own accusation. In this and in sharing descriptions of suffering, these two different genres are engaged as vehicles to convey

their victim and often forced to confess; *The Sanctified Church* (Berkeley: Turtle Island, 1983), 21. Jahnow suggests that in the Hebrew Bible in 2 Sam 3:33f with David's dirge for Abner, by not publicly expressing an accusation against nor identifying his murderer, David *undermines the foundation of public justice* by leaving the matter of the murder, the justice and the vengeance to YHWH; meanwhile the author has ('politically') presented a favorable impression of David with his act of mourning; *Hebräische Leichenlied*, 89–90. Cf. Deut 21:1–9 for the law and ritual requirement for an unsolved murder where the nearest city's elders must come forward and confess that they were not responsible for the death in order to absolve themselves and the city from bloodguilt; Moshe Weinfeld, *Deuteronomy and the Deuteronomic School* (Winona Lake, Ind.: Eisenbrauns, 1992), 210–11. Also cf. Nu 35 and legal stipulations for planned and unplanned murder, in relation to blood vengeance.

157 Jahnow, *Hebräische Leichenlied*, 54, 88. Indeed, such imagery emerges in the dirge speech of Lam 4:13–15 where the singer employs a midrashic fragment of the Cain and Abel story precisely to *accuse* the priests and prophets as murderers who have shed innocent blood; see below and my proposal of a Cain and Abel subtext already within the poetry of the book of Jeremiah; Nancy C. Lee, "Exposing a Buried Subtext in Jeremiah and Lamentations: Going After Baal . . . and Abel," in *Troubling Jeremiah*, eds., A. Diamond, K. O'Connor, L. Stulman, 87–122.

158 *Two Elegies on a Pushkin Museum Tablet: A New Sumerian Literary Genre* (Moscow: Oriental Literary Publ., 1969), cited in P. Ferris, Jr., *Genre of Communal Lament*, 71–72.

159 Many scholars suggest that the rhetoric of Lamentations essentially represents the voice of the people, and the dirge is certainly a popular mode of expression.

160 On this trend, see T. Linafelt, *Surviving Lamentations*, 9–13.

something of the magnitude of the devastation and injustices of the perpetrators. But the enormity of this 'freight' puts structural strains on the vehicles. Lamentations does also show a decided movement *from* the dirge genre at the outset *to* the lament genre across the five chapters, though this movement is not simply linear but is an interplay of voices between the two genres while moving to a final sustained communal lament prayer in Lam 5. Thus Westermann is on target in redirecting the scholarly conversation to emphasize lament (prayer) as well. That the book ends this way, with a plea to YHWH by a not-so-innocent 'Jobian' community, is altogether fitting as it leaves the ball in the court of the one who is both accused perpetrator and redeemer. Or to use the earlier metaphor, the end of the book like a dumptruck unloads its overbearing freight at YHWH's feet. Divine response or intervention, though not forthcoming, is desperately waited upon by the people, not primarily to complete a genre, but to buttress their debilitated vehicle for its next leg of the journey, if it will in fact be able to continue on down the road, that is, if indeed the entire journey thus far was not in vain.

Scholarship on other ANE Texts of Lamentations over Cities

Both Westermann's commentary (1990) and Delbert Hillers' revised commentary on Lamentations (1992)[161] include comparative discussions on lamentations over ancient cities, e.g., *Lamentation over the Destruction of Ur.*[162] As Hillers notes, in the 1950s, interest was renewed in comparing such ancient lamentations to the biblical book of Lamentations.[163] However, these older comparative studies, being

[161] D. Hillers, *Lamentations*, Anchor Bible, rev. ed. (New York: Doubleday, 1992).

[162] The critical edition is by Samuel Kramer, Assyriological Studies No. 12 (Chicago: Univ. of Chicago, 1940).

[163] D. Hillers, *Lamentations*, 32. Recently by F. W. Dobbs-Allsopp, *Weep, O Daughter of Zion: A Study of the City-Lament Genre in the Hebrew Bible* (Rome: Editrice Pontificio Istituto Biblico, 1993). In surveying this trend in scholarship, Dobbs-Allsopp notes that in 1959 S. Kramer proposed that Mesopotamian laments were the forerunners of the book of Lamentations. Those who saw parallels and followed his basic suggestion included C. Gadd (1963), H.-J. Kraus (1968), H. Vanstiphout (1983), W. Gwaltney, Jr. (1983), N. Gottwald (1988), C. Westermann (1990), and eventually D. Hillers (1992). On the other hand those who disagreed that there was any connection were led by T. Jacobsen (1946). They included W. Rudolph (1962), A. Weiser (1962), O. Eissfeldt (1976), and T. McDaniel (1968); see the summary in F. W. Dobbs-Allsopp, *Weep, O Daughter of Zion*, 2–10. The trend now toward moderating positions is evident among scholars. No one maintains a direct literary dependence of

preoccupied with the question of direct influence, had not yet clarified the important form-critical question of genre, either of the ancient lamentations over cities or of the biblical book. (It should be noted that the word "lamentation" is only a general term, not a technical genre, and means different things depending on its referent).[164] However, definition of genre is essential in any folkloric, literary, and/or historical comparison of cultures and their religions, especially in what were predominantly oral cultures.[165] Scholars of Mesopotamian lamentations do not consistently utilize biblical form criticism's definition of the "lament" genre as essentially *prayer* to the deity, as distinguished from the widely-attested "dirge" genre.[166] The general label of "city-lament" for the Mesopotamian texts is unclear, for example, as designation for the *Lamentation over the Destruction of Ur*, since most of that text is of the communal *dirge* genre, and very little of it is 'lament' prayer. At the least, it would be more accurate to call it a "city dirge."

Lamentations on the Mesopotamian laments, but in Mowinckel's words (1962), both Lamentations and Mesopotamian laments are part of "the common oriental culture"; cited by Ferris, *Genre of Communal Lament*, 175.

[164] Perhaps Hillers' recent comment about form criticism has been characteristic; citing Jahnow, Gunkel and Begrich's work, he states, "It is evident that we derive relatively little help from such form criticism for the interpretation of the book"; *Lamentations*, 32.

[165] See F. W. Dobbs-Allsopp's comparative study that explores the question of genre for the Sumerian lamentations texts and biblical Lamentations. He lists nine features that all of these texts share and thus proposes a single "city-lament" genre for them (see below). The nine features include "subject and mood, structure and poetic technique, divine abandonment, assignment of responsibility, the divine agent of destruction, the weeping goddess, lamentation, and restoration of the city and return of the gods"; F. W. Dobbs-Allsopp, *Weep, O Daughter of Zion*, 30. In the present study, an oral poetic method (that also contains a comparative element) asks if there are not two different genres within these works. Also, the last seven features listed above (except for 'lamentation') might be grouped together under a poet's use of "themes."

[166] However, recent works have carefully delineated the 'lament' element (as appeal/prayer to the deity) *within* Mesopotamian *balag* texts, thus analogous to the classical lamentations over destroyed cities; e.g., Mark E. Cohen's critical edition of *balag* laments, *The Canonical Lamentations of Ancient Mesopotamia* (Potomoc, Md.: Capital Decisions Limited, 1988) which also includes attention to *šuilla* and *eršahunga* types of lamentations; also Cohen's *Sumerian Hymnology: the Eršemma*, Hebrew Union College Annual Supplements, no. 2 (Cincinnati, Ohio: Hebrew Union College, 1981). Other critical editions and studies of ANE lamentation texts include Piotr Michalowski, *The Lamentation over the Destruction of Sumer and Ur* (Winona Lake, Ind.: Eisenbrauns, 1989); Samuel Kramer, "Lamentation over the Destruction of Nippur," *ASJ* 13 (1991): 1–26; Margaret Green, "The Eridu Lament," *JCS* 30 (1978): 127–67, and "The Uruk Lament," *JAOS* 104 (1984): 253–79.

The proposal to apply the label "city-lament" not only to the Mesopotamian lamentations over cities, but also to biblical Lamentations, and to prophetic texts which adapt the dirge for cities and lands is not a convincing argument.[167] The Hebrew term קִינָה, a genre term, is used by biblical texts themselves to label traditional dirges for the dead, *as well as* prophetic communal dirges, as well as biblical Lamentations (adopted by most of the ancient versions and traditions; but see the caveat below). Thus, "communal dirge" (communal קִינָה) for these kinds of texts remains, arguably, the best generic term as based on terminology, content, form, and purpose presented by these texts.

Yet the caveat is just as important, that both biblical Lamentations and the Mesopotamian lamentation texts also contain 'lament prayers,' another genre. If anything, the presence of at least two genres in these works makes the enterprise of labeling the entire work with a single generic term problematic anyway.[168] Indeed, scholars note that there has *not* been discovered *one genre term* used by ancient Mesopotamians inclusive of all kinds of communal 'lamentations.'[169] Thus, there is no sound reason presented to dismiss Lowth, Gunkel, and Jahnow—that prophetic texts and biblical Lamentations 'transfer' the dirge genre for use as a distinctive *communal* dirge genre. Obviously, other cultures used a similar communal dirge genre to describe the destruction of cities (and kingdoms and temples and land). Jahnow has brought wide-ranging evidence of the dirge and communal dirge among the cultures of the world (not just from the ancient Near

[167] D. Hillers, *Lamentations*, 32–39; Dobbs-Allsopp, *Weep, O Daughter of Zion*, 1–2, 8–10.

[168] Dobbs-Allsopp notes that the 'city-lament' features do not occur in most of Lam 3; ibid., 31.

[169] See P. Ferris's discussion on the problem of identifying genre; *Genre of Communal Lament*, 6–17. Ferris opts to use the genre term "communal lament" in a broad way to include those texts "used by and/or on behalf of a community to express both complaint, and sorrow and grief over some perceived calamity, physical or cultural, which had befallen or was about to befall them *and* to appeal to God for deliverance" (emphasis added; he also excludes pentitential psalms) ibid., 10. While Ferris's term is more inclusive, moving beyond the 'city' only to the larger community, his definition also appears to undercut Westermann's definition of "communal lament" which refers primarily to the *appeal* to the divinity (prayer/petition) element. Once again, the definition of 'lament' is used differently by these scholars. It should be added that the picture grows more complicated upon the recognition that scholars in folklore and oral tradition often use the word "lament" to refer to the "dirge."

East), and from ancient periods to the modern. On the question of genre, it remains only to extend and modify if necessary Jahnow's basic form-critical insights to these texts, not propose a 'new' genre.

For example, Jahnow presents (from Lübke) such a communal dirge from the Greek island of Khíos that was struck by an earthquake in 1881:

> O Khíos, once so highly praised,
> favored by all the world,
> How you are now so deathly pale,
> consumed by bitter grief!
> How withered the splendid blossom there,
> where now is your lasting loveliness?
> The daughter's charm of sweet ecstasy,
> the fresh vigor of the son? . . .
> O' Omnipotent, you are a greater God,
> Ah! Have pity on us!
> Allow yourself to grieve for the children,
> those fully innocent, in misery! . . .[170]

The last third of the communal dirge contains lament prayer to the deity. As already mentioned, the genre identification of Lamentations is *neither* lament *or* communal dirge alone; it rather holds the two in tension.

Rhetorical Criticism and Beyond

The several speaker(s) in Lamentations, as a rhetorical critical matter,[171] garnered attention with a 1974 study by William Lanahan,

[170] Translated by the writer from the German translation of the original Greek; cited by Jahnow, *Hebräische Leichenlied*, 178. Note the shift from communal dirge speech to lament prayer at the end.

[171] Already in his 1968 address, "Form Criticism and Beyond," James Muilenburg was discussing the issue of different speakers in poetry; *Hearing and Speaking the Word*, 13. The element of the speaking voice in biblical poetry has been largely overlooked in most of the *general* works on biblical rhetorical criticism (B. Anderson, 1974; Clines, 1980; Kessler, 1982; Wuellner, 1987; Barton, Warner, and Patrick and Scult, 1990; West, 1992; Gitay, 1993; Trible, 1994; Watson and Hauser, 1994). However, a number of scholars have referred to the element of the speaking voice (or speaker) in their more specific studies (Holladay, in a study of Jeremiah's rhetorical style, 1962; Lanahan's study on Lamentations, 1974; Lundbom, in a study of rhetoric in the book of Jeremiah, 1975; Niditch on the composition of Isaiah 1, 1980; Gwaltney in a comparison of Lamentations to ANE lament literature, 1981; Caspi, "The Speaking Voice and the Poem," 1982; Kessler, in a study of Psalm

"The Speaking Voice in the Book of Lamentations."[172] While Lanahan suggests his study is not about the authorship of the book but is a "stylistic concern" to identify the speaking voice, he goes on to say that "the poet" uses five personae to express different viewpoints of his world.[173] It appears that Lanahan regards 'the poet' like previous commentators have regarded the individual 'author' of Lamentations in a modern literary sense. Lanahan's approach is plausible, and along with other recent literary approaches it suggests that Lamentations is a kind of unified poetic drama.

Yet such approaches do not consider the possibility that Lamentations may reflect (and have crystallized in writing) the voices of several poets who performed their songs in an oral poetic context.[174] Indeed, more scholars are admitting the dialogical nature of the voices in Lam 1–2. Dialogue is integral to oral poetic contexts. First, as explained by A. B. Lord, a fundamental dialogical phenomenon is built into the oral poetic *composing/performance process*. That is, the skilled poetic singer engages in a composing process within the community that involves listening to his or her peers in the tradition (whether epic singers or dirge singers or prophets or psalmists) and then composing/singing his or her own songs in response.[175]

However, when the genre is a form of dirge, another dialogical dynamic may enter in, as Jahnow and researchers in South Slavic

18, 1983; Fishbane, in a few textual analyses in *Biblical Interpretaton in Ancient Israel*, 1985; Kaiser, in a study of Daughter Zion as speaker in biblical texts, 1987; Brueggemann in his Jeremiah commentary, 1988; Provan, in a recent commentary on Lamentations, 1991; Lenchak, in a study of Deuteronomy 28–30, 1993; Brenner and van Dijk-Hemmes in a study on gender in biblical texts, 1993; Dobbs-Allsopp in a comparative study of Lamentations to ANE lamentations, 1993; Stowers, using the Greco-Roman category, *prosopopoeia*, in a study of Romans, 1994; Beal's study on the voice of YHWH as the speaking subject of a *dirge* in Mic 1:8–9; Tull's published dissertation on 2nd Isaiah recollections of Lamentations, 1997; and Linafelt's *Surviving Lamentations*, 1997). Thus, the element of the speaking voice is regarded as a legitimate rhetorical category for analysis. However, a *thorough* analysis of the speaking voices in Lamentations has not been undertaken.

[172] William Lanahan, "The Speaking Voice in the Book of Lamentations," *JBL* 93 (1974): 41–49.

[173] Ibid., 41.

[174] For example, Lanahan says, "obviously, the city of Jerusalem cannot speak except in some figurative sense" (ibid.). This strict literary view requires Lanahan to have a single author or poet who creates Jerusalem and makes her speak. On the other hand, that Lamentations may reflect several oral poets' utterances crystallized in writing does not preclude the redacting process that would have changed the poems to some extent.

[175] A. B. Lord, *Singer of Tales*, 13–29.

contexts have shown. Dirges often involve a group of singers performing in response to one another, a kind of dialogue or antiphony (see above). Certainly communal dirges are being expressed in Lamentations, along with the psalmic-type lament. Recent research by Carleen Mandolfo has *also* demonstrated a *dialogue* of sometimes disagreeing musical voices in biblical lament psalms.[176] Thus, it may be proposed that the so-called speakers in Lamentations indicate different poetic singers who performed their composed songs in response to one another. Of course, an oral poetic approach also allows the possibility that a single poet *wrote* the text from within and reflecting an oral poetic context.

This study will take the approach that Lamentations has crystallized the oral dialogue of two lead poetic singers in Lam 1, 2, and 4, whose utterances would have followed on one another fairly immediately.[177] Thus, the initial poet describes the devastated city of Jerusalem and typically personifies it as a woman (perhaps the poet has been moved by witnessing women suffering around him). Another poet (a woman perhaps moved by his depiction) responds by singing about her individual suffering, loss of children, etc., such that the juxtaposition of their songs and interaction leads to her being identified as "Daughter Zion" (the city personified). Other voices enter the dialogue in Lam 3, and it is unclear whether they might have been part of this direct performance exchange, or offer a response after some time delay.[178] An oral poetic approach further suggests

[176] C. Mandolfo, "YHWH is Tzaddiq?: The Dialogic Theology of Lament Psalms." SBL paper, 2000 (forthcoming).

[177] Of course, this doesn't mean that the text represents some "original" performance, but simply may have crystallized the evolving songs at a certain point in the process. No one can ever prove such an oral performance happened in the context or proximity of the 587 destruction, yet there is no serious reason to doubt that singers would have gathered together in the midst of the crisis or its immediate aftermath. Such a scenario is just as plausible (even moreso) than the idea of an individual poet/author composing a literary work in isolation from the community, though an oral poetic approach must also allow for this possibility. In recent times, the phenomenon of poets gathering to compose and recite their work certainly happened in the aftermath of war, for example in Croatia, where poetry groups formed for the processing of trauma and grief (e.g., NONA in Zagreb, a women's refugee center).

[178] Traditional oral poetic performances can involve some time lag between each poet's composing/singing their songs; that is, a number of days or much longer may pass after the first poet utters his or her speech before another, having heard it, returns to perform orally their own composition and to some extent respond to the previously heard poet.

that songs composed and arising out of this communal dirge/lament context might have been sung/composed *line by line*,[179] and later resung by other singers in the group, as in refrains (thus much repetition), likely involving oral modification as they continue to be sung. In any case a scribe eventually crystallized two lead singers in dialogue and may also be the compiler who added the later singers' utterances. In my view such a scenario is suggestive of a traditional oral context in ancient Israel.

The oral poetic method, however, is *not* interested in a historical reconstruction of "the actual" or "original" poem or song performed behind the preserved text. Rather, according to John Miles Foley,[180] it is sufficient to recognize that a text has roots in oral tradition. Because such a poem (regardless of genre)

> depends on a specialized idiom that is both traditional and individual, we can speak of a singer of tales. Because that art depends for its expressive force on its emergence within a specialized context, we can speak of a realm of performance. Even when the discussion turns to texts, and even when those texts are not transcriptions but lettered works in the traditional idiom, rhetorically the singer persists and the performance goes on.[181]

Further, it should be noted that scholarship on oral dirges and laments recognizes that the performance of songs is not restricted to one social locale (such as in the temple or at the funeral bier). Moreover, in the context of the destruction of Jerusalem and its temple, amidst the chaos of the failure and absence of religious and political leadership, it makes sense that at least some of these songs in Lamentations were probably sung 'in the ruins,' and it is not surprising that a

[179] It is my view that such a line by line composing process lends itself to the acrostic pattern, especially when the first line of a dirge typically begins with the first א—letter: איכה. Or perhaps the acrostic was a technique of oral performance that re-shaped the previously sung dirges and lament songs. The same people could have re-sung their songs, or other singers may be performing them (including adding to/reshaping them as the context of suffering unfolds).

[180] Foley has carried forward, at times corrected, and expanded the Parry/Lord approach of oral traditional theory and analysis. See esp. *Oral-Formulaic Theory and Research: An Introduction and Annotated Bibliography* (1985), *The Theory of Oral Composition: History and Methodology* (1988), *Traditional Oral Epic: The Odyssey, Beowulf, and the Serbo-Croatian Return Song* (Berkeley: Univ. of California, 1990), *Immanent Art: From Structure to Meaning in Traditional Oral Epic* (Bloomington & Indianapolis: Indiana Univ. Press, 1991), and *The Singer of Tales in Performance* (Bloomington & Indianapolis: Indiana Univ. Press, 1995).

[181] John M. Foley, *The Singer of Tales in Performance*, xiv.

number of poetic voices emerge rather than a single authoritative voice.

Beyond Lamentations, in the book of Jeremiah[182] only recently have a number of scholars begun identifying "speakers" there,[183] especially Jerusalem/Daughter Zion's voice (John J. Schmitt,[184] Kathleen O'Connor,[185] Mark Biddle,[186] and Joseph Henderson).[187] In his commentary on Jeremiah, William Holladay had emphasized the need to deal systematically with this question. He suggested that other prophetic books do not contain anything quite like the multiple speakers in Jeremiah.[188] He disagreed that the voices of YHWH and

[182] Recent studies on the problem of how the book of Jeremiah might have been composed/redacted are included in the larger anthology, *Troubling Jeremiah*, eds., A. R. Pete Diamond, Kathleen M. O'Connor, Louis Stulman, *JSOTS* 260 (Sheffield: Sheffield Academic Press, 1999).

[183] Commentators traditionally presumed the merging together of the voice of YHWH and the voice of the prophet without distinguishing them as different speakers, though the texts usually implicitly indicate they are different speaking subjects. Cf. W. Holladay's attention to the question of who is speaking, albeit brief, in his analysis of Jer 4; Holladay also notates the interchange of speakers in his commentary translations, *Jeremiah*, vol. I, Hermeneia (Philadelphia: Fortress Press, 1986), 137–38, 338.

[184] John J. Schmitt, "The City as Woman in Isaiah 1–39," in *Writing and Reading the Scroll of Isaiah: Studies of an Interpretive Tradition* (New York: E. J. Brill, 1997). Schmitt also suggests "Daughter Babylon" speaks in Isa 21:3–4; ibid., 107.

[185] K. O'Connor, "The Tears of God and Divine Character in Jeremiah 2–9," in *God in the Fray*, 172–85.

[186] M. Biddle, *Polyphony and Symphony in Prophetic Literature: Rereading Jeremiah 7–20* (Macon, Ga.: Mercer Univ. Press, 1996), 1–13, has been developing a methodology that includes identifying speakers. His method includes (1) identifying speakers; (2) analyzing characterization of the figures identified; and (3) the dialogue between these figures. He states, "The canonical text has captured voices in perpetual dialogue. This dialogue must be heard on its own terms" (11). Biddle suggests his method is literary, canonical, and redaction critical (5–9). It is not clear exactly how he integrates the redaction critical elements with the literary findings in the text. While I affirm Biddle's contribution toward such a method, I believe his analysis of the characterization of Jerusalem/D. Zion in Jer 7–20 (*Polyphony and Symphony in Prophetic Literature*, 100–01) is incomplete, if not misleading, because he does not identify the speech in Jer 10:23–25 as 'D. Zion's' (see below). Similarly, B. Bakke Kaiser overlooks the importance of Jerusalem's speech in Jer 10:23–25 for her characterization in "Poet as 'Female Impersonator': The Image of Daughter Zion as Speaker in Biblical Poems of Suffering," *JR* (1987): 164–82.

[187] J. Henderson, "Who Weeps in Jeremiah 3:23 (9:1)?" (forthcoming).

[188] Only Micah and Habakkuk contain "hints of a dialogue" with YHWH; W. Holladay, *Jeremiah*, vol. I, 137. Holladay suggested a parallel of Jeremiah's poetic use of multiple speakers to the works of Aeschylus and Sophocles (ibid.), yet these were Greek playwrights (a different genre) whose works obviously spelled out the different characters' speaking parts in the text. What is the traditional Hebrew prophetic way of introducing characters/persona? Does Jeremiah (or the compiled book) ever diverge from this pattern and why? (see below).

Jeremiah simply blend together, and maintained that distinct voices can be identified with a high degree of probability, based on the evidence of "internal clues of diction and analogies of such clues in comparable passages."[189] Holladay maintained that Jeremiah historically uttered the poetry and asks,

> How did he make plain in his recitation or his chanting who was speaking a given sequence of cola? Was it a shift of rhythm, or the pitch of his voice, or were there different modes or harmonies or gestures associated with the different speakers? . . . One must assume that such shifts were apparent to Jrm's audience, however painfully we ourselves must tease them back to life.[190]

However, what Jeremiah performed was not the compiled text we have in front of us. It is evident that Holladay's view of Jeremiah is much like Lanahan's single poet/author who presents different personae. However, Holladay may overstate Jeremiah's need to perform oral interpretation of speaking characters, since even Holladay suggested that the rubrics "oracle of YHWH" and "for thus YHWH has said" usually match the voice identified, with minor exception. Indeed, when Jeremiah presents a speaking persona in his poetry, he invariably *introduces* it quite simply, for example, with "Israel said" or "Judah said" or "Rachel weeps." However, when Jeremiah speaks, he does *not* introduce himself, and when a voice speaks whom scholars (noted above) have identified as Daughter Zion/Jerusalem, neither is she introduced. Could a scribe/compiler have included the poetic songs of others within the book of Jeremiah? As will be seen below, the present study maintains the possibility that the poetry of both Lamentations and Jeremiah reflects a prophet residing in a traditional oral poetic context in which he is not the only singer.

The Present Study

The oral poetic approach in the present study will analyze the poetic speeches in Lamentations as composed and performed by poets participating not only in their culture's rhetorical traditions (communal

[189] Ibid. Holladay notes that the rubrics "oracle of YHWH" and "for thus YHWH has said" usually match the voice identified, but are not always reliable, since they "stand outside the poetic structure of the lines"; ibid.

[190] Ibid., 137–38.

dirge and lament prayer), but who, as poetic singers, infused these genres with their own, individual artistry in *response* to their context, the destruction of their city Jerusalem. Dialectical insights will be drawn by comparisons of oral poetic traditions from former Yugoslavia and other cultures. A socio-rhetorical approach will also be integrated in the analysis, since the poetry at hand not only reflects a traditional world (and its collapse), but just *how* the poets are reshaping a crumbled world shall be explored.

The study will consider whether Jeremiah as a prophetic, oral poet can be identified as one of the speakers in Lamentations. The exploration will be based not on the Septuagint's superscription, or on traditions' attribution to him, but on oral poetic grounds, on whether one of the poetic singers in Lamentations might use *formulaic* language characteristic of Hebrew prophets, *as well as* peculiar artistic rhetoric identifiable as Jeremiah's individual style in response to the context.[191] This latter individual style of Jeremiah will be sought by a synchronic reading between the poetry of the books of Lamentations and Jeremiah, both works falling within the same general context of Jerusalem's destruction.[192] At the same time, a poetic voice often identified as personified Jerusalem appears and has speeches in the book of Lamentations and, it shall be argued, in the book of Jeremiah. These speeches by "Jerusalem's poet," as I shall call her, will also be analyzed in this study.

[191] Scholars pursuing the 'authorship' question of Lamentations in terms of common language therein and in Jeremiah tended to focus upon concordance studies and simply listed which terms appeared in both books, but did not analyze these terms as to how they were used by poets in context; e.g., Max Löhr, "Der Sprachgebrauch des Buches der Klagelieder," *ZAW* 14 (1894): 31–50; William W. Cannon, "The Authorship of Lamentations," *BSac* 81 (1924): 42–58.

[192] Since scholars generally agree that most of the poetry of the book of Jeremiah comes from the prophet (notwithstanding its redaction).

CHAPTER TWO

POETIC SINGERS IN THE BOOK OF JEREMIAH: THE PROPHET (RENDERING THE CITY AS FEMALE) AND THE CITY'S FEMALE POET[1]

My proud Bosnia,
Must you go the way of Slovenia and Croatia?
Does there not exist a hand in the world
  that will stop your war-fire and destruction?
Is your way of the cross too long?
When will you stop bleeding?
What will become of your bloody wounds?
Who will heal the countless broken hearts?
Who will raise again the countless demolished houses,
  sanctuaries, factories, bridges and tunnels?
Before all these questions one is left mute.
One finds no answers.

Marija Koprivnjak, "Jeremianic Lamentations over Bosnia and Herzegovina" (1992)[2]

[1] Biblical texts use a variety of appellatives to refer to the city of Jerusalem: Jerusalem, Zion, Daughter Jerusalem, Daughter Zion, virgin Daughter Zion, Daughter of My People (e.g., in Mic 4:8–11; Jer 4:14–31; Lam 1:6–7; 2:10–13). For studies of traditional views of the city as female in the ANE, including ancient Israel, see Peggy L. Day, "The Personification of Cities as Female in the Hebrew Bible: the Thesis of Aloysius Fitzgerald, F. S. C.," in *Reading from This Place*, 284–302; Mark E. Biddle, "Lady Zion's Alter Egos: Isaiah 47.1–15 and 57.6–13 as Structural Counterparts," *New Visions of Isaiah*, ed. Roy F. Melugin, Marvin A. Sweeney, JSOTS 214 (Sheffield: JSOT Press, 1996), 124–39; F. W. Dobbs-Allsopp, "The Syntagma of *bat* Followed by a Geographical Name in the Hebrew Bible: A Reconsideration of Its Meaning and Grammar," *CBQ* 57 (1995): 451–70; M. Biddle, "The City of Chaos and the New Jerusalem: Isaiah 24–27 in Context," *Perspectives in Religious Studies* 22 (1995): 5–12; John J. Schmitt, "The Virgin of Israel: Referent and Use of the Phrase in Amos and Jeremiah," *CBQ* 53 (1991): 365–87; Elaine R. Follis, "The Holy City as Daughter," in *Directions in Biblical Hebrew Poetry*, ed. E. Follis (Sheffield: JSOT Press, 1987), 173–84; John J. Schmitt, "The Motherhood of God and Zion as Mother," *RB* 92 (1985): 557–69.

[2] Transl. N. Lee; "Jeremijine tužaljke nad Bosnom i Hercegovinom" in *Ratni Blagoslovi* (Osijek: Izvori, 1996), 135, first published in *Izvori* magazine, 1992. The biblical influence on this poet is obvious, as she renders a striking parallel to the prophetic 'warning' function of communal dirge, suggesting (in 1992) that Bosnia was headed for the same devastations of war already experienced by Croatia (1991). The primary difference is that this poet refrains from using retributive justice that claimed such devastation was God's punishment.

Heavily damaged farm, Eastern Slavonia, Croatia (N. Lee, 1996)

Scholars have noted that, besides Jeremiah, different voices appear in the book of Jeremiah,[3] including one 'identified' as "Daughter Zion" = "Jerusalem". This figure might also be identified as a singer in Lamentations. As shall be seen, this identification of the voice as "D. Zion" is perceived by modern readers due to the *juxtaposition* of the voice (by a scribe or compiler or redactor) next to Jeremiah's references to the personified city. Such identification is not explicitly stated in the text by Jeremiah's voice or by prose headings. An oral poetic approach now proceeds to explore three initial questions within the larger analysis: (1) Is there evidence that the two different voices in the specific texts under consideration may actually represent different *poets* who composed their utterances in relation to the original and larger context of the destruction of Jerusalem in 587 BCE?[4]

[3] The primary text analyzed will be the MT (BHS) in light of variants in LXX, DSS, and other manuscripts.

[4] There must obviously be a *diachronic* element in the poetry in the book of Jeremiah (and Lamentations), since numerous poetic speeches, which could not have

(2) Is it possible that *one* of the poetic voices *in Lamentations* is Jeremiah or at least re-sings his utterances? (3) Is it possible the 'D. Zion' poet in Jeremiah reappears 'with him' in Lamentations? In this analysis, it will not be necessary to determine the dating of the composition of the poems, since with this method, there is no such thing as "the original" poem or text, only multiple performances which are variations from an individual singer and those who come after him or her. Even Jeremiah would have modified an utterance of his own as the days went by, adapting it to the evolving context. Moreover, poets referring to a historical event may compose some time after the fact (even years later) as the event remains painfully real for those who experienced it. It is obvious here that I accept the basic premise and traditional claim that Jeremiah was an important creative voice and historical figure in Israelite tradition, and that the books of Jeremiah and Lamentations primarily reflect the context of the 6th c. destruction of Jerusalem. But I aim to reveal how this second poet also makes a most extraordinary contribution in response to the context. Thus, following S. Niditch, it is not necessary to demonstrate whether biblical Lamentations was originally oral or written; it is traditional literature coming from an oral context; it is analysis of the poetry as reflective of that dynamic that might shed greater light on its meanings and impact.

Following the basic Parry/Lord approach, oral poets used "formulas" and "themes" common to their cultures as well as innovated them according to each poet's individual, creative style in response to immediate context.[5] A poet's 'favored uses' of certain formulas, as well as his or her apparent innovations may help identify the individual poet responsible for a work. Lord explains,

all been uttered at the same time, have been compiled into a whole. Yet the compilation, upon close examination, seems to reflect a growing dialogue prompted by the context and by Jeremiah's rhetoric in it, even as the compilation crystallized their oral performances or utterances into a synchronic piece.

[5] Lord following Parry defined a poetic "formula" as "a group of words which is regularly employed under the same metrical conditions to express a given essential idea." Examples of formulas include brief phrases giving the names of characters, the main actions, their time, and place. Lord defines "theme" in epic poetry as the variable but "repeated incidents and descriptive passages in the songs." Examples include a 'council' scene, the arrival of a messenger, an arming scene, a journey and return (including disguise, deception, and recognition); Lord, *Singer of Tales*, 4, 34, 68–98.

> The picture that emerges is not really one of conflict between preserver of tradition and creative artist; it is rather one of the preservation of tradition by the constant re-creation of it.[6]

As will be seen, biblical prophetic and psalmic lament genres, by their 'disputatious' nature,[7] tend to challenge tradition just as much as they preserve it, are interested less in aesthetics of story-telling than they are in socio-political realities. The oral poetic method used here shall modify epic categories of "formula" and "theme" to suit Hebrew prophetic and psalmic poetry. It asks whether one of the poets in Lamentations uses *formulaic language* characteristic of Hebrew prophets (specific genres, terms, imagery, themes) as well as exhibits a *peculiar* rhetoric in these same areas (but 'favored use' of stock terms, *how* he/she uses imagery to build themes, modify, or extend them in response to context). The findings may enable identifying one of the poets in Lamentations as the prophet Jeremiah, or at least a re-singing of his perspective.[8]

Moreover, the same analysis will be applied to the other poet, whom I shall hereafter designate (not as Jeremiah's rendered persona, 'D. Zion'),[9] but critically as 'Jerusalem's poet,' the integrity of whose

[6] Ibid., 29.

[7] See especially, W. Brueggemann's emphasis on the importance of "dispute" (from legal and justice concerns and adjudication) as a consistent component of thought and life in the Hebrew Bible; *Theology of the Old Testament: Testimony, Dispute, Advocacy*, xvii.

[8] As noted, little work has been done by scholars to explore the peculiar characteristics of Jeremiah's poetry within standard prophetic style. Jack Lundblom's study was an exception (*Jeremiah: Study in Ancient Hebrew Rhetoric* [Missoula, Mont.: SBL & Scholars Press, 1975]), but even his analysis of the pervasive use of inclusio and chiasm in the book and his claim that these are especially characteristic of Jeremiah the prophet is no longer tenable, since such devices have been found to be common in other biblical and ANE works. A folkloric/oral poetic method would categorize these devices as *formulaic* rhetorical techniques typical of poets in the ANE, not peculiar characteristics of Jeremiah the poet. Yet, it remains to be seen whether Jeremiah used inclusio and chiasm in a characteristic way, as distinct from other poets' and prophets' use of these techniques.

R. Carroll suggests that it is only by the prose editorial pieces in the book of Jeremiah that Jeremiah can be identified in the poetry; that is, he claims the poetry in no way identifies Jeremiah as speaker; *Jeremiah*, 47. *Literally* this is true if one begins from a historical and redaction critical approach, but *poetically*, scholars in oral poetry claim that, given a large enough body of material (and this might be debated), an individual poet may be identified by his or her favored uses of formula and themes and peculiar modifications of them.

[9] Many scholars use a modern literary poetic approach in dealing with the persona, thus Norman W. Porteous, "Jerusalem-Zion: The Growth of a Symbol," in *Verbannung und Heimkehr* (Tübingen: J. C. B. Mohr, 1961), 235–52.

voice, I shall propose, has been preserved by the compiler[10] *in juxtaposition to* the prophet's voice,[11] not subsumed by it.[12] In the book of Jeremiah, Jerusalem's poet renders in song her experience in the threatened city, and her songs expand exponentially in Lamentations. Indeed, these and a couple of other texts at least (in Mic 7:8–10 and Isa 61:10–11),[13] may point to *a tradition of women singers in performance dialogue* with the prophets,[14] whose lament songs artistically rendered the experience of these capital cities especially in crisis. Such a role here for women singers would relate to their pervasive role as dirge and lament singers in Israel, across cultures, and through history.[15]

[10] I am not aiming to investigate the process of how the text came to be as it is, but perhaps this oral poetic analysis might suggest some aspects implicitly. Instead of compiler, others might prefer to use the term scribe or redactor for a person responsible for pulling the text together; for helpful insights, see R. Culley, "Orality and Writtenness in the Biblical Texts," 45–64; idem, "The Confessions of Jeremiah and Traditional Discourse," 69–81; Raymond F. Person, Jr., "A Rolling Corpus and Oral Tradition: A Not-So-Literate Solution to a Highly Literate Problem," in *Troubling Jeremiah*, 263–71.

[11] Otherwise, *on what methodological basis* is it claimed that the prophet himself speaks as the persona of female Jerusalem (is there evidence that this prophet, or traditional prophetic discourse, *takes on* other personae and *utters their speech* in this way)? This is a different question from the obvious personification and even address of cities by prophets. Here is where an oral poetic method challenges a possible 'reading in' of modern literary poetic understandings as if there were no difference in the way poets composed their work then and now.

[12] Obviously, there were numerous singers in the city, but Jerusalem's poet's songs were deemed significant for some reason to have been intentionally preserved in the written text. Cf. 'Mother Jerusalem's' speech in Baruch 4:9–29.

[13] In Mic 7:8–10 (and perhaps 14–20), a poet renders (her?) experience in (speaking as) the city (in this case, Samaria). That this poet speaks from the perspective of Samaria, not Jerusalem, is suggested by the surrounding context. A later example may be seen in a poet's speaking of her experience as D. Zion/Jerusalem in 2nd Isaiah (61:10–11), a later context. I am grateful to John J. Schmitt for calling to my attention the Micah 'city speech,' which he alternatively identifies as the speech of Jerusalem/D. Zion; John J. Schmitt, "The City as Woman in Isaiah 1–39," in *Writing and Reading the Scroll of Isaiah: Studies of an Interpretive Tradition* (New York: E. J. Brill, 1997), 95–119, esp. 106 (note 37).

[14] Thus preserved and valued by the biblical prophetic tradition.

[15] Indeed, such singers' 'juxtaposition' in the preserved texts may be suggestive of their *social juxtaposition* with the prophets in context. So 2 Chronicles 35:25 may be helpful not in literally locating a historical text referred to but in suggesting these singers' and prophets' *social association*: "Jeremiah also uttered a lament for Josiah, and all the singing men and singing women have spoken of Josiah in their laments to this day. They made these a custom in Israel; they are recorded in the Laments." Rachel's lament (31:15) and its expansion in legend suggest a valuing of women's laments; L. Ginzberg, *Legends of the Jews* (NY: Simon & Schuster, 1956), 628.

Thus, those blocks of texts wherein Jerusalem's poet speaks, in conjunction with Jeremiah's poetic speech, will be the basis for the comparative analysis below (in Jer 4, 8, 10, and Lamentations).

A clue to the possible presence of a female poetic singer in the book of Jeremiah is that the above speeches, like Jeremiah's own speeches typically, are *not introduced* or *explicitly* identified in the poetry. 'D. Zion's' speech is never introduced, but suddenly appears. Yet elsewhere, throughout the poetry of the book of Jeremiah, the prophet usually explicitly refers to YHWH, the people, false prophets, priests, the wise, Rachel, etc., as the voices of the speech he cites.[16] If Jeremiah were employing the city persona, why would he not identify Jerusalem's speech directly, as he does with these other speakers whose personae he renders? A second, important clue resides in the fact that one of the speeches under consideration, Jer 10:23–25, is a *lament* prayer song, which a lyricist who was a temple singer/psalmist might have composed. (Note, the song cannot be Jeremiah's perspective as the singer admits needing YHWH's 'correction', while Jeremiah consistently claims his innocence.) Indeed, the speech in Jer 10:25 is *nearly matched* in Ps 79:6–7, a *communal lament* psalm likely describing the destruction of 587. That the singers of lament songs strongly influenced Jeremiah (note his well-known personal laments in the book) associates him to some extent with them, possibly leading to the inclusion of their own songs in his book.[17]

Again, key questions are these: Does a comparison of Jeremiah's poetic speeches with those of any of the poets in Lamentations suggest he is one of them giving utterance? Does a comparison of the speeches by 'Jerusalem's poet' in both books suggest she is a sepa-

[16] Notably, what appears to be the first direct speech by the people of Judah to YHWH in the entire book, at 14:7–9 (and vs 19f), is also *unintroduced*, suggesting perhaps that it was merely recorded as part of the rhetorical context. While I am less concerned about YHWH's speeches in Jeremiah (though the divine perspectives rendered are important), since none are found for comparison in Lamentations, one must face the peculiar nature of Hebrew prophecy in which the messenger of the deity also speaks poetically *for YHWH*. Then one must ascertain, beyond the use of formulaic rhetoric, *how Jeremiah* characteristically renders YHWH's speech, different from prior or later prophets. Hereafter, I will refer to YHWH's speaking with the implicit understanding, obviously, that they are mediated through the prophet.

[17] This is suggestive for Jeremiah's potential input into the compilation of the book (and sympathy for such other singers) perhaps in association with his scribe Baruch.

rate poet, and moreover, does she reappear in Lamentations? But beyond this and more importantly, how do the singers of Lamentations participate both in their culture's formulaic poetic traditions (e.g., communal dirge and lament prayer), but also infuse these genres and formulas with their own, individual artistry in response to their context, the imminent and unfolding destruction of their city Jerusalem?

The Songs of Jerusalem's Female Poet

In the Hebrew Bible, speech related to Jerusalem/Daughter Zion is found in four categories:

(1) a poetic voice *briefly quotes* Jerusalem/D. Zion's direct discourse, calling her by name (quoted by YHWH as in Isa 49:14, 21; or by a prophet, like Jeremiah, in Jer 4:31);
(2) a poetic voice *refers* to her speaking (Isa 3:26; 29:4; 51:3; Mic 4:10; Jer 8:8; 12:8; 30:15);
(3) a poetic voice *beseeches* or *calls her to speak* in various ways (to mourn: Jer 6:26; to lament: Lam 2:18; to lift up her voice: Isa 40:9; to sing: Isa 52:9; 54:1; to rejoice: Isa 66:10; Zech 9:9); and,
(4) unintroduced *direct discourse* by a poet in texts have been identified by scholars as speeches by 'Jerusalem/D. Zion.'[18]

Of this last category, such speeches are found in Lamentations 1:9c, 11c–15b, 16, 18–22; 2:20–22; 3:42–47, three are in the book of Jeremiah–4:19–21;[19] 8:18;[20] 10:19–20, 23–25,[21] and only one other

[18] In contrast to most of the Mesopotamian lamentation texts, in the Nippur lamentation a poet *speaks as the city* itself (noted by Dobbs-Allsopp, *Weep, O Daughter of Zion*, 77), but that voice does not offer a lament prayer to the deity (though encouraged to do so; rather the goddess Ninlil is referred to as interceding on the city's behalf to Enlil and securing response and restoration). This is in contrast to Jerusalem's poet esp. in Lamentations with her ready expressions of such lament prayers, which yet go unanswered. The city also speaks in the *balag* lament ELUM DIDARA; Mark E. Cohen, *The Canonical Lamentations of Ancient Mesopotamia* (Potomac, Md.: Capital Decisions Limited, 1988) 73, 79–81, 183.

[19] Long ago, P. Volz identified Jerusalem/D. Zion's speech in Jer 4:19–21 in *Der Prophet Jeremia: Übersetzt und Erklärt* (Leipzig: A. Deichertsche Verlagsbuchhandlung, 1922), 56, cited in B. Bakke Kaiser, "Poet," 168. This was also recognized by F. K. Kumaki (1982; see note below). While Kaiser recognized the persona of D. Zion in the Jer 4 and 10 texts and briefly compared them with Lamentations, her basic suggestion that the historical Jeremiah (or the male poet) *imitated* or impersonated

speech identified as Jerusalem's is found thus far, and it is in Isa 61:10–11 (see above).[22] In the blocks of text in Jer 4, 8, and 10, Jeremiah's speeches appear in conjunction with Jerusalem's.[23]

The analysis here will proceed to compare the speeches of Jeremiah in Jer 4:3–31, Jer 8:18–9:2; Jer 10:17–25, and the poetic speech in Lam 1. Likewise, the speeches of Jerusalem's poet will be analyzed in those same texts.

Evidence for specific congruences in each poet's speeches between the books will be sought in the following key areas:

(1) use of genres
(2) use of imagery and themes
(3) use of terminology
(4) use of rhetorical techniques
(5) expressions of content

As will be seen, the oral poetic method reveals that congruences appear not only within each poet's *formulaic* expressions (e.g., of genres, images, content, etc.), but also in each poet's *peculiar* develop-

the female D. Zion for an intensifying, emotional effect in the book of Jeremiah needs methodological support; neither does Bakke Kaiser delineate the speaking voices thoroughly, apart from 'the poet'; see Christl Maier, "Die Klage der Tochter Zion," *Berliner Theologische Zeitschrift* 2 (1998): 176–89.

[20] R. Carroll unconvincingly identifies the city as the voice of all of 8:18–9:1; *Jeremiah*, 235–36. Joseph Henderson has offered the most convincing evidence in identifying voices in Jer 8:18–9:1. While I disagree that the people speak in 8:18 (rather it is 'D. Zion'), I concur that Jeremiah speaks in 8:19a, YHWH in 8:19bc, the people in 8:20, Jeremiah in 8:21–9:1 [E], then YHWH in 9:2f; J. Henderson, "Who Weeps in Jeremiah 8:23 (9:1)?", article forthcoming.

[21] W. Holladay noted that in Jer 10:19–20 Jerusalem is speaking, "Style, Irony, and Authenticity in Jeremiah," *JBL* 81 (1962), 47; F. K. Kumaki identified Jerusalem as the speaker in Jer 4 and 10 texts, "A New Look at Jer 4,19–22 and 10,19–21," *AJBI* 8 (1982): 113–14, cited in and followed by M. Biddle, *Polyphony*, 21; Robert Carroll identified Jer 4:19–21 as Judah or Jerusalem's speech and 10:19–20, 23–24 as speech of the city or community, *Jeremiah* (Philadelphia: Westminster, 1986), 167, 261–65.

[22] For this and other 2nd Isaiah texts' relationships to Lamentations, see Patricia Tull, *Remember the Former Things*.

[23] In a survey of Jer 2–23, I find 24 speeches (including his laments) that can be identified as Jeremiah's voice *distinct from YHWH's* (Jer 4:10; 5:3–6; 6:10–11; 6:26; 8:19a; 8:21–9:1 [E]; 9:11; 9:19–21; 10:21; 11:18–20; 12:1–4, 12–13; 13:15–17; 14:1–6; 14:13; 14:17–18; 15:10, 15–18; 17:14–18; 18:18–23; 20:7–18; 22:28–29; 23:9–10; 23:18–20). I am following J. Henderson's identifications of Jeremiah's speech in Jer 4:10–12, 8:19a and 21–23, and 14:17–18; "Who Weeps in Jeremiah 8:23 (9:1)?".

ment of those areas. Here is an outline of all the 'speakers' identified in the four textual units:

Jer 4:3–31[24]		*Jer 8:18–9:1 (9:2)*		*Jer 10:17–25*		*Lam 1*	
3a	[intro.]	8:18	*Jerusalem*	17–18	YHWH	1–9b	Jeremiah
3b–9	YHWH	19a	Jeremiah	19–20	*Jerusalem*	9c	*Jerusalem*
10–12	Jeremiah	19b	People	21	Jeremiah	10–11b	Jeremiah
13	People	19c	YHWH	22–25	*Jerusalem*	11c–15b	*Jerusalem*
14–18	YHWH	20	People			15c	Jeremiah
19–21	*Jerusalem*	21–23	Jeremiah			16	*Jerusalem*
22	YHWH	9:1	YHWH[25]			17	Jeremiah
23–26	Jeremiah					18–22	*Jerusalem*
27–28	YHWH						
29	Jeremiah						
30–31	YHWH						

In the following analysis, it will be necessary to briefly summarize the relationship between the figures of YHWH and Jerusalem as it is characterized by speeches attributed to YHWH *preceding Jer 4*. In the Jeremiah texts under consideration, one may note that the devastation of Jerusalem and surrounding Judah is *unfolding*; we do not have to wait until Lamentations to see texts that depict this.

Across Jer 2–3, the divine point of view rendered toward Jerusalem is that figuratively she is his wife but is no longer loyal to him (2:2; cf. 3:10–13); she has instead acted like a prostitute[26] and does not serve her 'husband' (2:20). Moreover, in Jeremiah's poetic rhetoric, the voice of YHWH accuses Jerusalem of claiming innocence and of being more concerned with the removal of divine anger (2:35; 3:4–5). Yet YHWH continues to accuse Jerusalem of wrongdoing (2:35; 3:5).[27]

[24] Jer 4:1–2 may be treated separately since it is the conclusion of a contrasting discussion about the northern kingdom of Israel begun at 3:6.

[25] This is 9:2 in English versification.

[26] "For long ago you *broke* (שׁבר) your *yoke* (על) . . . you played the whore" (2:20, NRSV following LXX). Other prophetic voices critique Jerusalem as being like a prostitute (e.g. Isa 1:21, by YHWH/Isaiah; Ezek 16 and 23:40–42 by YHWH); thus the imagery is not unique to Jeremiah's rendering of YHWH's rhetoric, but is a recurring formula (nonetheless striking) in the prophetic tradition.

[27] Both the themes of unfaithful Israel/Judah/Jerusalem depicted as a prostitute, as well as the *anger* of YHWH and subsequent punishment of the people are not uncommon in prophetic books (e.g., Isa 1:24; Hos 5:3; Ezek 7:3, 8).

Jer 4:3–31[28]

After YHWH's numerous references to Jerusalem as a persona, continuing into Jer 4, direct discourse by Jerusalem's poet appears in 4:19–21, the first in the book of Jeremiah. She responds first, however, to the ongoing military invasion: "My insides! my insides (מעי מעי)! I labor in anguish!"[29] Commentators have traditionally identified this speech as Jeremiah's personal lament. However, it cannot be, when the flow of the whole section is read.

That is, just prior to her speech, at 4:10–12 Jeremiah intercedes with YHWH on behalf of the people and Jerusalem: "Aha! Adonai, YHWH, but surely you have truly deceived (נשׁא) this people and Jerusalem. . . ."[30] At 4:13 *the people* interject with a description of the coming disaster. At 4:14 YHWH exhorts Jerusalem, even though the siege is imminent: "Wash your *heart* of evil, Jerusalem, so that you may be saved!" And YHWH explains that she is besieged "because against me she has *rebelled* (כי־אתי מרתה)" (16–17).[31] Then YHWH speaks directly to the personae of Jerusalem and Judah:

Your ways and your doings have brought these things upon you.

> This is your evil—how *bitter* (מר) it is!
> Indeed, it has reached your *heart* (לבך). (4:18)

It is here that 'Jerusalem' speaks:

> *My insides! my insides* (מעי מעי)! *I labor in anguish* (אחולה)!
> The walls of *my heart*![32]

[28] Cf. the treatments by M. Biddle, *Polyphony*, 17–22, and K. O'Connor, "The Tears of God," 175–79.

[29] One word: אחולה, reading with K and LXX; the same root is used in the same image of a woman in travail later in vs 31.

[30] The verb is the same as used by Eve in Gen 3 to say that the snake "deceived" her. That Jeremiah wrangles with whether to empathize with the people or critique them is evidenced elsewhere, as in his lament of 18:18–23 in which he calls upon YHWH to punish those against him, especially the leaders, among his own people. That 4:9–12 is also poetry (not prose as NRSV) as some scholars and translations suggest is convincingly demonstrated by R. Althann, *A Philological Analysis of Jeremiah 4–6 in the Light of Northwest Semitic*, Biblica et orientalia 38 (Rome: Biblical Institute Press, 1983), 58–72. J. Henderson makes a convincing argument that Jeremiah continues speaking through 4:11 and 12 since they lack the formula, "thus says the Lord" and contain Jeremiah's characteristic use of the term of endearment, 'Daughter of My People' (בת־עמי); J. Henderson, "Who Speaks."

[31] This rhetorical claim with the verb מרה will be important in 'Jerusalem/D. Zion's' speech in Lam 1.

[32] The phrase "walls of my heart" (קירות לבי) is used only here in the Hebrew

My heart is in turmoil;
I cannot keep silent;
for the sound of the *shofar* I hear—O my soul!—
the alarm of battle.
The clamor of *destruction upon destruction*—
(שבר על שבר; "crushing upon crushing"),
indeed!—the whole land is devastated.
Suddenly *my tents* are devastated,
my curtains in a moment!
How long must I see the signal,
hear the sound of the *shofar*?! (19–21)

This poet responds from her experience in the city, thus in juxtaposition to Jeremiah's renderings of YHWH's judgments against the city, her voice comes across *as the city's*. Her speech resembles a communal dirge, because it contains the element of the description of disaster, distress, and mourning speech. Essentially, Jerusalem's poet responds to the imminent danger of the context and possibly to Jeremiah's already-voiced rhetoric. Not only does she echo YHWH's reference to the city's "*heart*," she also echoes YHWH's earlier speech about the "*shofar*" signaling war (cf. vss 5) and the coming "*destruction*" (שבר; vs 6).[33] Is there a singer in the context responding to Jeremiah's utterances, whose songs have been inscribed in the final form of the text?

Another indication that in vss 19–21 the poet speaks as the city Jerusalem is that she says, "my tents (אהלי) are destroyed, my curtains (יריעותי). . . ." She refers to these also in Jer 10:20, which are suggestive, perhaps in addition to humble habitations, of the Jerusalem

Bible (BDB: 885), yet it is fitting, since the city is like a person whose being ('heart') is contained within the city (and temple) walls. The phrase also works if the voice refers to all of Judah, since "wall" is often used to denote a city, thus, ". . . the 'cities' of my heart."

[33] While it may be proposed that this speech is by YHWH who is suffering the effects of seeing the city threatened, this interpretation is not as convincing, in my view, because the dramatic flow has suggested that YHWH has just vociferously *called for* the sounding of the shofar so that the invasion is unmistakable to Jerusalem, has been castigating Jerusalem, and in the previous verse has just said that everything coming upon Jerusalem has now "reached *your heart*" (vs 18). YHWH's tone, expressed in the texts, has been one of anger, not anguish, about what is happening. Moreover, YHWH would not likely say "my tents are devastated," but "my *tent* is devastated" (vs 20). As we shall see in Lam 1–2, the first poet there uses much of the same specific terminology again to describe, not YHWH, but Jerusalem; moreover, Jerusalem's poet uses first-person speech in Lam 1–2 with some of this same rare, peculiar terminology.

'sanctuary' (cf. Exod 25:8; 26:1, 7).[34] As will be seen below, in Lam 2:4 another poet echoes her speech: "Like an enemy [YHWH] has killed all those who were the 'pride of our eyes' in the *tent* (אהל) of D. Zion . . ."[35]

Here in Jer 4, there is no dialogue that ensues with YHWH after Jerusalem's poet's speech,[36] but YHWH instead condemns *the people* (22).[37] (This may be suggestive that Jerusalem's poet speaks from the people's point of view.)

How *foolish* (אויל)[38] are my people!
Me they do not *know* (ידעו; or, 'acknowledge');[39]
Children of *stupidity* (סכלים) they are,
without understanding they are.
(But) skilled they are for doing evil (להרע)—
yet for doing good (להיטיב)
they do not *know* how (ידעו).

Jeremiah next utters a 'cosmic' communal dirge about the death of creation and the destruction of the land (4:23–26).[40]

I *look* upon the *land/earth* (הארץ), and *behold!* (הנה)—'*waste and void*' (תהו ובהו),
and unto the *heavens* and their *light is not* (ואין אורם)![41]

[34] BDB: 438. In Isa 54:2, in contrast, YHWH addresses and *encourages the destroyed city* of Jerusalem as a barren woman who will have so many children that she will need to enlarge her *tent* and stretch out the *curtains* of her habitation (noted also by B. Bakke Kaiser, *Poet*, 169). Cf. Jer 49:28–29 and the taking of the *tents* and *curtains* of the people of Kedar and Hazor when their settlements are attacked.

[35] Note that the poet(s) of Jer 4, 10 and Lam 2:4 do not use the term 'temple' (היכל). What might the poet(s)' choice of rhetoric say about their social location, vis-a-vis the 'temple' leadership? Cf. Jer 7:4, where YHWH says, "Do not trust yourselves to the lying words: 'the temple (היכל) of YHWH, the temple of YHWH, the temple of YHWH.'"

[36] Yet, just prior to a salvation oracle in Jer 30:16–17, YHWH responds to Jerusalem, "Why do you cry out over your *brokenness/crushing* (שברך) . . .?"

[37] R. Carroll notes that the LXX renders this text condemning not the people, but the leaders, as in Jer 10:21; *Jeremiah*, 167. Since both groups are critiqued in Jeremiah texts, the LXX is suspicious in perhaps bringing this text in line to match the parallel one in Jer 10:21, especially since that text suggests Jeremiah as speaker (who typically blames the leaders).

[38] LXX has אילי ('rams') here, likely harmonizing with the parallel, but different, speech in Jer 10:21 which has 'shepherds'; see discussion in R. Althann, *A Philological Analysis of Jer 4–6*, 92–94.

[39] For this meaning of ידע in a covenantal context, paralleled in Ugaritic texts, see R. Althann, ibid., 93, and M. Dahood who cites it in *KTU* 2.39:12–14.

[40] That Jeremiah is the speaker is evident from the third person reference to YHWH in vs 26, as well as his characteristic prophetic use of the communal dirge, here applied to the land/creation.

[41] Whether intentionally or not, B. Arapović uses this communal dirge motif (also

I *look* to the mountains, and *behold*! they are quaking,
and *all* the hills shaking.
I *look* and *behold*! there is *no 'adam'* (אין האדם)!
and *all* the *birds* of the heavens flee.
I *look* and behold! the *garden-land* a desert!
and *all* its cities are pulled down (> נתץ),[42]
on account of YHWH,
on account of his burning *anger* (חרון אפו). (4:23–26)[43]

Jeremiah's peculiar poetry depicts an ironic reversal of the creative power of YHWH's speech in the Gen 1 tradition, a reversion to chaos. Jeremiah has raised the contrast motif of the social dirge to a cosmic level. The emphasis on complete destruction by the repetition of "*all*" echoes Jerusalem's poet's previous speech (vs 20): "The clamor of destruction upon destruction, *all* the land/earth (כל־הארץ) is devastated."[44]

In vss 27–28 YHWH takes up the same topic from the preceding lines, summarizes and affirms it: ". . . Because of this the earth shall mourn, and the heavens above grown black."[45] Then in vs 29, Jeremiah brings down the dirge description of the *heavens and earth* (23–26) *to the land of Judah* and *all its cities*:

At the noise of horse and archer,
all the cities (כל־העיר) flee;
they go into thickets,[46]
and they climb among rocks;
all the cities are forsaken,
and there is *no man* (אין־יושב . . . איש) dwelling in them. (vs 29)

If the parallel between *all* creation and *all* the cities of Judah destroyed is not clear enough, Jeremiah also echoes his "no *adam*" from vs 25 above with "no *ish*" here.[47]

contrast) in his war poem "Codex Criminalis, I": "Lord–You said: 'Let there be light!'/but who was it who said 'Let there be darkness'?; transl. I. Pozajić Jerić, in *Between Despair and Lamentation*, 35.

[42] נתץ is an important verb; it is one of the four destroying verbs in the prophet's call narrative (Jer 1:10).

[43] YHWH also expresses the coming destruction of Jerusalem as a pouring out of divine anger in Ezek 7:3, 8.

[44] See below the pervasive repetition of "*all*" by the two poets of Lam 1.

[45] W. Holladay notes a similar pattern in Am 7:7–9 of the prophet's vision report followed by YHWH's confirmation of it; *Jeremiah*, vol. I, 148.

[46] NRSV.

[47] For an analysis of Jeremiah's use of Genesis rhetoric in YHWH's speech in Jer 2:2–9, including "no *adam*" and "*hevel*," see N. Lee, "Exposing a Buried Subtext

Compare the contrast motif of the Croatian communal dirge, "Vukovar", cited earlier, rendering war's impact upon the natural order/created world. Slavica Crnjac, like Jeremiah, uses the same images of birds fleeing, a hovering black cloud (of mourning), and an empty, forsaken city:[48]

A black cloud hung
over the ancient town of Vukovar
beautiful lime-trees fell,
"tambura" were silenced.

Now the ghastly ruins stand.
And the white doves fly far away
and tell the sad tale:
"Oh world that was Vukovar. . . ."

Returning to Jer 4, in vs 30 Jeremiah renders YHWH directly addressing again personified Jerusalem as the "Devastated One" (שׁדוד). Is this YHWH's (or the redactor's) response to Jerusalem's poet's complaint that her tents are "devastated" (שׁדדו; vs 20)? The tone of YHWH's speech here matches the divine anger and judgment expressed pervasively in Jer 4 and in prior texts. Here YHWH, using the same imagery of the prostitute as before, describes personified Jerusalem's gawdy clothing and denigrates her vanity. Finally, YHWH's speech closes the section in vs 31 as though he has *only just heard* Jerusalem's poet's cry of travail, rendered back in vs 19 above:

Indeed! A cry like *a woman in labor* (כחולה) I hear![49]
  distress like one bringing forth her first child,
the voice of Daughter Zion gasping,
  stretching out her hands (יפרשׂ כפיה),
"Woe is me, for my being faints before killers!" (4:31)

YHWH links the image of the prostitute with the other common prophetic formula of a woman in travail to describe Jerusalem. This text implies Jeremiah has rendered YHWH 'hearing' Jerusalem's prior speech, but YHWH's description of her, while she is suffering

in Jeremiah." W. Holladay also links the האדם אין in Jer 4:25 to ואדם אין in Gen 2:5, and the הכרמל ("fruitful land") in Jer 4:26 to "creation" in Gen 1–2; *Jeremiah*, vol. 1, 148.

[48] Translated by Dalia Kuća, "Vukovar," in *Pismo iz rasapa* [Writing from Turmoil], ed. Đurđa Miklaužić (Zagreb: Multimedijski ženski centar NONA, 1995), 16.

[49] Same root as utilized in vs 19 above when Jerusalem cried, "I labor in anguish!"

destruction, is one of angry contempt, not compassion or comfort. Jerusalem does not speak again in Jer 4. She is left at the mercy of killers.

In summary, what role do *Jeremiah's speeches* play in this text? The passage shows Jeremiah's point of view interjected at vss 10–12 with a complaint against YHWH (lament genre) for deceiving Jerusalem and the people. The prophet tries to intervene on their behalf and shows empathy. He also uses the communal dirge typical of prophets, but infuses it with his individual poetic style, drawing upon rhetoric similar to that found in Genesis 1.

Just as striking is the role of Jerusalem's poet, who in expressing her own suffering in the city, is heard as the city's voice, rarely heard in the Hebrew Bible, a first person account of its suffering. Second, Jerusalem's poet reflects the course of events moving forward. Her expressed suffering is a result of the destruction which has ensued after Jeremiah's/YHWH's threats and warnings in the previous verses. Third, her speech responds immediately and precisely to elements in YHWH's speech ("heart," "*shofar*," "destruction"). Fourth, *what she does not say* is also significant. She does not respond to YHWH's repeated judgment speeches about her transgressions (4:4, 12, 14, 17, 18, 22, 30). Jerusalem's poet is preoccupied with suffering, not sin, and alludes to the suffering of women in the devastation of war.

Before moving to Jer 8, several texts between chapters 4 and 8 shed light on the points of view of the speakers. In the very next text, Jer 5, there is an ironic development. YHWH tells Jeremiah in 5:1:

> Go to and fro through the streets of *Jerusalem*;
> look now and notice!
> Search in her squares, (see) if you can find a man,
> if (you can find) a doer of *justice*, a seeker of truth—
> so that I may pardon (סלח) *Jerusalem*.

This is reminiscent of Abraham and YHWH discussing the fate of Sodom and Gomorrah.[50] An irony is that the fate of Jerusalem, personified as a sinful woman in YHWH's metaphors, now hangs

[50] Cf. the use of this theme by M. Koprivnjak in her poem about the destruction of Mostar in Bosnia in 1992, "Mostar, the Vukovar of Herzegovina," transl. Janet Berković and Ružica Pađen, in *Ratni Blagoslovi* (Osijek: Izvori, 1996), 138–39.

in the balance upon finding *one man* who is *just* or *truthful*. More irony will be seen in Jer 10:24 below, where Jerusalem's poet admits needing "correction" (יסרני), but this has no effect on YHWH's response. Here in Jer 5, the prophet gives an equally ironic, even amazing, response about the people (in light of Jerusalem's outcry of anguish in chapter 4 above):

> O Lord, your eyes, do they not (look) for truth?
> You have struck them,
>   but they *felt no anguish* (לא חלו);
> You have consumed them,
>   they refused *to take correction* (מוסר; from יסר). (5:3ab)

Yet Jerusalem's poet above said precisely that she *was* 'feeling the *anguish*' (4:19, 31). Thus in his poetry here, Jeremiah is *unaware* of Jerusalem's expressed "anguish" in her prior speech; if Jeremiah is the poet of all the speeches, he presumably would know his character Jerusalem. This non sequitur (or seam) in the text is one of the first textual evidences that we may have *a poet other than Jeremiah* speaking as Jerusalem. YHWH concludes in 5:7, 9a, saying to the persona of Jerusalem through Jeremiah, "How can I pardon you for these things? Your children have forsaken me . . . Shall I not punish (them) for these things?"[51] And in 6:6c, 8, YHWH explains why Jerusalem will be punished: "There is only oppression within her . . . *Be corrected* (הוסרי), Jerusalem. . . ."

While the preceding discussion has not intended to present a thorough analysis of Jer 2–6, it has set forth the larger rhetorical context within which Jerusalem's poet's first speech appears in Jer 4. It has characterized the poetry of both Jeremiah and Jerusalem's poet in the context. And it has highlighted the dialogical nature of the discourse (rather unusual in a prophetic book), as different voices echo one anothers' terminology, themes, and concerns. The second key text where Jerusalem's poet speaks will now be considered.

> To Mostar—my beloved town . . .
> the dark clouds of war,
> of destruction and decay have covered you.
> And could not God find even ten righteous men
> within your walls for whose sake
> he would save you from this evil?

[51] See K. O'Connor, "Tears of God," 178, for the identification of D. Zion whom YHWH addresses: "How can I pardon you?"

My eyes today are as hundreds of springs,
my voice a whistling wind from the glen.
If only my arms were wings above the village
that I might fly and fly, fly without cease.[52]

Jure Kaštelan, from *Pjetao na krovu*

Jer 8:18–9:1 (9:2)

In Jer 8:18 Jerusalem's poet speaks again. This identification is evidenced by the combination of several rhetorical features. She uses first person singular speech to refer again to her *heart*, reminiscent of Jer 4:19.[53]

> My joy has gone; *grief* (יגון) is upon me; *my heart is faint* (לבי דוי).[54] (Jer 8:18)

"My heart is faint" recurs verbatim in Lam 1:22, where I shall consider her poetic voice there. Immediately here in 8:19, Jeremiah responds to her outcry with his favored term of endearment for Jerusalem—"*Daughter of My People.*"[55]

[52] Ante Kadić, "Postwar Croatian Lyric Poetry" [i.e., post-WWII] *American Slavic and East European Review* 17 (1958): 523. It is fascinating to compare Kaštelan's speech here similar in form to YHWH's speech below, and wish to flee from the people, a theme modified perhaps from Ps 55 (see below).

[53] J. Henderson identifies Jer 8:18 as speech of "the people (בת־עמי)," though not explaining the shift from first person singular to plural later in the passage. However, Henderson's identification of the speakers in 8:19–9:1, based on a subtle and sophisticated reading of the text (esp. the speakers' different uses of עמי and בת־עמי), is most convincing: Jeremiah (8:19a); YHWH (19bc); people (20); Jeremiah (8:21–23); YHWH (9:1); J. Henderson, "Who Speaks."

[54] YHWH had also described Jerusalem as "*fainting*" (עיפה) before killers in Jer 4:31. Compare "*my heart is faint*" in Lam 1:22 to Isa 1:5, and the poet of Lam 1:4 describing Zion's daughters as "*grieving*."

[55] The appellative בת־עמי appears only 15x in the Hebrew Bible (MT; 14x if Jer 9:6 is excluded, LXX). YHWH as speaker prefers the term "My People" (used 29x in the book of Jeremiah; 25x in Ezekiel). In Lamentations בת־עמי is used only by the speaker I identify below (for various reasons) as Jeremiah (Lam 2:11; 3:48; 4:3, 6, 10). I was aware of the peculiar use of this term in poetry in the book of Jeremiah. J. Henderson convincingly argues from the use of the phrase בת־עמי in Lamentations where YHWH does not speak that *YHWH cannot be the speaker in the book of Jeremiah in texts using this appellative* (Jer 4:11; 6:26; 8:11, 19, 21, 22, 23; 9:1, 6; 14:17). Henderson proposes that Jeremiah is the speaker of those texts, and his argument helps further my own (that Jeremiah speaks as a poet in Lamentations). However, one of these Jeremiah texts poses a difficulty for Jeremiah as speaker. It is Jer 8:11 (MT), which contains the speaker's use of בת־עמי in what appears to be

Listen! A sound! A cry for help from *Daughter of My People*,
  those being removed from the land. . . . (8:19a)

One may already ask here whether "*Daughter of My People*" is the prophet's favored term of endearment for the personified city Jerusalem, or *for Jerusalem's poet*. Jeremiah's previously detached attitude (in Jer 4 and 5) about 'Jerusalem' shifts to one of *empathy*, as his speech seems to be a direct response to Jerusalem's poet's speech above. A few lines later, Jeremiah speaks again, and *subjectively mourns* for the first time in the book, over the devastations unfolding against Jerusalem and the people.[56] Note his echoing of Jerusalem's poet's earlier double use of שֶׁבֶר (שֶׁבֶר עַל שֶׁבֶר; 4:20).

For the *crushing* (שֶׁבֶר) of the *Daughter of My People* I am *crushed* (הָשְׁבַּרְתִּי);
  I mourn; dismay has seized me.
Is there no balm in Gilead?
Is there no physican there?[57]
Why is the wound of the *Daughter of My People* not healed?
O that my head were a spring of water,
  and my eyes a fountain of tears (מְקוֹר דִּמְעָה),[58]
that I might cry day and night
  for the slain of *Daughter of My People*. (8:21–23)

a doublet of YHWH's speech from Jer 6:14 (MT; wherein YHWH uses the term "my people," עַמִּי). Yet, if YHWH does not use בַּת־עַמִּי, why would it appear in 8:11, a doublet of YHWH's prior speech?

It is precisely here that an oral poetic approach clarifies the matter. For 8:11 is not a mere "doublet" (*literary* term) of 6:14, *but rather* it may be argued, is Jeremiah's (oral poetic) re-utterance of YHWH's speech in 6:14. Jeremiah's use of a different appellative may be evidence of a different speaker/poetic composer. Instead of YHWH's עַמִּי of MT 6:14, Jeremiah allows his own characteristic appellative, בַּת־עַמִּי, to slip into the re-utterance. A careful examination of 6:12–15 and 8:10–12 reveals that these are not duplicate texts, but the second pulls together the pieces of the prior speech in a slightly different configuration, and in this case, still true to the intent of YHWH's speech. This phenomenon well accords with A. B. Lord's description of how oral poets composed 'new' poems from previous phrases and themes, producing agreements and differences in two, resulting, performed poems; *Singer of Tales*, 30–98.

Thus, we may conclude that בַּת־עַמִּי *is emerging as an epithet characteristically favored by Jeremiah as poet*. Likely Jeremiah built upon its single usage by Isaiah in Isa 22:4, where it is also a term of endearment when Isaiah weeps for the 'devastation' (שֹׁד) of Jerusalem.

[56] See the same unusual shift by the poet from communal dirge in Lam 1 to mourning in Lam 2:11.

[57] Vs 22a: NRSV.

[58] Vs 8:23a: NRSV. See also Jeremiah's similar tone and terminology in Jer 13:17 ("my eyes will run down tears," וְתֵרַד עֵינִי דִּמְעָה). J. Henderson notes the frequent connection of weeping (and other) terminology to the use of בַּת־עַמִּי, used by Jeremiah in his poetry; "Who Speaks."

By contrast, YHWH's speech in this text still conveys a tone of frustration, anger, and condemnation, beginning at 19c: "Why do they provoke me to *anger* with their images, with their foreign idols?!" Scholars differ in their identification of intermingling voices in Jer 8:18–9:1 and often indicate that the pathos of the voices of Jeremiah and YHWH here are indistinguishable.[59] I would suggest that a careful reading reveals more subtlety in their points of view than this. It cannot be denied that Jeremiah must convey the full range of YHWH's emotion in addition to his own, and that YHWH at certain places in the entire discourse feels pain at the deaths of the people. The specific text here, however, is not primarily aiming to convey this divine pain, nor has the flow of the larger text *yet* conveyed YHWH's expression of grief for the people's suffering. That vss 21–23 expresses *Jeremiah's* grief is evident in his use of "Daughter of My People," not "My People," YHWH's favored term.

Instead, Jeremiah and YHWH are grieving for two different reasons. The passage suggests that where Jeremiah's grieving for the people leaves off at 8:23 (note his repeated use of בת־עמי, Daughter of My People, in vss 19, 21, and 22),[60] YHWH's speech begins (9:1; using עמי):

> O that I had in the desert a wayfarer's hut;
> let me forsake *my people* and go away from them!

YHWH expresses grief for [him]self out of serious *complaint* about the people's behavior; it is a grief rooted in their lost relationship, that the people have forsaken YHWH.[61] YHWH's grief is that of a wounded lover or spouse who is not dealing with [his] partner's pain. Unlike Jeremiah, YHWH's speech does *not* convey grief *because of* the people's *suffering*.[62] Brueggemann has incisively noted that YHWH's speech above is a poetic reworking of a psalmic theme (Ps 55:7–8):[63]

[59] Thus W. Brueggemann, yet who also suggests that YHWH in this passage is both grieving and angry, *A Commentary on Jeremiah: Exile and Homecoming* (Grand Rapids: Wm. B. Eerdmans, 1998), 91–95.

[60] See J. Henderson, "Who Speaks."

[61] W. Brueggemann, *A Commentary on Jeremiah*, 94–95.

[62] This analysis differs slightly from K. O'Connor's reading that identifies YHWH as the principal speaker in 8:18–9:3; "Tears of God," 179–183. I would not agree that YHWH is a "weeping God" in the book of Jeremiah but a grieving God, cf. 12:7–11.

[63] W. Brueggemann, *Commentary on Jeremiah*, 94.

O that I had wings like a dove! Let me fly away and rest!
See! I would flee far away; I would lodge in the desert.

But this speech falls within a lament where the psalmist grieves and complains of his or her mistreatment by enemies and longs to escape. YHWH identifies with that view in relation to the people who are like his enemy.

YHWH's litany of angry accusations follow (9:2–8). Not until 9:9 does YHWH call for the mourning women to raise a dirge, first however, for the devastated land, and then, in 9:16, to raise a dirge for "us." The God characterized elsewhere in the Hebrew Bible as "slow to anger" might well be characterized in the book of Jeremiah as angry, and "slow to show compassion" in comparison to Jeremiah. Yet YHWH's point of view reflects 'where YHWH is,' at a stage in a broken relationship. Jeremiah's compassionate mourning (Jer 9:1) "leads" YHWH to compassionate mourning (Jer 9:10f and 9:17).

Jer 10:17–25

Jerusalem's poet's *third speech* in the book of Jeremiah appears in two parts in 10:17–25, alongside speech by Jeremiah and the prophet's rendering of YHWH's speech.[64]

Jer 10:	17–18	YHWH
	19–20	*Jerusalem's poet*
	21	Jeremiah
	22–25	*Jerusalem's poet*

YHWH speaks to the persona of Jerusalem, with second person singular imperative, in vs 17:

"Gather up your bundle from the ground,[65]
O you who live under siege!" (17)
For thus says the Lord:
"Look! I am slinging out
  the inhabitants of the land at this time,
and I am pressing them out,
  so that they may be detected." (18)[66]

[64] Most commentators treat 10:1–16 as a separate section focusing on idols.

[65] NRSV; LXX has "from the street."

[66] Contra NRSV, the translation of והצרותי in vs 18b is the hip'il of one sense of צרר (to restrict, make narrow, BDB:864) and suggests a purpose and consequence of a siege upon inhabitants who are holed up within a town: to cause such distress

Since chapter 4, the rhetorical situation has moved forward such that the previously anticipated siege has now been reality long enough for YHWH in Jer 10:17 to refer to Jerusalem *living under* siege. Jerusalem's poet's speech that follows (vss 19–20 and 22–25) is longer than her first speech in Jer 4. In both, the poet begins with mourning speech due to the intensifying attack and picks up some of the same terms and themes.

> Woe is me because of my *crushing* (שׁבר)!
> My wound gushes.[67]
> But I say, "Truly this is my piercing (חלי),
> and I will bear it."[68]
> My *tent* (אהלי) is *devastated* (שׁדד)
> and all my cords are snapped;
> my children have gone out from me,[69]
> and are no more.
> There is no one any more to stretch out *my tent* (אהלי),
> or set *my curtains* (יריעותי). (Jer 10:19–20)

Jerusalem's poet speaks further about the *destruction* or *crushing* (שׁבר; 4:6, 20) of the siege. In 4:20 she had said, "*destruction upon destruction* (שׁבר על שׁבר)—the whole land is *devastated* (שׁדדה)." But here in 10:19, the terror of distant destruction has drawn near. The widespread שׁבר is now "*my* שׁבר!": "Woe is me because of my *crushing/brokenness* (שׁבר)! My wound gushes . . . this is my piercing." Repeating the *devastation* of her *tents* (4:20 and 10:20), the 'body' of the city (of the poet?) receives and feels the blows of violent impact. An important related text is *Jeremiah's* response to her crushing blow in Jer 14:17b–18:[70] "Let my eyes run down with tears day and night . . . with

that they are 'pressed' or forced out; that YHWH intends to create vulnerable refugees is a stunning statement. The LXX phrase used here, εν θλίψσει, is also suggestive of both 'compression' and 'distress' (BAG, 362); 'that they may be detected' translates ימצאו as a nifal imperfect, foll. LXX.

[67] An unusual use of a verbal form of the noun נחל ("torrent" or "wady" that flows), rather than from חלה (as W. Holladay, *Lamentations*, 342; to be "weak, sick"; nifal fem. sing. participle); cf. Jer 14:17 and Lam 2:18.

[68] Implicit in this statement is her understanding that the suffering is punishment she must bear.

[69] LXX has the term for "flock" instead of the verb, יצא: καὶ τὰ πρόβατά μου ("my children and my flock are no more").

[70] The identification of this text as *Jeremiah's* mourning speech, not YHWH's, follows J. Henderson, "Who Weeps." Henderson follows Holladay's argument (*Jeremiah*, 436–37) that 14:17a really is a summary statement to YHWH's speech preceding it, and that several key terms in the mourning speech are Jeremianic, based on several texts elsewhere.

what a great *crushing* (שֶׁבֶר) is Virgin Daughter of My People *crushed* (נִשְׁבְּרָה), (her) *wound gushes forth* (מַכָּה נַחְלָה מְאֹד)." While the line "the wound gushes/flows" is not unique to these poets—it appeared/was perhaps coined by the poet of Nah 3:19 regarding Assyria—it is elaborated upon several times by these poets (Jer 10:19; 14:17; 30:12).[71]

Jerusalem's poet then adds another aspect of her suffering: "My children have gone out from me, and they are no more. There is no one any more who will stretch out my tent, or set my curtains" (10:20b–c). She is a *mother* alone, wounded, with her habitation in ruins around her, and her children gone who would help her restore it. This poet's image of Jerusalem is a suffering mother, which differs greatly from YHWH's image of her as an unfaithful wife or prostitute.

The text shifts away from this image of the suffering city, perhaps indicating a new speaker, to the prophetic *judgment* genre about the "shepherds" or leaders who are reponsible for the loss of the children and 'scattering of the flock' (21).[72] Is this Jerusalem still speaking, or Jeremiah?

a *How* (כִּי) *stupid* (נִבְעֲרוּ; like beasts) are the shepherds!
b because *YHWH* (אֶת־יְהוָה) *they did not* seek;
c so they have not been *prudent* (הִשְׂכִּילוּ),
d and all their flock is scattered! (21)

The speech is not a non sequitur, but a *reponse* to YHWH's parallel critical speech against the whole people in Jer 4:22 at virtually the same place in that text (also foll. the city's speech about tents). I quote it again here for comparison:

a' *How* (כִּי) *foolish* (אֱוִיל) are my people!
b' *Me* (אוֹתִי) *they did not know* (יָדָעוּ);
c' children of *stupidity* (סְכָלִים) they are,
without understanding they are. (4:22a–b)

Just prior to this text in 4:22, YHWH had also blamed *Jerusalem* in 4:18a: "Your way (דַּרְכֵּךְ) and your doings have brought these things

[71] See discussion of Lam 1 and 2 below, however, for the poets' continued rendering of these terms, esp. Jeremiah's transforming "wound flowing" to "eyes flowing with tears" because of the wound.

[72] R. Althann and others suggest there is linkage of meaning between vss 19–21 and 22; *A Philological Analysis of Jer 4–6*, 94.

upon you." That the poet in 10:21 *shifts the criticism away from Jerusalem* and the people *to the "shepherds"* is suggestive of Jeremiah's point of view. As mentioned earlier, he had intervened to defend the people in 4:10. In numerous places in the book of Jeremiah he is sympathetic to the people over against the rulers, priests, and prophets.[73] Note the striking wordplay he uses with שׂכל (*shepherds* not 'prudent'; 10:21) in response to YHWH's סכל (*people's* 'stupidity'; 4:22). Jeremiah is responding *precisely* to YHWH's judgment speech with *more nuanced* judgment speech. They have different points of view about who is to blame.

The above dialogue is interrupted in the text by a distant sound from the north Jerusalem's poet notices and mentions. Previously (4:19, 21), she had spoken of hearing the *shofar* sounding the alarm of the approaching enemy. Now she hears the enemy itself drawing near:

> —a sound is heard! listen! it is coming—
> a great rumbling from the land of the north,
>   to make the cities of Judah a *desolation* (שׁממה),
>   a lair of jackals. (10:22)

While this speech might be attributed to Jeremiah, the poet's use of the term "*desolation*" occurs elsewhere in this section only in Jerusalem's poet's later speech in vs 25 (referring to the *desolation* of Jacob's pastures).

Then Jerusalem's poet shifts back to the previous topic: the failings of human beings for not seeking YHWH's guidance. That it is Jerusalem's poet still speaking is evident from her directly asking YHWH to *correct* her (יסר) in 24 below, suggesting admission of guilt. Ironically, the poet's lament is a daring act, because further lament is the genre YHWH has forbidden in this dialogue and scenario (e.g. 7:16, 11:14, 14:11).[74]

[73] E.g., 5:4, 12–13; 13:15–17; 14:13; 18:18; 20:2; 23:9–10; 25:35–38; 28:15; 36:32; 37:18–19; 38:6.

[74] It is also ironic since it is the very genre (lament) through which the people typically *confess*. Jerusalem's poet's lament is also significant in that in the book of Jeremiah the people as a whole do not lament to YHWH until Jer 14:7–9. Indeed, her lament in Jer 10 *precedes* Jeremiah's individual laments in the final shape of the book, yet they both lament to YHWH in spite of YHWH's prohibitions. *This same ordering of laments, first by Jerusalem's poet and then by Jeremiah, is also followed in Lamentations* (see below).

I *know* (ידעתי), YHWH,
that the *path* (דרך) of humans is not their own,
and it is not for a man, as he walks, to direct his own steps. (vs 23)[75]

The above address of YHWH is an ironic theological midrash, since YHWH had said to Jerusalem in Jer 4: "your *path* (דרך) and your doings have brought these things upon you" (4:18a); and, "my people are foolish, they do not *know* me . . . they do not *know* how to do good" (4:22). But the poet has uttered a formulaic *confession*, but modified it with wisdom rhetoric (Prov 20:24) to respond to YHWH's terms and concerns ("knowing," "path"), in order to convey a subtle dispute (ריב) with YHWH. She does not entirely agree that her path has caused the disaster, but *implies* that unknowing humans depend upon YHWH to direct them!

Jerusalem's poet goes further and utters, I propose, *one of the most stunning theological challenges to YHWH in the Hebrew Bible*,[76] in the guise of a formulaic plea of lament and confession.

Correct me (יסרני), YHWH, but with *justice* (משפט),
and *not* with your *anger* (באפך), lest you diminish/belittle me. (10:24)[77]

A confession like this is unprecedented in the psalms.[78] Moreover, *nowhere* does the prophet Jeremiah make this particular theological

[75] Contra M. Biddle, who does not identify 10:23–25 as spoken by 'Jerusalem', though based on unconvincing text critical and redaction critical reasons. He misses the mark with this statement: "the phenomenon of Mother Jerusalem commenting on the vagaries of human nature or referring to Jacob in the third person has no obvious parallel" (*Polyphony*, 100–101). Apart from what sounds like Biddle's questionable critique of the mother/woman city being *able* to make such insights (!), the idea that "mother" Jerusalem might comment empathetically on the fate of Jacob as a lost son (who also represents the destruction and exile of the northern kingdom) is anything but far-fetched. See Jer 30 where YHWH addresses precisely these two individuals, *Jacob/Israel* and *D. Zion*, with consolation speech. Also note J. Schmitt's analysis of Zion as mother in Jer 31 who receives and embraces exiled *Jacob*; "Virgin," 383–86.

[76] Cf. Jerusalem's poet's theology in Jer 10:24 with the daring intervening laments by Abraham for Sodom and Gomorrah (Gen 18:23–33) and Moses for the people in the wilderness (Nu 11:11–15) and at Sinai (Exod 32:11–13).

[77] YHWH's speech in the book of Ezekiel is suggestive of the very action that Jerusalem in Jer 10:24 speaks against. Because Jerusalem "has rebelled (< מרה) against my *judgments* (משפטי) . . . [I will] carry out *judgments/justice* (שפטים) against you *with anger and fury* (Ezek 5:6, 15; cf. Ezek 20:8–9, 13–14, 21–22, 33–38).

[78] The only psalmic confessions that come close to this plea in Jer 10:24 are in Ps 38 ("O YHWH, do not reprove me with your wrath or *correct* me [תיסרני] with your *anger* [בחמתך]"), and similarly Ps 6, but they fall short of asking YHWH to correct instead according to *justice*.

appeal to YHWH in this book.[79] Indeed, Jeremiah and YHWH in the book of Jeremiah do not question the general prophetic theological theme of a deity who punishes out of excessive anger. These points provide further evidence for the argument that we have here *a different poet*. Also unprecedented in this confession is the absence of explicit admission of "transgression" or "sin", etc., found in all the confessional psalms.[80] Jerusalem's poet admits needing correction, but her plea has a hoped-for condition as to how YHWH will deal with wrongdoing. She does not ask for mercy, but simply that YHWH will correct or punish according to justice, not anger.[81] The request implies that *justice puts limits on YHWH's response*, while YHWH's *anger* can be all-consuming. The poet's lament prayer is thus a window into her view of YHWH's character and also her own human character.[82] Who would offer such a challenge in the guise of 'Jerusalem,' being familiar with lament psalms and claiming some authority in theological matters? A modest proposal is that this poet is a temple singer, an 'oral poet' who composed and sang psalms. However, as was evident from previous texts that YHWH did not believe 'Jerusalem' had confessed, it is possible that neither is her "contrite" speech in Jer 10 regarded as wholehearted by YHWH. But the text does not give YHWH's immediate reaction, either to her contrition or to her challenge.

[79] Rather, a key theological development conveyed by Jeremiah and YHWH is a move away from the traditional theology that children suffer for the sins of their parents (e.g., Jer 2:2–9; 18:21; 31:29).

[80] Cf. the confessional laments: Pss 6, 25, 32, 38, 39, 40, 41, 51, 90, 106, 107.

[81] Thus similarly R. Carroll, who says she asks YHWH for "discipline in due proportion" and who notes the appearance of this phrase again in Jer 30:11 in YHWH's answering consolation, only *to Jacob* (*Jeremiah*, 263): ויסרתין למשפט, 'I will *correct* you *with justice*.' But *to Jerusalem* in the very next lines YHWH says (!): "I have struck you with the blow of the enemy, with cruel *correction* (noun form of יסר), because your inquity is great . . ." (30:14). It is as though YHWH has heard Jerusalem's earlier challenge and followed through on the idea *for Jacob*, but not her. LXX renders in 10:24: "Correct *us*, YHWH"! (noted by M. Biddle, *Polyphony*, 100, see above, and cited as one reason for discounting D. Zion as speaker here). Yet the rhetorical context in which D. Zion has been speaking supports the MT rendering of her confession here, moreso than the people's. Perhaps the LXX rendering reflects a later liturgical usage, or a connection with the communal lament of Ps 79.

[82] Following S. Balentine: "Prayer as a means of characterization . . . reveals both the prayer and his or her conception of God," *Prayer in the Hebrew Bible* (Fortress Press, 1993), 25; Balentine draws from M. Greenberg's study, *Biblical Prose Prayer, as a Window to the Popular Religion of Ancient Israel* (Berkeley: Univ. of California Press, 1983), 15. Greenberg's category includes prayers in prophetic oracles in addition to narratives (7).

Jerusalem's poet ends her lament with a typical, formulaic call for YHWH's just vengeance on her enemies,[83] but it too is modified to current terms and issues.

> *Pour out* (שְׁפֹךְ) your *wrath* (חמתך)
> on the peoples that have not *known* you,
> and upon the clans that have not called on your name;
> for they have devoured Jacob;
> they have devoured him and consumed him,
> and have desolated his *pasture-abode.* (10:25)[84]

Jerusalem's poet suggests YHWH's anger should instead consume the people 'consuming' Jacob (figurative of those destroyed/exiled in the north) who do not *know* YHWH! Note that her rendering of the desolation of the *pasture-abode* of Jacob echoes the scattering of the *flock/pasturage* of Judah (vs 21 above).

Summary

We may now sum up the purposes and characteristics of Jerusalem's poet's speech (formulaic and peculiar) in Jer 10. First, her use of the genre of mourning speech, yet stressing some of the same terms and imagery set forth in Jer 4, continues to move the poetic drama forward (scenario of invasion and destruction). She introduces into her mourning speech the matter of *her children* (10:20) who are victims of invasion and exile and uses the *image of mother* to describe herself (as opposed to YHWH's images of prostitute and wife). Second, she continues to respond specifically to *terms in YHWH's speeches* (4:5–6, 14, 18, 22, 30), suggesting that this poet has heard Jeremiah's poetic performances of YHWH's speech. YHWH's speeches in Jer 4, 5, and 10, however, have shown no evidence that YHWH responds *to*

[83] Several elements of the lament genre are here: the address of God, imperative pleas, a confession (sometimes part of a lament), and a call for YHWH to deal with her enemies. Her previous descriptions of suffering in first person (19–20) serve also as the element of 'complaint,' as does the condition appealing to YHWH not to exercise anger against her. For the standard discussion of elements of the lament genre, see C. Westermann, *Praise and Lament in the Psalms* (Atlanta: John Knox Press, 1981).

[84] Several scholars have suggested that vs 25 is a quote of Ps 79:6–7, a communal lament whose content is about the destruction of Jerusalem (e.g., R. Carroll, *Jeremiah*, 261; M. Biddle, *Polyphony*, 96), yet it is just as possible that that song is influenced by this poetic singer's speech in Jer 10:25.

Jerusalem's poet. Third, Jerusalem's poet attempts to make direct contact with YHWH through the *lament prayer* genre (10:23–25). In this lament, she significantly alters a formulaic element of confession, omitting the usual technical terms indicating transgression, but including her admission of a need for correction. This is a move beyond her speech in Jer 4. Yet Jerusalem's poet uniquely modifies a formulaic confession by challenging YHWH in *how* to respond to the people's wrongdoing, with justice and not anger.[85]

The above analysis suggests how Jeremiah and Jerusalem's poet in the book of Jeremiah participate both in their culture's formulaic poetic traditions, but also infuse this formulaic poetry with their own individual artistry in response to their context, the unfolding devastation of their city and land. The analysis now moves to the book of Lamentations, chapter 1, where the speech of the first poet of that book will be compared to Jeremiah's speeches in order to assess whether Jeremiah can be identified as the poet of Lam 1–9b and of speeches later in Lamentations. Moreover, the speeches by the poet beginning at Lam 9c, and later in the chapter, will be compared to Jerusalem's poet's speeches in Jeremiah to determine whether she might be the same poet.

[85] Jerusalem's poet's challenge evokes pressing theological questions. Can the execution of justice be separated from YHWH's anger? If the people of Jerusalem and Judah violate covenantal justice, can they still appeal to that justice with regard to YHWH's treatment of them? If YHWH's people are not living covenantly, can they expect YHWH to keep their covenant and defend them against other nations? How can YHWH's justice be fairly meted out to the guilty and the innocent among them when punishment comes through wholesale destruction by an outside nation?

CHAPTER THREE

LAMENTATIONS 1

... but between the shivering barefooted bosnian woman
or the vukovar madonna with her headless child
and the palace of justice there lie
a million miles a million millionaires
and a billion paragraphs of toothless resolutions

our beautiful homeland is furrowed with graves
where the living sing to the dead
and the dead laugh at the living
where the dead listen and the living do not hear
and bonebreaking prayers
from each side
are faxed into celestial databases
to the tricolor Christ and the other one
for peace on earth
for us to be on it for them to be under it
when offered bread they offer cannonballs...
is God or is baal the leader of croatians?
stop heaven save at least the young ones....

Borislav Arapović, "Codex Criminalis, I" (1993)[1]

The analysis now moves to the book of Lamentations.[2] The poetic singers of Lamentations 1 will be analyzed for their use of *formulaic language* characteristic of Hebrew prophets and/or psalmists as well as their individual modifications of it.[3] Thorough comparisons have

[1] Transl. Ivana Pozajić Jerić. Written in the midst of war, Arapović in this selection fills his lament with ironies and parallels the poetic lamenter of Lam 2 below and her concerns for lack of justice for those suffering, futility of prayer, plea for the children, and accusation of God (Arapović: "why have you also abandoned us"); in *Between Despair and Lamentation*, 37.

[2] See Alan Mintz, *Hurban: Responses to Catastrophe in Hebrew Literature* (New York: Columbia Univ. Press, 1984).

[3] For such formulaic elements, see esp. Robert C. Culley, *Oral Formulaic Language in the Biblical Psalms*; idem, "The Confessions of Jeremiah and Traditional Discourse," in "'A Wise and Discerning Mind,'" 69–81; and William Whallon, *Formula, Character, and Context*.

Borislav Arapović

been made between the terminology of Lamentations and all the other prophetic books, psalms, and other ANE lamentation texts, in order to determine whether what appears to be a poet's peculiar rendering in Lamentations 1 is not already formulaic in other texts. However, only occurrences elsewhere that are relevant to the argument, pro or con, will be brought into discussion. Then, comparisons will be made with the previous findings in Jeremiah 4, 8 and 10 to determine whether peculiar renderings by Jeremiah as poet there, and by Jerusalem's poet, also recur with the poets of Lamentations.

This oral poetic analysis of formulaic poetry and its modification in Lamentations explores each poet's response to the *context* of the destruction of Jerusalem. The analysis of every poetic line in Lamentations asks how each poet makes use of the following elements: genre(s), imagery/themes, terminology, rhetorical techniques, and content. These criteria were applied to Jerusalem's poet's speeches in the book of Jeremiah to produce a characterization of this poet. Jeremiah's poetry as well, located in proximity to Jerusalem's poet in Jeremiah 4, 8, and 10, was analyzed using these criteria to characterize him as prophetic poet. Now Lamentations 1 will be thus analyzed where Jerusalem's poet appears in proximity to another poet. Just as other poetic texts in Jeremiah were garnered to help fill out the rhetorical context there, points of view, and overall style of the poets, so too may additional Jeremiah texts be garnered below that illumine a poetic relationship to Lamentations.

In Lamentations there are no oracular formulas indicating YHWH's speech; neither are there implicit textual evidences that YHWH speaks anywhere in the book.[4] Here is an outline of alternating poetic singers, and the genres they employ, in Lam 1.

Poetic Singers in Lamentations I; Lament and War, Ancient and Contemporary

Lam 1:	
1–9b	First poetic singer (communal dirge)
9c	*Second poetic singer: Jerusalem's Poet* (lament)
10–11a	First poetic singer (communal dirge)
11b–15b	*Jerusalem's poet* (lament → communal dirge)
15c	First poetic singer (communal dirge)
16	*Jerusalem's poet* (mourning speech)
17	First poetic singer (communal dirge)
18–22	*Jerusalem's poet* (communal dirge → lament)

First Poetic Singer in Lamentations 1 (vss 1–9b)

Let us now consider the first poet in Lam 1:1–9b, focusing on the first segment of this speech, vss 1–6. In third person, the poet *describes* personified Jerusalem (vss 1–2), personified Judah (vs 3), and the sufferings of different inhabitants (vss 4–6), before returning to personified Jerusalem again in vs 7.[5] In the Jeremiah texts previously considered, YHWH had described personified Jerusalem, but usually with *second* person address (4:7, 14, 18, 30; 10:17),[6] whereas Jeremiah referred to Jerusalem in *third* person speech (4:11; 8:19). Both formulaic

[4] F. W. Dobbs-Allsopp contrasts the absence of YHWH's speech in Lamentations to Mesopotamian lamentations that contain the deity Enlil's speeches; *Weep, O Daughter of Zion*, 37.

[5] Dobbs-Allsopp notes the parallel between this poet as an 'impartial narrator' or 'reporter' to the poet's usual role as a reporter in the Mesopotamian lamentations; ibid., 33. This third-person descriptive style is typical of the communal dirge genre.

[6] YHWH speaks of personified Jerusalem in third person in Jer 4:17 and 31.

expressions and their modifications will now be traced in these verses in terms of the poet's uses of genre(s), imagery/themes, terminology, rhetorical technique, and content.

Use of genre. Lam 1 begins with the aftermath of destruction of Jerusalem (and Judah) described with the *communal dirge* genre. This follows most scholars' identification of such a genre here, found also in prophetic judgment speeches, which adapts a traditional funeral song (*Leichenlied*)[7] or dirge and applies it to the city or land.

The opening cry of a dirge (e.g., 'Alas!', 'How!', איכה) is *formulaic* for the genre, appearing regularly.[8] As noted earlier, the basic elements of the dirge include associated weeping/mourning speech,[9] often a proclamation or referral to death,[10] followed by a narration of the death; a complaint (*Klage*) about the death/destruction; melancholy over the transitoriness of the deceased/destroyed; an accusation (*Anklage*) against the perpetrator, perhaps with a provocative motif, i.e., a call for justice, revenge, or a curse; a call and response performance style that allows for different singers, including perhaps

[7] H. Gunkel, "Klagelieder" in *RGG*, 1500; H. Jahnow, *Das hebräische Leichenlied*, 162.

[8] See esp. Susan Niditch on this point, "The Composition of Isaiah 1," *Biblica* 61 (1980): 509–29.

[9] C. Westermann, *Lamentations*, 7.

[10] While Jahnow had observed that the proclamation of death is missing in Lam 1–2, Westermann suggests the texts assume that "death has already occurred"; *Lamentations*, 7. Actually while there is not a literal proclamation of just one death, there are the following proclamations of *multiple* deaths within these communal dirge speeches in Lam 1–2 (in Lam 1:15: "my young men" and "virgin daughter Judah"; in Lam 1:19: "my priests and elders"; in Lam 2:4: "all in whom we took pride"; in Lam 2:11–12: "infants and babies"; and additional deaths are enumerated in the 'lament' portions of the text); this expansion of deaths "proclaimed" is entirely fitting for the "transferred" use of the dirge for the entire community. Moreover, personified Jerusalem, as a mother, is typical of a mourning "survivor" (Jahnow) for whom the effect of the deaths is described by *another mourner*. Tod Linafelt discerns profound irony regarding death and D. Zion in Lam 1:

> The dirge, which should properly signal her death, takes place while she is yet alive . . . The import of this really only becomes apparent in the second half of chapter 1. It is here that Zion emerges most forcefully as a speaking subject, and it is here that elements of the funeral song increasingly give way to the elements of lament. The scene of death implied by the dirge, already undercut by the presence of Zion, begins to open out toward life even more. Not only is the one who should be dead alive, but she is speaking and speaking vigorously.

T. Linafelt, *Surviving Lamentations*, 77–78.

a direct address of the dead or the dead speaking; a brief question; a summons to mourn; mourning over the incomprehensibility of the event; impact of the death/destruction on the survivors; mention of the manner of death, especially if unexpected or due to some violence; a reconciling motif (reference to the death being brave or noble and the burial honorable); praise for the deceased; a contrast motif; and occasionally a prayer to God.[11]

In Jer 4 and 10, Jeremiah rendered YHWH's communal dirge speech as a warning to announce the imminent destruction of the city, describe the coming enemy, and unfolding destruction (4:6–8, 11–17, 27–28). YHWH is said to have explicitly *called for* such discourse—the communal dirge and related mourning speech (Jer 9:18, 20; 10:17–18; 25:34–38).[12] This adaptation of the dirge to predict communal death and destruction is related to the prophetic concern and punishment for *injustice*. That is, prophetic judgment speeches invariably critique social injustice in the community, based on legal precedents. In the book of Jeremiah, there is explicit critique of injustice in the community of Jerusalem and Judah involving violence and bloodshed (killing) (2:34; 5:1; 6:7–8; 7:6; 22:15–17). Thus, Jerusalem and Judah's own forewarned death/destruction conveyed through the communal *dirge* is a legal sentence, their "just" punishment for the murders they have perpetrated, yet which could have been commuted had they shown remorse/repentance.[13]

In the book of Lamentations, YHWH does not speak. On the other hand, in the book of Jeremiah, the prophet often expressed communal dirges (e.g., Jer 4:23–26, 29)[14] and mourned for Daughter My People (e.g., Jer 8:19a, 21–23).[15] In Lam 1:1–9a, the destruction

[11] H. Jahnow, *Das hebräische Leichenlied*, 98–178.

[12] See Timothy K. Beal's related study, in which he reads YHWH as lamenting with dirge speech in Mic 1:8–9, "The System and the Speaking Subject in the Hebrew Bible: Reading for Divine Abjection," *Biblical Interpretation* 2/2 (1994): 171–89. R. Salter's statement with regard to dirge elements in Lamentations 1, 2, and 4 ("however, a dirge is not a dirge when the deity is involved or even when petition is implied") misses YHWH's 'involvement' with communal dirge in the book of Jeremiah and misses the point that the performance of the dirge cross-culturally can *include* petition within its very structure; "Searching for Pattern in Lamentations," *Old Testament Essays* 11/1 (1998): 101.

[13] Nu 35:16–21, 30; Deut 19:10–12; cf. Deut 21:1–9; Gen 9:6.

[14] In other texts as well, Jeremiah uses communal dirge rhetoric (e.g., Jer 12:12; 13:19; 14:1–6; and 25:34–38).

[15] In Jer 16:4–7, YHWH finally forbids Jeremiah even *to mourn* the people's destruction, explaining, ". . . because I have removed my peace from this people . . .

of Jerusalem is accomplished fact and the first poet describes it with a communal dirge. Thus, we must raise the possibility that, though this is a different biblical book, the first poet speaks much like a prophet and may be Jeremiah, because the poet engages in one of Jeremiah's previously identified prophetic roles in this context—communal dirge discourse.

The objection may be raised, however, that the prophet Ezekiel also voiced a dirge (YHWH's) over the people of Jerusalem/Judah in this context, in Ezek 19:1–14.[16] Yet, different prophets use genres differently, due to their individual artistry and context. Ezekiel's dirges show two important differences from Jeremiah's. Ezekiel raised YHWH's dirges over the *princes* of Israel/Judah in Ezek 19. These dirges are similar, therefore, to the type in 2 Sam 1:17–27 (David's dirge over Saul and Jonathan), since they focus on the *individual* fates of kings. The dirges of Lamentations on the other hand bewail the *communal* destruction of Jerusalem and Judah.[17] Ezekiel also uses *second* person address in his dirges, not third as in Lamentations. However, other types of rhetorical evidence besides genre will be compiled to identify the poets in Lam 1.

In the book of Jeremiah (7:16; 11:14; 14:11; cf. 15:1 and Zech 12–13), YHWH had also *prohibited* the offering of *lament prayers*,[18] nevertheless both Jerusalem and Jeremiah persisted in lamenting to YHWH (Jer 4:10 and 10:20–22 respectively). In Lam 1, the first

my loving kindness, and my mercy" (vs 5); YHWH also forbids Ezekial to mourn for the death of his wife as a symbol of the coming destruction of Jerusalem (Ezek 24:15–27).

[16] Ezekiel also voiced dirges over other nations, their cities and kings (Tyre in Ezek 27; king of Tyre in Ezek 28; king of Egypt in Ezek 32).

[17] The only reference to the fate of a king in Lam occurs in 4:20 where the speaker simply refers to the capture of a Judean king. Cf. Jer 22:10–12, 18–19.

[18] In this and other contexts, biblical texts portray YHWH as refusing to hear prayer because of rampant injustice, including Isa 1:15, Mic 3:4, Ezek 8:18, and Zech 7:8–13. See S. Balentine's study, *The Hidden God: the Hiding of the Face of God in the Old Testament* (Oxford: Oxford Univ. Press, 1983). See also Biddle, *Polyphony*, 13; yet, in employing the vague category "lament/confessional material," Biddle does not make the important distinction between 'lament' as mourning or dirge speech, and 'lament' as prayer to the deity; *Polyphony*, 13, 15–17. Also, using the traditional term "confession" for the prophet's speeches (which are really lament prayers to the deity) is problematic since Jeremiah is not depicted in the book as being sinful, thus not 'confessing,' but rather 'complaining.' P. Re'emi also blurs the distinction of different lament genres; *Amos and Lamentations: God's People in Crisis*, ITC (Edinburgh: Handsel Press, 1984), 84. See Westermann for a clear explanation of genres and terminology, *Praise and Lament in the Psalms*.

poetic voice restricts himself at least initially, to using the *communal dirge* genre through the chapter; however, the poet rendering Jerusalem/D. Zion's speech begins (and ends) with *lament prayer*, as did the poet rendering her speech in Jer 10. However, by Lam 2:18–19, the first voice directly addresses D. Zion, imploring her to *keep lamenting* to YHWH. Thus these two singers' attitudes about the use of genres in this context *match Jerusalem's and Jeremiah's* in Jer 4 and 10, and elsewhere in the book, over against YHWH.[19]

Lam 1 opens with איכה, formulaic of a dirge: "Alas! she sits alone." The particle איכה (and איך) appear more often in the book of Jeremiah than in any other prophetic book (18x),[20] and are used most often by the voice of YHWH in judgment speeches and communal dirges.[21] However, in Lam 1:1 the poet uses איכה at the outset, not primarily to warn or condemn Jerusalem, or to proclaim her death, but to express *sympathy* by describing her distress in the aftermath.[22] That the communal dirge is here turned to sympathetic use echoes Jeremiah's earlier defense of and empathy for the people. In the implied social and oral poetic context of the performance of a dirge, this poet's dirge contains speech, as is traditional, which *comforts a surviving mourner*. The poet's repeated line "there is no one comforting (from נחם) her" is more than just thematic[23]—it is *contextual*, an expression in song

[19] In Lam 1 below, Jerusalem's poet, lacking a response from YHWH to her first two laments (vss 9c and 11c), returns to mourning and communal dirge speech (vss 12–16, 18–19).

[20] These terms are used in the book of Jeremiah 7x in accusation speeches (Jer 2:21, 23; 3:19; 8:8; 9:6; 47:7; 48:14) and 9x in communal dirges (Jer 9:18; 48:17, 39 (2x); 49:25; 50:23 (2x); 51:41 (2x); Mandelkern, *Veteris Testamenti Concordantiae* (Jerusalem: Sumptibus Schocken, 1955), 42–43. Also, in Jer 12:5, YHWH uses the term to question, if not judge, Jeremiah himself; in Jer 36:17, the term is used in a question by the people, within a narrative. When one adds to this number the three occurrences of the term איכה opening each of the communal dirges in Lamentations (Lam 1, 2 and 4), then the 21 occurrences of the terms in these two books comprise nearly one third of all those in the Hebrew Bible. By comparison, Ezekiel uses only one form, איך, and it appears *only two times* in that entire book (26:17 and 33:10). First Isaiah uses the terms 5x in communal dirges and accusations.

[21] איכה and its abbreviated form, איך, are used in the Hebrew Bible also in individual dirges (like David's lyric for Saul and Jonathan: "*Alas!* (*how*) the mighty have fallen!" [2 Sam 1:19f]).

[22] Cf. this poet's *empathetic* opening with איכה in Lamentations to the *angry judgmental* use of the term in the communal dirge of Isaiah in 1:21 ("*Alas!* [*how*] she has become a whore, the faithful city!").

[23] Though commentators invariably read the "no one comforting" refrain as simply literarily thematic. Yet a refrain is typical of lyrics—and here, of a dirge song.

of his empathetic comforting. The importance of this term, "comfort," used especially for mourners is also implied in Job 29:25.[24]

Uses of imagery/themes. The distinction between poetic 'imagery' and 'theme' is often a fine line. For example, as will be seen below, the poet emphasizes the general 'theme' of the destruction of the sanctuary, but he *builds* this theme by rendering specific 'imageries,' including the devastation of the "tent." How a poet builds imageries into themes helps characterize the peculiar artistry of that poet.

An analysis of the artistry of the first poet of Lam 1 reveals that his technique in the use of imagery to build themes virtually *matches* the prophetic poet Jeremiah[25] in the following six instances:

(A) Sufferer 'sitting alone'

> Oh how (!) she *sits alone* (ישׁבה בדד),
> the city (once) full of people. (Lam 1:1)

The *contrast motif* of the communal dirge[26] is evident here and in the following verses, comparing Jerusalem's former glory with her present hardship. The term "lonely" or "alone" (בדד) is used *only 11 times* in the Hebrew Bible,[27] but twice in Jeremiah[28] and twice in Lamentations. What makes the poetic uses of the term unique in these two books is not the term by itself, but how in *all four instances* it is paired with ישׁב to create an image. In one of Jeremiah's personal laments, he says, ". . . under the weight of your hand I *sat alone*" (בדד ישׁבתי, Jer 15:17). בדד is used again in Lamentations, in 3:28, by a poet lamenting, sitting alone (ישׁב בדד). Jeremiah and Lamentations contain *four of the only five* instances in the entire Hebrew Bible where these two exact terms, "sit alone," are used.[29] If the image in Lam 1 implicitly suggests that Jerusalem is sitting *on the*

[24] "I lived . . . like one who comforts mourners (אבלים ינחם)" (Job 29:25).

[25] That is, Jeremiah's poetry especially in Jer 4, 10, and other texts in that book.

[26] Dobbs-Allsopp notes the use of the contrast motif, and the associated reversal motif, also in Mesopotamian lamentations over cities; *Weep, O Daughter of Zion*, 38–39.

[27] Mandelkern, 163–64.

[28] The other occurrence in Jeremiah is 49:31, a prophetic oracle against Hazor; a people "sit alone," also under attack by Nebuchadrezzar.

[29] The other is Lev 13:46, wherein persons who suffer from leprosy shall "live alone." Such persons also were required to cover the upper lip, a mourning custom; *EJ*, 485–93.

ground, elsewhere emblematic of mourning,[30] the theme fits the context of the communal dirge quite well (e.g., Lam 2:10).[31]

Who, we may ask, might have a personal, yet 'metaphorical' bond with the city of Jerusalem, suffering alone, without a spouse, responsible for its children/inhabitants? Indeed, Jeremiah was charged by YHWH in his call narrative (Jer 1:18) to *identify with the city*:[32]

> See!—now I make you today *a city* fortressed . . . against the whole land, the kings of Judah, its princes, its priests, and the people of the land.

I propose that the overlapping pyscho-social experiences of Jeremiah (as prophetic poet in the context, isolated in his calling) and *the city* abandoned after war (like the women around him), both anguished by YHWH, *merge* in his vision of the city as a widow weeping alone in the night.[33]

(B) The suffering woman

Alas! she sits alone,
  the city (once) full of people,[34]
  she has become like a widow;
    (once) great among the nations,

[30] See Xuan Huong Thi Pham on mourning motifs in Lamentations, *Mourning in the Ancient Near East and the Hebrew Bible*, JSOTS 302 (Sheffield: Sheffield Academic Press, 1999).

[31] *EJ*, 485–93 (cited above, also in Ezek 26:16, Jonah 3:6, and Job 2:8, 13). Another form of בדד—לבד—also appears with ישב: in Ex 18:14 (of Moses judging all the people: "why do you sit by yourself . . .?"), in Ju 20:15 ("apart from/besides the inhabitants of . . .", NJPS), and in Is 5:8 ("you are caused to live alone in the . . . land"); Mandelkern, 164.

[32] B. Bakke Kaiser also draws this connection, "Poet," 173. Note also her incisive suggestion that YHWH's promise of protection to Jeremiah as a city *displaces* YHWH's perceived protection of Zion in the 'inviolability of Zion' tradition/ideology (ibid.).

[33] It may be argued that the prophet Ezekiel could be the poet here who identifies with the widow, since his wife died ("the delight of your eyes," Ezek 24:15f). Yet YHWH directed Ezekiel *in exile* not to mourn initially or weep over her, but to keep silence; his loss, YHWH explains (24:21f), is analogous not to the city as a whole, as with Jeremiah, but to the profaning of "my sanctuary" ("the delight of your eyes"), and to the deaths of "your sons and daughters whom you left behind." YHWH draws analogies with both Jeremiah (who is not married; Jer 16:1f) and Ezekiel (who loses his wife) to the suffering and loss of family members in the destruction of Jerusalem and exile. This connection alone is insufficient to identify Jeremiah or Ezekiel as the poet of Lam 1:1f. What adds to the argument in favor of Jeremiah as poet is the point of view of someone *in Jerusalem*, describing the destruction, not of one in exile.

[34] NRSV.

'Princess among the provinces,'
  she has become a slave.
She weeps and weeps in the night,
  with (her) tears on her cheeks;
she has no one comforting her (אין־לה מנחם)[35]
  among all her lovers . . . (Lam 1:1–2b)

The poet compassionately develops a picture of the city *as a suffering woman*—a widow. It conveys the plight of women left in the aftermath of siege and war. Tradition suggests Jeremiah was left behind in Jerusalem to witness the aftermath and later went to Egypt (Jer 39–44). This image of the suffering city is in empathetic agreement with Jerusalem's poet's *own image of herself* in Jer 10:20 as a suffering woman—an abandoned mother. That the poetic theme of the city personified as a woman is not unique,[36] was common in oral poetry of the ANE, is a different matter from *the specific rhetoric of the city this poet chooses* to describe her. His purpose in expressing *empathy* through the image of the *widow*, not judgment, is a peculiar development of it not seen heretofore in the Hebrew Bible.[37] This is especially the case since YHWH is the implied husband (a prophetic theme), yet this (prophetic) poet is saying *YHWH* has abandoned *her*. It may be noted that in an oracle against Babylon for a later context, Jeremiah says, "For Israel is not widowed, nor is Judah, from his God" (Jer 51:5). This theme of the Lamentations poet has been picked up and reshaped for later contexts. The poet of Isa 47:8–9 perhaps borrows this image when rendering a judgment oracle against the city of Babylon who says, "I will not sit (as) a widow or know the loss of children"; the prophet rejoins, "but . . . loss of children and widowhood will come upon you. . . ." Then, the 2nd Isaiah poet uses the same image *for Jerusalem* in a later context than Lamentations, in a salvation oracle where YHWH consoles the city (Isa 54:4): "The disgrace of your widowhood (אלמנותיך) you will no longer remember."

[35] The "no one comforting" refrain in Lam 1:2 recurs in vss 9, 16, 17, and 21, uttered by both poets. Cf. the "comfort" terminology/theme in Ezek 14:22–23 and Isa 40:1f; for a treatment of Second Isaiah texts' responding directly to Lamentations, see P. Tull, *Remember the Former Things*.

[36] Also the phrase, 'the city will sit on the ground,' symbolic of her downfall and/or mourning is a recurring oral poetic formula (see Isa 3:26; 47:1).

[37] Cf. Is 1:8: "Daughter Zion is left *like a booth in a vineyard* . . ."; and Is 47:1: "Come down and sit on the dust, virgin daughter Babylon . . . *without a throne*."

Returning to Lam 1:1, another theme appears that is typical of prophets in the Hebrew Bible when they name cities with appellatives. For example, the poet of Lam 1:1 calls Jerusalem "'Princess among the provinces' (שׂרתי במדינות), she has become a vassal" (Lam 1:1c). The prophet of Isa 47:5, 7 says, "You [Babylon] will no longer be called 'Strong Woman of kingdoms'" (גברת ממלכות; Isa 47:5). The common prophetic theme has to do with naming the city, and it is used in the 'contrast motif' of the communal dirge genre, normally by prophets, to depict the fallen state of the city. The *purpose of the communal dirge* speech, however, must be clarified as two different things in these texts: the former speech expresses *empathy*; the latter speech expresses *judgment.*

The empathy of the poet in Lam 1 is also in stark contrast to YHWH's rhetoric in Jer 4:31 where YHWH linked the image of the city suffering in labor[38] to the harsh image of her as a prostitute.[39] By contrast, this poet in Lam 1 *refrains* from any terminology suggesting she is *either prostitute or adulterous wife.* Indeed, the image of Jerusalem as bereaved *widow* contrasts with YHWH's image of Jerusalem as a disloyal wife abandoned by her husband. Thus the first poet of Lam 1 is a prophetic voice, as indicated by his use of the communal dirge and attention to the city, yet it is a prophetic voice who empathizes with and implicitly defends the city.[40]

In fact, in Lam 1:8–10, this poet will go on to depict Jerusalem *as a victim* of violence/rape (see below). Rendering her plight, the poet echoes YHWH's compelling image from Jer 4 of "*Zion stretching out her hands*" for help, but poignantly adds here, "*yet there is no one helping her*" (Lam 1:7). In Lam 1:9c, the second poet of Lam 1 will appear and she shall be identified as Jerusalem's poet, speaking for the city.

[38] Also a formulaic prophetic image, found in Isa 13:6–8; 21:3–4; 23:4; 26:17–18; Mic 4:10; Jer 6:24; 13:21; 48:41; 49:24; 50:43; cf. Isa 66:7–10; cited in M. Biddle, "City of Chaos," 8–10.

[39] Also a formulaic prophetic image/theme not isolated to Jeremiah texts, and used by YHWH's voice in Jer 2:20–25, 33; 3:1–5; 13:27.

[40] Thus, with significant additional evidence compiled below, I shall propose that this first poet of Lamentations is Jeremiah, who in texts in both the book of Jeremiah and Lamentations is "participating in his people's sorrow and anguish" by his empathetic portrayal of Jerusalem (contra Biddle, *Polyphony*, 22).

Into the Danube, Mother, throw the white flower,
Let the whole world know, down the length of the river
Of your grief and of your pain . . .
Decorate the unknown grave of your children![41]

(c) Children going away

Another image from Jer 10:20 reappears in Lam 1. Jerusalem's poet had said: "*My children* (בני) *have left* me (יצאני) and are no more."[42] (Jer 10:20)

The poet of Lam 1:5 empathetically echoes Jerusalem:

Her children (עולליה) *have gone* (הלכו),
captive before the face of the foe.[43]

In Lam 1, the rapid juxtaposition of images (children in vs 5c; empty roads to Zion and ravaged gates in vs 4) is suggestive of the chaos of a war zone. Compare the following excerpt from the poet Borislav Arapović about the siege of Osijek, Croatia in 1991; note he also renders the same images as the poet of Lamentations of destroyed buildings and suffering children, and the absence of children who when possible were evacuated from war zones:

night midnight fire slaughter hell
....
. . . 994471/81..........99331...............99468.............
. . . dialing..............dialing..............dialing...........
. . . london.............paris.................stockholm
. . .—lines dead—no connection—

[41] From "I Forgive the Enemy, but I Cannot Forget the Pain!" *Izvori* 3/4 (1996), 32. In the contemporary context of Croatia, Kata Šoljić, a mother who lost four sons in the war, wrote her own lament. Not knowing where their bodies were or where they might have been buried, she scatters flowers for them. Dominick A. Varga laments the loss of his child in "A Thousand Words and an Occasional Hand," transl. Duška Radosavljević, in *Prayers Unheard*, 23–27.

[42] The combination of phrases "her children are no more" in Jer 10 and "no one comforting her" in Lam 1 are likely rhetorical precursors to YHWH's speech about Rachel in Jer 31:15 just before YHWH's empathetic oracle of salvation to her: "A voice is heard in Ramah, mourning, bitter weeping. Rachel weeping for her children (בניה); she refuses to be *comforted* (להנחם) for her children, because *they are no more* (איננו)." (NRSV). The comparison with Jer 31:15 is also noted by S. P. Re'emi, *Amos and Lamentations*, 84.

[43] See section below for a discussion of Jeremiah's preference for the less common term for "child," עולל, used here, whereas the poet speaking for Jerusalem uses the common term בן (Jer 10:20 and Lam 1:16).

but I would like to transmit to them by fax
. . . the pictures of . . . the calm silence of gaping shop windows
and the ghostly rows of houses along empty sidewalks
and sketches of unexploded bombs
and the labor of a birthing mother in a hospital on fire
and holes in the children's clinic walls
and voices never born . . .
and why not also human words—children's voices?
ah yes—no children's voices are to be heard around osijek
they've been swallowed by the city cellars
I can only transmit their silence. . . .[44]

(D) LOSS OF TENT/SANCTUARY AND RELIGIOUS LEADERSHIP

In Jer 4:20b, Jerusalem's poet said, "Suddenly my *tents* (אהלי) are devastated, my *curtains* in a moment." She had said in Jer 10:20,

> My *tent* (אהלי) is devastated,
> and all my cords are snapped;
> . . . there is no one any more to stretch out my *tent*,
> or set my *curtains*.

Since the terms "tent" and "curtains," in a technical sense, are suggestive of the Jerusalem sanctuary, those who would attend to setting them up would be the priests and 'temple' workers, but now there is no one.[45] Though the topic of the sanctuary is important to Jerusalem's poet in Jer 4 and 10, nevertheless she gives only a few lines about it. The poet in Lam 1:4, however, echoes her basic imagery of destruction and absence in relation to the sanctuary but renders, at length, the poignant impact upon persons and personified city structures who suffer the loss of cult and festival life:

> The roads to Zion mourn (אבלות),
> (empty) of anyone coming to festival (מועד);
> all her gates (שעריה) are ravaged (שוממין),
> her priests are groaning,
> her young women *grieving* (נוגות),[46]
> and she is *bitter* (מר). (Lam 1:4)

[44] Borislav Arapović, from "Telefax from Croatia," transl. I. Pozajić Jerić, in *Between Despair and Lamentation*, 28–31.

[45] See e.g., Exod 25:8; 26:1, 7; and F. K. Kumaki ("A New Look," 115–16) for suggestion of a "tabernacle tradition" referred to here.

[46] Occurrences of the verb and noun forms of יגה (*to grieve; misery*) are not common, occurring only 26x in the Hebrew Bible, but 4x in Jeremiah and 5x in

The poet goes on in Lam 1:8–10 (see below) to *detail* the violation of Jerusalem's sanctuary (מקדש). The same poet in Lam 2:4–7 (see below) continues expanding the imagery: "In the *tent* (אהל) of Daughter Zion [YHWH] has poured out his *wrath* like fire" (4c); "he has broken down his booth . . . destroyed his tabernacle (מועדו) . . . he has erased from memory in Zion festival and sabbath" (6), "disowned his sanctuary (מקדשו)" (7).

And these walls speak
  to future generations and ages,
They know every living trauma, shame, and grief,
  despised and gray with grief:

  "Don't forget that
    children's play was shattered
    loved ones slaughtered
    sisters wounded
    mothers killed."
1.12.1941–7.5.1942

(inscription on a wall at the site of the WWII concentration camp in Dakovo, Croatia)

(E) City structures mourning

The first poet's expanding of imagery in support of earlier themes in the book of Jeremiah continues in Lam 1:4. Before discussing his *peculiar* modification of the imagery of city structures mourning, we must consider his poetry's *formulaic* aspects. First, he uses a formulaic style found in other prophetic poetry in the Hebrew Bible and in the ANE. More than merely describing the destruction of specific city structures, he also *personifies* them.[17] The "gates" are "ravaged" as a person might be.

The roads to Zion *mourn* (אבלות) . . .
all *her gates* (שעריה) are *ravaged* (שוממין). . . . (Lam 1:4ab)

Lamentations; Mandelkern, 449–50. Cf. the similar use of the term in the salvation oracle (Jer 31:13) that describes the *misery* of the young woman, young and old men. In the book of Jeremiah, the term also refers to Jerusalem's *misery* (8:18), Jeremiah's *misery* (20:18), and Baruch's *misery* (45:3) which Baruch attributes to YHWH as the cause (see also Lam 1:12 below). The root appears only twice in 2nd Isaiah, used generally, not for specific individuals (51:11).

[17] Cf. the style of Jerusalem's poet who had simply stated that her tents were devastated (in Jer 4 and 10).

Compare this poetic style to a strikingly similar one by Jeremiah in Jer 14:2 where personified structures mourn:[48]

> Judah *mourns* (אבלה),
> and *her gates* (שעריה) *collapse* (אמללו),
> they are black (with remorse; קדרו) upon the ground,[49]
> a cry of Jerusalem goes up. (Jer 14:2)

The above texts, at first glance, demonstrate that the poet of Lam 1:4 participates in *prophetic* poetry of the Hebrew Bible, not necessarily that that poet is also Jeremiah. That is, four texts in the Hebrew Bible (two prophetic) use the term אבל to describe city structures *mourning*: Zion's "doorways/city gates will groan and *mourn*" in Isa 3:26; Judah *mourns* and her cities' gates collapse in Jer 14:2; the "roads to Zion mourn" in Lam 1:4; and "rampart and wall *mourn*, together they collapse" in Lam 2:8. Thus *only* first Isaiah and Jeremiah use this *particular* formulaic imagery of city structures mourning (using the term אבל) among all the prophetic literature in the Hebrew Bible, and then sparingly.[50] That is, only first Isaiah and Jeremiah, *besides the poet* of Lam 1:4 and 2:8. A further explanation of these poets' artistry, based only on the few texts we have, is that in Jer 14:2 Jeremiah appears to have inherited Isaiah's phrase of Zion's *city gates* "mourning" and expanded it by adding another act of mourning to them; they *collapse* (אמללו) to the ground: "Judah mourns and her city gates *collapse*."[51] If this is the case, this poetic phrase by Jeremiah in Jer 14:2 (the specific image of the structure "collapsing" in mourning) *reappears* in Lam 2:8c–9a: "rampart and wall *mourn*, together they

[48] In Jer 14:2–6, Jeremiah utters a communal dirge prompted by YHWH; A. W. Streane briefly noted the connection of the Lamentations imagery to Jer 14:2; *The Book of the Prophet Jeremiah together with the Lamentations* (Cambridge: Cambridge Univ. Press, 1913), 331; C. Westerman notes that Jer 14:1–6 and Lam 1:1–6 are basically the same type of discourse: the "description of misery" after the fact of destruction; *Lamentations*, 123; see also W. Holladay's study on this text, "Style, Irony, and Authenticity in Jeremiah," *JBL* 81 (1962): 51–52; cf. Jer 23:10 where Jeremiah also speaks of similar matters, including a drought: "indeed, on account of these, the land mourns, the pastures of the desert have dried up."

[49] That קדר refers to the blackness of mourning in parallel to אבל is also suggested by YHWH's speech in Jer 4:28 (because of the devastation of creation and Judah): "the earth shall mourn (תאבל), and the heavens above grow black (קדרו)."

[50] The other prophets use the term אבל to describe *persons* mourning (the only use of the term by 2nd Isaiah) or often to say *the land or earth* mourns (Isa 24:4; Hos 4:3; Amos 9:5; Joel 1:10; Jer 4:28).

[51] For this imagery with a person, see Ps 35:13–14; 38:6; cited in W. Holladay, *Jeremiah 1*, 430.

collapse, her gates have *sunk into the ground*." The poet here, like Jeremiah in Jer 14:2, employs the peculiar phrase with both "mourn" and "collapse" and even returns to the original structure of city gates, further elaborating their collapsing: they sink to the ground. In Lam 2:8c–9a, the poet's careful, nuanced rendering of an older prophetic phrase (Isa 3:26) and his attention to its recent expansion by Jeremiah (Jer 14:2), I propose, very likely comes *from Jeremiah himself as poet*.[52]

The exact phrase "her gates" appears only nine times in the Hebrew Bible (twice in Lamentations [1:4, 2:9] and three times in Jeremiah [14:2, 17:27, 51:58]. That Jeremiah, in Jer 14:2, 'sees' a blackened visage of gates, equated with their mourning, may suggest that a siege is underway, or imminent, in which the gates and city walls were typically burned, thus blackened. Indeed, in every one of the six other usages of "her gates" in the Hebrew Bible, there is reference to the *burning* of city gates.[53]

We may pause here to consider lamentations poetry outside biblical Lamentations from the recent wars (1991–95) in Croatia and Bosnia. One of my first encounters there was on a night train moving through Slavonia and in my compartment was a woman sitting quietly intently reading a little book in the dim light. After some time she shared with me what it was, a book of poetry by Helena Rinklin, and her favorite poem she had been meditating on was called "Slakovci".[54] Only 16 lines long, it began "In these empty nights/I remember bygone days,/and then my heart hurts/like an angry, bitter wound . . ." and it ended like this: "O Slakovci, little village! How much I think of you, and in my heart now are all these: every farm and lane." The woman, Gojka, had become a refugee, lived in Germany, and traveled back to see her relatives still in their home village.

Cities and villages under siege were left ravaged and empty, often burned shells. I can attest, having seen many such destroyed cities and villages in Croatia and Bosnia, that when one passes before their 'visage,' one cannot help but feel that the town's 'persona' is somehow in anguish, mourning. Consider the excerpts below that show

[52] Indeed, the imagery of *every part* of the city falling down, and being *brought down* by YHWH, pervades Jeremiah's poetry of Lam 2:1–10 (see below). Pamela Jean Owens 1998 SBL paper, "Charts of Semantic Fields in Lam 2" reveals this poetic pattern.

[53] Jer 17:27; 51:58; Neh 1:3; 2:3, 13, 17.

[54] In *Pjesme* (H. Rinklin, 1994).

Mostar, Bosnia-Herzegovina, 1997 (N. Lee)

how poets there drew on personal experience and used similar imagery to describe their towns, with which they identify and personify.[55] In the first example, Marija Koprivnjak conveys the devastation of Mostar in Bosnia:

> To Mostar—my beloved town . . .
> The dark clouds of war,
>   destruction and decay have covered you . . .
> The beautiful spring in you is now cloaked in black.
> It weeps, moans, and sobs.[56]

Consider an excerpt from Ljubica Ostojić's poem about Sarajevo that opened this study, "Record of the City in Blank Verse":

[55] Another example is in the poem by Lidija Mahovlić, "Za Vukovar" (For Vukovar), in which she personifies that town and uses the typical contrast motif of the dirge to describe how it once was and is now; in *Suze boli-za slobodu* (Tears of Anguish—For Freedom). [No editor, not translated.] Našice: Siječnja, 1992), 68–69.

[56] M. Koprivnjak, from "Mostar, the Vukovar of Herzegovina," in *Ratni Blagoslovi* (Osijek: Izvori, 1996), 138–39, first publ. in 1992. English translation, first three lines of selection by J. Berković and R. Papen, last two lines by N. Lee.

> . . . The City full of hollow silence:
> With just the church bells shivering
> And the wounded minarets
> Speaking quietly with the heaven,
> Pianos in the shattered chambers . . .
>
> The freezing City in the deep darkness,
> tired to death, parched, lonesome,
> the monster sticks its teeth into it. . . .
> The City is numb. Its tears freeze
> in the whirlpools of dark horizon.[57]

While Jeremiah developed an image of grief-stricken, collapsing city structures, other biblical prophets and ANE poets rendered the *weeping* and *mourning speech* of city structures.[58] Isaiah called for city structures to *vocalize* their grief (Isa 14:31): "Wail, O gate; cry, O city," and similarly Habakkuk: "the very stones will cry out from the wall, and the beam will respond from the woodwork."[59]

Similarly, poets of Mesopotamian lamentation texts personify city structures weeping and call them to express grief, as in *Lamentation over the Destruction of Ur* (ca. 2000 BCE): "O thou brickwork of Ur, a bitter lament set up as thy lament . . . O thou shrine Enunkug, a bitter lament set up as thy lament" (*LU* 46–62); and "Thy brickwork of the righteous house like a human being cries thy 'Where, pray?'" (*LU* 365).[60] This vocalizing of grief by personified structures is also found in later *balag* lamentations.[61] In URU AŠERA (The City in Sighing), "the cella [part of temple] cannot hold back its tears."[62]

We may conclude from the previous examples that the poetic formulae of personifying cities and their mourning is common through history and across cultures, as is the human suffering behind it. What

[57] L. Ostojić, selection from "Record of the City in Blank Verse," *Sahat Kula*, 91.

[58] As will be seen below, Jeremiah calls for Jerusalem, not to weep only, but to cry out in lament prayer to YHWH.

[59] NRSV.

[60] Samuel N. Kramer, *Lamentation over the Destruction of Ur*, 23, 63.

[61] The balags could be dated closer to Jeremiah's time, that is, possibly used in neo-Assyria, since some were found in Ashurbanipal's library in the 7th c.; Mark E. Cohen, *The Canonical Lamentations*, 15. See also "IMMAL GUDEDE" ("the brickwork . . . cries out all day long"), ibid., 36.

[62] Lines 20–23; ibid., 70–71; also reconstructed lines 3–12 in URU AŠERA (The City in Sighing) possibly have other structures, like 'brickwork' and 'the shrine,' 'sighing' (ibid.).

remains to be noticed is how individual poets uniquely develop such imagery in their own contexts, and what those poets' developments suggest about those contexts and their human suffering and need.

(F) Leaders flee like starving animals

If the first poet in Lam 1 is Jeremiah, in Lam 1:6 he also echoes his own imagery in Jer 10:21 of the people, the flock, being scattered like animals:

> . . . therefore, the shepherds were not prudent,
> and all their *pasturing* (מרעיתם; 'flock')[63] has been scattered. (Jer 10:21)

Also in Jer 25:36–37, Jeremiah says, "A sound of the cry of shepherds, and howling of the lords (אדירי) of the flock, for YHWH is devastating their pasturing (מרעיתם; flock)." In the first part of that passage however, vss 34–35, Jeremiah reverses the image: shepherds who allowed their flock to be scattered are now scattered themselves by YHWH:

> The shepherds wail and cry out—
> but roll in ashes, you lords of the flock!
> For the days of your slaughter are fulfilled,
> and you will be scattered. . . .
> Flight will perish from the shepherds,
> and escape from the lords of the flock. (Jer 25:34–35)

In Lam 1:6 Jeremiah resumes the imageries of the scattering of the human flock like animals of Jer 10:21 and of the *leaders* in 25:34–37, only in Lam 1:6 the leaders, like animals, cannot even find pasture (food) for themselves and flee slowly, without strength. Thus Jeremiah in Lam 1:6:

> From D. Zion has gone out all her *nobility* (הדרה);
> her princes (שׂריה) have become *like deer* (כאילים; stags);[64]
> they *find* (מצאו) *no pasture* (מרעה);
> weakly they go[65] before the face of the pursuer. (Lam 1:6)

[63] Following BDB's understanding of the usage (945). Two of the nominal forms of רעה (מרעה and מרעית) are not common in the Hebrew Bible (23x), but in a lengthy speech in Jer 23:1–6, YHWH speaks a woe oracle: "Woe to the shepherds who destroy and scatter the sheep of *my pasturing* (מרעיתי). . . ."

[64] MT. LXX reads "rams" by vocalizing *'ālîm*; cited in I. Provan, *Lamentations*, 41.

[65] Literally, 'without strength,' but Westermann's translation here ('weakly') captures the effect of starving animals; *Lamentations*, 110.

The poetic imagery of *humans* being *specifically* likened to "deer" ("stag," איל, or "doe," אילה) can be found in just *six* places in the Hebrew Bible[66] In the poem of Deut 49:21, Naphtali is described as a "*doe* sent out." In the song attributed to David in 2 Sam 22:34 (quoted in Ps 18:34 and Hab 3:19), the singer says, YHWH "made my feet like (those of) *deer* (כאילות)."[67] The *only other use* of this specific imagery, besides that in Lam 1:6, is in Jer 14:3–6, a text just shown to have similarities to Lam 1. Across several verses of that text, again Jerusalem's *nobles* are paralleled by Jeremiah to the desperate animals fending for their lives, *finding no food or water* (cf. Lam 1:6) in the conditions of the siege.

> Their *nobles* (אדריהם) send their servants for water;
> They come to the pools, they *find* (מצאו) *no water*,
> their vessels return empty;[68]
> They are ashamed and humiliated, and cover their heads . . .
> For even the *deer/doe* (אילת) of the field gives birth and forsakes,
> because there is *no grass* (דשא).
> And the wild asses stand on the bare hills;
> they pant for air like jackals, their eyes fail,
> because there is *no herbage* (עשׂב). (14:3, 5–6)

Note that in both texts Jeremiah uses the imagery of the *nobles* (Jer 14:3: אדר; Lam 1:6: הדר) like *deer* who find *no pasturage.*

Use of key terms. A number of key terms appear both in the poetry used by Jeremiah in the book of Jeremiah and in Lam 1:1–6, suggestive of the same poet's terminology and concerns in the context.

(a) "betray" (בגד)
The poet of Lam 1:2 says of Jerusalem:

> All her friends have *betrayed* (בגדו) her;
> they have become her enemies.

[66] D. Hillers and J. Rimbach note similar imagery in one of the curses of Esarhaddon's vassal treaty, though it does not refer to leaders (ANET, lines 576–78, p. 540): "Just as a stag is chased and killed, so may your avengers chase and kill you . . ."; cited in D. Hillers, *Lamentations*, 85.

[67] Qere. Individuals are likened to "rams" (singular, איל, *'ayil*) in the poem of Ex 15:15, "trembling seized the *leaders* [literally, "*rams*" (אילי)] of Moab." Cf. the use of the phrase, the "chief leaders of the land" (אילי), in the prose of Ezek 17:13, and the ram as representing the Persian empire in the apocalyptic prose of Dan 8.

[68] Following Holladay, *Jeremiah*, 430.

The term for "betray" ("be unfaithful," בגד) appears in the Hebrew Bible 52x, and *most* often in the book of Jeremiah (8x in poetry and 4x in prose, and once in Lamentations, totaling one fourth of all occurrences).[69] In Jeremiah the term is *always* used by YHWH to refer to Israel and Judah's unfaithfulness, *except once, in Jeremiah's lament* in Jer 12:1, where he asks: "Why are all the '*betrayers in betrayal*' at *ease* (כל־בגדי בגד שלו)?" YHWH responds to Jeremiah by saying, "Indeed, even your brothers and the house of your father, even they *betray* you . . ." (12:6). Jeremiah, in Lam 1:2 above, *rather* than saying Jerusalem *has betrayed* YHWH, *empathizes* with her, who is like himself, and says: "all her friends have *betrayed her*." Moreover, he describes *her* enemies (in Lam 1:5 below) with the same term he also used in Jer 12:1 to describe *his* enemies. In Lam 1:5: "her enemies are *at ease*" (שלו).[70]

(b) "grieve" (ינה)
In Lam 1:5, Jeremiah uses the *same uncommon term*[71] Jerusalem's poet used in her speech of Jer 8:18 where she said: "My joy has gone; *grief* (ינון < ינה) is upon me. . . ." In Lam 1:5, he says "Indeed, YHWH makes her *grieve* on account of her many transgressions." In Lam 1:12 below Jerusalem will again express YHWH's "*grieving*" her. Jeremiah had used this term to describe himself in another of his own *laments*, 20:18: "Why did I come forth from the womb to see toil and *grief* (ינון)?"

(c) "bitter" (מר)
Jeremiah's last sentence in Lam 1:4 ("and she [Zion] is *bitter* [מר]") echoes the picture of her given in Jer 4 and 10. In Jer 4:18, YHWH had addressed Jerusalem directly: "This is your evil—how *bitter* (מר) it is!" Of the approximately 30 occurrences of forms of מר in poetic and prophetic texts, *only* 3x does it refer to Jerusalem: (1) in Jer 4:18; (2) in Lam 1:4; and (3) in Jer 2:19 in YHWH's speech to the city ("know and see that it is evil and *bitter* (מר) for you to forsake the Lord your God"). Thus, the term *bitter* is used by YHWH's voice in the book of Jeremiah to describe Jerusalem and is echoed here

[69] The term does not occur at all in Ezekiel and only once in 2nd Isaiah (48:8).
[70] Forms of שלה/שלו occur 24x in the Hebrew Bible. This term in Lam 1:5 and Jer 12:1 is cited by D. Hillers, *Lamentations*, 67.
[71] The root ינה occurs only 26x in the Hebrew Bible; among those related to this study are five occurrences in lament psalms; in Ezek 23:33 where YHWH says to 'Oholibah' (Jerusalem): "You shall be filled with drunkenness and *grief* (ינון).

in Lam 1:4 by the voice of Jeremiah. Note that the prophet stresses only the bitterness, not the "evil" of Jerusalem thus far. This is consistent with his attitude of empathy in some texts, over judgment.[72]

(d) "Children" (עוללים)
As noted above, in Lam 1:5, Jeremiah echoes Jerusalem's poet's reference to her children in Jer 10:20, but uses an unusual term: עולל. This term is not very common in the Hebrew Bible (~23x), but is utilized 3x in the book of Jeremiah by the voice of YHWH and 5x in Lamentations by Jeremiah and Jerusalem (2:11, 19, 20–21; 4:4; see discussion below on Lam 2). In five of these eight instances, in both books, the term is found in a recurring phrase describing suffering of "*child(ren)* (עולל) *in the street(s)* (חוץ)."[73] The only other use of this term for children (עולל) in connection with 'streets,' a prophetic formulaic phrase, is in Nahum 3:10 (ca. 626–612). Nahum says of Assyria, "even her infants were dashed in pieces at the head of every street." Nahum's poetry is just prior to that of Jeremiah and Lamentations, in fact, likely overlaps with Jeremiah's early prophetic activity.

It is apparent from analysis of the four terms above that Jeremiah is not the only poet to ever use them, but he does characteristically use them to describe Jerusalem, *in response to their context* (with its sociological, rhetorical, historical aspects). The term "*betray*" he uses to describe Jerusalem in terms of his own *social* experience of "betrayal." Likewise, he uses the term "*grieve*" to describe Jerusalem with the same *rhetorical* term she uses to describe herself, as well as the term he uses in his own personal lament. The term "*bitterness*" he uses to describe Jerusalem as an echo of YHWH's *rhetorical* use of that term

[72] Jeremiah at times expresses anger and judgment against the people of Judah (e.g., Jer 5:3–5, 6:10) and sometimes defends and empathizes with them, over against YHWH. See Mark Biddle's helpful point that distinguishing voices also includes distinguishing the different viewpoints of the voice of the same character [or poet] (e.g., "one hears various Jeremiahs—the indignant prophet, the plaintive sufferer, the hopeful visionary. One hears various YHWH's, the various incarnations of the people, various personifications of Jerusalem . . . Without some method for discerning the distinctiveness of these voices, the reader risks hearing their dialogue as cacophony instead of the intricate polyphony intended . . .," Symphony, 7).

[73] "Child(ren) in the squares/street(s)" is used in Jer 6:11 (by YHWH); 9:20 (by YHWH); Lam 2:11, 19 (both by Jeremiah), and 20–21 (by D. Zion, after being encouraged with the phrase by Jeremiah). This term for 'children' also is used in Jer 44:7 (by YHWH) and Lam 4:4 (by Jeremiah); the term does not appear at all in Ezekiel. Second Isaiah uses the term בניך for children fainting in the streets (51:20).

about her. And finally, Jeremiah echoes his and YHWH's use of the less common term for "*child*" (עולל) to describe their *historical* suffering in the context of war and destruction. To summarize, the findings of this analysis thus far point toward a preliminary conclusion about the first poet of Lamentations (1:1–9b). In his attitude toward Jerusalem, in his use of the communal dirge genre, in his use of specific imagery in support of six previous themes and four key terms found in the poetry in the book of Jeremiah, this poet's oral poetic style all point toward identifying him as the prophet Jeremiah. While this evidence is suggestive, next we move to a feature of this poetry that further solidifies such a conclusion.

Use of double meaning. W. Holladay has noted the prevalence in the book of Jeremiah of the rendering of double meanings from single terms.[74] He suggests this device is Jeremianic; while many of Holladay's examples are spoken by YHWH's voice in the book of Jeremiah, the other instances of the prophet's peculiar use of the device are, importantly, entirely in his personal laments: Jer 11:18; 17:14; 20:7.[75] However, R. Gordis notes that the repetition of identical roots (which may employ the use of double meaning as well) is a widely attested rhetorical phenomenon, appearing also in Ugaritic poetry. Yet, Gordis also suggests it can be characteristic of some "writers" (e.g., in Job and Lamentations, esp. Lam 2).[76] Thus, we cannot assume that the simple use of double meaning in Lam 1:1–9b reflects Jeremiah as poet, yet a careful analysis of *how* the poet uses the technique here may provide clues and evidence in a larger argument. In the first verse of Lamentations, the poet twice uses רבתי:

> Oh how she sits alone,
> the city (once) *full of* (רבתי) people,
> She has become like a widow;
> (once) *great* (רבתי) among the nations. . . . (Lam 1:1a–b)

The double use of רבתי utilizes two of its meanings, both "full of" people and "great" among the nations (from רבב). What supporting evidence might there be that this poet is Jeremiah? Jeremiah also uses *this same root* for double meaning in Jer 51:13, *also* within a contrast

[74] Holladay notes ("Style, Irony, and Authenticity," 45–47) that S. R. Driver had noticed this device in Jeremiah (*An Introduction to the Literature of the Old Testament*, 276).
[75] Holladay, "Style, Irony, and Authenticity," 46.
[76] R. Gordis, *The Song of Songs and Lamentations* (New York: KTAV, 1974), 121–23.

motif of a communal dirge over *another city*—Babylon: "You reside beside *great* (רבים) waters, *full of* (רבת) riches." (Jer 51:13) It appears likely that the same poet composed these lines in Jer 51:13 and Lam 1:1. There is no doubt about the congruences here, in context. Other examples of Jeremiah's poetic use of double meaning, and in contrast to the second poetic voice in Lam 1, will be brought out below (see esp. Lam 1:7–9).

Content

(a) The empty city and its enemies

Jeremiah's poetry is preoccupied with the desolate *emptiness* of the city, the absence of inhabitants, as well as the *enemy* invasion (in Jer 4:25–26, 29, in Jer 10:21, and in Lam 1:1, 3c, 4ab, 5ac, and 6c).

(b) Suffering for transgression/sin

In Lam 1:5, Jeremiah introduces the prophetic idea of Jerusalem's *transgression* as bringing on the suffering/destruction, entirely consistent with the basic theology of YHWH's judgment oracles in the book of Jeremiah. Here, after the invasion/destruction, this theme is part of the prophet's communal dirge explaining a cause of distress:

> Her foes have become the head,
> her enemies prosper,
> for YHWH has caused her grief
> on account of her many *transgressions* (פשעיה).

This verse follows Jeremiah's mentioning Jerusalem's "bitterness" in Lam 1:4 and *specifically echoes* YHWH's speech in Jer 4:18 to Jerusalem, *associating* her wrongdoings (her "*rebelling*," מרה) with bringing the "bitterness" upon her. Here in Lam 1:5, YHWH does not speak, but the prophet echoes YHWH's theology of Jerusalem's suffering on account of her wrongdoing. Daughter Zion will also echo this theological understanding, and challenge it to a degree later, in chapters 1, 2 and 3.[77] Related to this, in Lam 1:18 and 20, Jerusalem will answer YHWH's charge that she has "rebelled" (see below).

To sum up, the above analysis of Lam 1:1–6 alone reveals an intimate connection between the poet responsible for it and Jeremiah's poetry in Jer 4, 8, 10 (and other texts of that book). The poetry shows such strong congruences, in terms of both prophetic formulaic poetry and its unique modifications, in all the areas of genre, imagery/

[77] Lam 1:14, 18, 20, and 22.

themes, terminology, rhetorical technique, and content, that it may be proposed that this first poet of Lamentations is the poet Jeremiah of the book of Jeremiah. Further analysis will support this claim.

Lam 1:7–11c

In the continuing exegetical analysis of the rest of Lam 1, formulaic poetry and modifications of it will be considered in terms of genre(s), imagery/themes, terminology, rhetorical techniques, and content. However, these aspects will be addressed as they appear in the unfolding of the chapter's sections and verses.

In Lam 1:7–9b the first poet, whom the textual evidence thus far suggests is Jeremiah, shifts attention back to the 'persona' of Jerusalem whom he rendered in vss 1–2. Still using the communal dirge genre, he describes her taking account of her lot as she considers events of the fairly recent past:

> Jerusalem is preoccupied with (זכרה; MT)[78]
> the days of her *suffering/rape*[79] and *wandering*[80] (עניה ומרודיה),[81]

[78] The verb can be translated in two ways: (1) it is a qal perfect, third fem. sing. (*zākᵉrā*); the above translation aims to render the psycho-social state of one who has been traumatized, who constantly remembers, relives, and is preoccupied with the violence that still causes her suffering; (2) it is an imperative to YHWH about Jerusalem ("Remember Jerusalem"); this is corroborated by a Qumran variant (4QLam[a]; זכורה יהוה [כו]ל מכאובנו): "Remember, YHWH, all our pain." F. M. Cross suggests מכאובנו corrects or revises the original rare מרודיה; "Studies in the Structure of Hebrew Verse: The Prosody of Lamentations 1:1–22," in *The Word of the Lord Shall Go Forth* (Winona Lake: Eisenbrauns, 1983), 134, 140. See also Cross' recent revision of this article, "The Prosody of Lamentations 1 and the Psalm of Jonah," in *From Epic to Canon: History and Literature in Ancient Israel* (Baltimore: Johns Hopkins Univ. Press, 1998), 135–47. 4QLam[a] drops out the phrase "days of her rape/suffering and wandering." Yet, Cross keeps the מרודיה of MT and posits from 4QLam[a] an original text: "Remember, YHWH, her troubles. . . ." on the basis that it "begins a long-range sequence of addresses to the deity" (*Studies*, 140). However, this basis alone does not work with the MT when thorough note is taken of who is speaking. Only D. Zion addresses the deity with the lament prayer genre across Lam 1 and 2 (though cf. the 'aside' by Jeremiah to YHWH in vs 10). More likely, the Qumran variant reflects an adaptation of the speech for liturgical purposes in another oral poetic context (note the shift to the first person plural possessive, "our pain," nowhere else found in MT Lam 1). LXX follows MT in reading Jerusalem as the subject who remembers/is preoccupied.

[79] That the noun עני can carry the more specific meaning of rape is clearly evident in other texts where the verb form is used: Deut 22:25–27; Ju 19:24; 2 Sam 13:12, 14, 22, 32; Ezek 22:10, 11; and possibly in Gen 34:2.

[80] Forms of the verb רוד occur only 7x in the entire Hebrew Bible, twice in Lam, once in Jer (2:31), and in Gen 27:40; Ps 55:3; Hos 12:1; and Is 58:7.

[81] In Lam 3:19 the individual lamenter echoes Jeremiah's phrase "suffering and

all her precious things
  that were from days of old,
when her people fell into the hand of the foe,
  and there was no one helping her.
The foes looked upon her[82] and mocked over her end. (Lam 1:7–9b)

Jeremiah's depiction of Jerusalem "remembering" or "being preoccupied with . . . her precious things" (מחמדיה) signals the *contrast motif* of the communal dirge. "Precious things" may refer to Jerusalem's children, other persons dear to her, and/or the treasures of the temple and city.[83] Jeremiah sums up her losses, referring to those "things precious" to Jerusalem that are external to her (and again in 1:10 and 11), but then redirects focus to the *foes* hovering over her, a recurring topic which he already alluded to in vss 2, 3, 5, and 6. He now renders their specific actions.

Jeremiah says the foes "*mock*" or "*laugh*" (שׂחק) at Jerusalem. This uncommon root appears 7x in the book of Jeremiah,[84] yet *never* is it used in the lament psalms to describe the enemies' behavior, even though in that genre lamenters very often speak of enemies within the community who ridicule them.[85] However, this term for 'mock' (שׂחק) is *peculiarly favored by Jeremiah as poet*, unlike any other prophet.[86] He uses it in his own lament in Jer 20:7: "I have become a *mockery* (לשׂחוק) . . . they all deride me (לעג)."[87] Here in Lam 1:7c, Jeremiah

wandering" (Lam 1:7) for his own first person lament (to YHWH): "*Remember my suffering and wandering*, to wormwood and gall!" The terms are paired *only in these two texts* in the entire Hebrew Bible, and *in both cases* as the direct object of the verb זכר ('remember'). The two sufferers are in dialogue.

82 Third masculine plural plus third feminine singular direct object suffix; contra NRSV.

83 See also Lam 1:10, 11; 2:4; cf. Ezek 24:16; I Ki 20:6.

84 Found twice in Lamentations and in Jer 20:7; 48:26, 27, 39, all with Jeremiah as speaker; and also in the sense of 'make merry' in Jer 15:17 (Jeremiah as speaker); 30:19 (YHWH as speaker); 31:4 (YHWH as speaker).

85 For an outline of lament elements, see C. Westermann, *Lamentations*, 129.

86 The *only* other prophets to use the term are Habakkuk in 1:10 to describe the Chaldean enemy: "rulers are an object of mockery (משׂחק) to him" and "he will mock/laugh at (ישׂחק) every fortress" to be attacked; and in Zech 8:5, YHWH predicts "boys and girls will be playing (משׂחקים) in [Jerusalem's] squares."

87 Six lament psalms favor the root לעג to express 'mocking' (Ps 22:7; 35:16; 44:14 = 79:4; 80:6; 123:4) as well as Isaiah in 28:11; 33:19; 37:22; Hos 7:16; and Ezek 23:32; 36:4. The lamenter of Lam 3:14 also uses the term: "I have become a *mockery* (שׂחק) of all my people. . . ." This fact can be used as a piece of argument supporting Jeremiah as the man of Lam 3, or, as suggestive that another poet/singer listening to Jeremiah uses his term to describe his own suffering.

uses this term "mock" in his (third person) communal dirge to describe how the effect of Jerusalem's downfall affects those around her, a typical element in this genre.[88]

The poetry of Lam 1:7 describes not only the loss of "things precious" *external* to Jerusalem, but also those things that are a part of her person: she is a victim of rape, as suggested by the term עני above, carrying double meaning (also "suffering").[89] Jeremiah's sympathy is evident here for two key reasons. First, he *refrains* from rendering Jerusalem in the negative imagery of a prostitute[90] or a faithless wife. This is in striking contrast to that in Ezek 16:38–41 where YHWH judges that the punishment of prostitute/adulteress Jerusalem is to be death by stoning (and even mutilation).[91] Second, Jeremiah adds to his sympathetic picture of Jerusalem by saying "no one is helping her" (אין עוזר לה) when the enemy attacked; this also recalls how she was *at the mercy of killers* in Jer 4:31. By employing the phrase in vs 7, "*no one helping her*" in the context of rape, Jeremiah invokes the legal case of Deut 22:23–27 where a woman is threatened with rape (ענה; vs 24). Though she cries out, no one may hear, and that text offers a similar formula: there is "*no one saving her*" (אין מושיע לה). The Deuteronomy text goes on to say that if a woman is threatened outside the town, not only is she blameless, but it is the same as if a man rose up against his neighbor and killed him. Likewise, if the woman was threatened within the town, her social and legal fate, not to mention her immediate welfare, depended on whether or not she cried out for help. Jeremiah's allusion to the legal case implies Jerusalem is the victim who must cry out for help.[92]

[88] See the discussion of formal elements of the dirge in the introduction.

[89] See B. Bakke Kaiser, "Poet," 175; K. O'Connor, "Lamentations," *The Woman's Bible Commentary*, eds. C. Newsom and S. Ringe (Louisville: Westminster/John Knox, 1992).

[90] And from any reference to its legal punishment (Deut 22:22; Lev 20:10).

[91] Likewise, see YHWH's scathing critique of "all" her "lovers" (Ezek 16:33, 37). Cf. Jeremiah's reference to Jerusalem's "lovers" in Lam 1:2; it is recast in empathy rather than judgment: "Among all her lovers she has no one comforting her." This is especially striking in light of the fact that *every* use of the term אהב in the book of Jeremiah (13x) is uttered by YHWH's voice, including the critiques of Jerusalem's "lovers" (Jer 20:4, 6; 22:20, 22). Yet, note in the larger rhetorical context YHWH's own empathetic recasting of the phrase "all your lovers," as well, in the divine consolation to Jerusalem in 30:14.

[92] For a recent focus on literal and figurative rape describing the suffering of a city, see Iris Chang, *The Rape of Nanking: The Forgotten Holocaust of World War II* (Penguin Books, 1997).

A troubling aspect is that elsewhere YHWH as speaker explains that Jerusalem, as a prostitute, suffers violent attack as punishment for sin ("iniquity," עונך), as in Jer 13:22:[93]

> It is for the greatness of your iniquity
> that your skirts (שוליך) are removed
> and your heels (עקביך) suffer violence. . . .
> (נחמסו; "are rudely exposed")[94]

In Lam 1:7–9, however, Jeremiah, *refrains* from connecting punishment for sin with rape. It is necessary to distinguish singers and viewpoints. YHWH nearly aligns himself with the violating enemies in Jer 13 and elsewhere. Yet, Jeremiah's rhetoric here is primarily compassionate toward Jerusalem. While Jeremiah does *not* say, in general, that Jerusalem has not sinned (vs 8), he certainly portrays her as the *victim* in rape. Jeremiah's poetry, more than YHWH's speeches, presents an agonizing ambiguity—and an important theological development: personified Jerusalem represents *corporate sin* as well as the *innocent individual* sufferer.

While Jeremiah's empathizing identification with the powerlessness of the woman figure is evident in Lam 1:7, this sensitivity may be found already in one of his personal laments. Indeed, in the same verse just noted above (Jer 20:7), Jeremiah uses terminology that carries undertones of sexual conquest in describing YHWH's treatment of him: "O Lord, you have seduced me[95] (פתיתני; or 'enticed'), and I was seduced (ואפת); you seized me and overpowered me. I have become a *mockery* all day long . . . For whenever I speak, I cry out, I shout: 'Violence (חמס) and destruction!' (Jer 20:7–8a)."[96] These

[93] Note that while YHWH is *not* a party to the violence (חמס) described in vs 22, a few verses later, in Jer 13:26, YHWH says, yet "I myself have stripped off (חשפתי) your skirts (שוליך) over/upon your face, and your shame is seen. I have seen . . . your adulteries . . . your aim of harlotry . . . Woe to you, O Jerusalem! How long will you *not* be *clean*?" (13:26). This text suggests to make naked is to humiliate and reveals wrongdoing (note Jer 49:10 where YHWH strips [חשף] Esau bare).

[94] Thus BDB: 784. NJPS has "your limbs exposed." Mandelkern includes 'rape' as one of the specific connotations of the noun חמס (404). Cf. the imagery in Nah 3:5 about Ninevah.

[95] See the use of the piel of פתה in Ex 22:15.

[96] Von Rad, *Genesis*, transl. J. Marks, OTL (Philadelphia: Westminster Press, 1961), 206, suggested that the term חמס ("violence!") may have been used as a cry for help by those in trouble (e.g., Hab 1:2, Job 19:7), and S. Berridge (*Prophet, People, and the Word of YHWH, An Examination of Form and Content in the Proclamation of the Prophet Jeremiah*, 153–54) suggested the term may have been voiced by women threat-

lines suggest that Jeremiah identifies with Jerusalem's being treated violently.

Indeed, in the next line (Lam 1:8) Jeremiah describes Jerusalem with the rare word "*despise*" (זלל; adjective: "*worthless*")[97] to suggest how she is treated. It is *the same rare word* YHWH employed to label *Jeremiah's* lament speech to YHWH: "*Surely you* [YHWH] are to me like a disappointing (deceptive) stream, unreliable" (Jer 15:18b). YHWH responded to Jeremiah: "If you utter . . . not what is *worthless* . . ." (Jer 15:19b). Yet, in spite of his empathy with Jerusalem conveyed in the term "*despise*" below, Jeremiah as prophet must reiterate the theology that she suffers for her sin:

> Jerusalem has indeed sinned; on account of this
> she has become a wanderer (Q: נוד; MT: נידה).[98]
> All who honored her *despise* (הזילוה) her,
> for they see her nakedness (ערותה).
> Indeed! she groans,
> and has turned away. (Lam 1:8)

Commentators often interpret the *hapax legomenon* נידה as meaning either 'impurity,' misintepreting it as 'menstruant' (as a variant of נדה),[99] or as one mocked, about whom people shake/wag their heads.[100]

ened with rape (as in the context of Deut 22:27); cited in W. Holladay, *Jeremia*, vol. I, 553.

[97] Forms of זלל occur only 11x in the Hebrew Bible (including 2x in Jeremiah [2:36; 15:19]; 3x in Proverbs, and in Deut 21:20, the 'worthless,' rebellious son about to be stoned in the gate).

[98] NRSV and NJPS have "mockery." While this translation appears to work in the context, there is little evidence that this nominal form of the root means this elsewhere.

[99] Thus W. Fuerst, *The Books of Ruth, Esther, Ecclesiastes, the Song of Songs, Lamentations* (Cambridge: Cambridge Univ. Press, 1975), 218; B. Bakke Kaiser, "Poet," 175–76; A. Brenner and F. van Dijk-Hemmes, *On Gendering Texts*, 85; I. Provan, *Lamentations*, 44–45; C. Westermann, *Lamentations*, 129; Shalom M. Paul, "Polysensuous Polyvalency in Poetic Parallelism " in *"Sha'arei Talmon": Studies in the Bible, Qumran, and the Ancient Near East Presented to Shemaryahu Talmon* (Winona Lake: Eisenbrauns, 1992), 162–63; while D. Hillers prefers reading "object of scorn" (thus Ibn Ezra, Löhr, Rudolph), less so "wander" (4QLam[a], LXX, Rashi), he also limits the several potential meanings of unclean, נדה, to only *one* meaning, "menstruant" (yet see Milgrom's clarification below); Hillers, *Lamentations*, 70.

[100] For a discussion of this meaning and commentators who follow it, see S. Paul, "Polysensuous Polyvalency," 162–163, and reference to the verbal form of the root נוד in the phrase "to shake/wag the head" in Jer 18:16 (YHWH's voice) and 48:27 (Jeremiah's voice). See the discussion of נדה by Jacob Milgrom, *Leviticus 1–16*, AB (New York: Doubleday, 1991), 38, 744–46, 948–53. He suggests נדה is derived from either נדד (to depart, flee, or wander) or נדה (chase away, put aside), yet he does not note (38) that this is a *different* term in Lam 1:8 (נידה from נוד).

However, little evidence for either of these interpretations is available. The term is, nevertheless, pivotal for the passage of vss 7–11, and its intended meanings must be more carefully explored. It is another of Jeremiah's characteristic uses of *double meaning*.

First, the other, general term נדה can have several meanings, depending on context: it can refer to impurity caused by menstruation, by sexual crimes, by contact with a corpse, or later metaphorical meanings of impurity caused by idolatry or immorality.[101] The key in the Lam 1:8 text is its emphatic claim that Jerusalem has become a נידה *because of her sin*. This *rules out* a meaning of נידה as menstruant, wherein impurity stems from a natural state, *not* from sin.[102] Milgrom has noted that the later priestly tradition (the H school) especially used נדה metaphorically to refer to impurity *caused by sin*.[103] *To the extent* that this Lamentations rhetoric using נידה echoes the sound and meanings of נדה, it most likely refers to a priestly tradition *concerned with sin*. That tradition is reflected in Lev 20:21 (within the 'Holiness Code') and is concerned with the *victim of a sexual transgression* and her resulting impurity (נדה). This connection will be important for the larger interpretation of the passage (see below).

The translation of נידה in vs 8 suggesting "an object of mockery" draws from another meaning of נוד, to shake/wag the head in derision about someone.[104] This meaning would work in the context, as the

[101] Milgrom also notes the meaning of the term as "lustration" in Nu 19:9 and Zech 13:1 which indicates the cleansing of impurity; *Leviticus*, 744.

[102] A similar misreading/poor translation is typically seen in Ezek 36:17 where YHWH uses the term נדה, differently than Jeremiah uses it in Lamentations, to describe the house of Israel: "they made (the soil) unclean (טמא) with their ways and their doings; like the uncleanness of a נדה is their way before my face." In my view, this line is too specifically translated by NRSV ("their conduct in my sight was like the uncleanness of a woman in her menstrual period"!; similarly in NJPS), since a נדה *does not have to be* a menstruant, but someone in a state of impurity for various reasons. Indeed, in this text *sinful action* is clear, including killing and contact with a corpse and blood, since "they have shed blood" (Ezek 36:17; see Nu 35:33–34; Lev 19:13; Isa 59:3, 6–7; Isa 63:3; Lam 4:13). Cf. J. Galambush's drawing a parallel between *niddah* in Lam 1:17 and Ez 36:17 without unpacking its meaning in context, *Jerusalem in the Book of Ezekiel: The City as Yahweh's Wife*, SBLDS 130 (Atlanta: Scholars Press, 1992), 146. Translators too quickly presume that the image of the menstruant is always a meaning here, rather than the possibility of resulting impurity caused by sin, the shedding of someone's blood. Must translators be so narrow in their focus on translating this term, נדה?

[103] J. Milgrom, *Lamentations*, 38, 952.

[104] Yet another meaning of the verb נוד is to bemoan or mourn (e.g. Jer 15:5; 16:5; 22:10; 31:18; all YHWH as speaker).

term parallels vs 7 where the foes *mock* (שׂחק) Jerusalem, except that there is no evidence for this syntactical use of the root as a noun alone, rather than the normal verb with object ("shake the head").

I would suggest, instead, that the primary meaning of נידה in Lam 1:8 is "wanderer." A 'female wanderer,' like Cain (vs 8b, from נוד),[105] being banished/punished because of sin (vs 8a) also parallels the image of "her wandering" in vs 7 (מרוד).[106] This meaning is confirmed by Qumran scroll 4QLam[a] which has the unexpected masculine form of the noun (נוד), though it describes female Jerusalem! This reading is also confirmed by the MT's spelling of the *hapax* נידה, the feminine form of נוד, which aims to distinguish it in writing from the secondary meaning of the homophon, נדה, 'impurity.' This is also given as the interpretation by Lamentations Rabbah '35: "Israel, however, sinned and [was] . . . punished. Therefore she is become as one unclean (le-nidah): i.e. she was doomed to vagabondage" (the editor noted: *niddah* is explained as *nadah* 'a wanderer').[107]

Yet, נידה carries more than the primary meaning of 'wanderer.'[108] As implied in Lamentations Rabbah, the sound and meaning of 'impurity' (נדה) is also suggested here. The next bicolon states, "All who honored her belittle her, for they see her *nakedness* (ערותה)." That is, sexual impropriety or violence against Jerusalem is unfolding in the rest of the verse; indeed, ענּי in vs 7 already suggested rape (see Lev 18 and 20 on 'nakedness' and sexual crimes or impropriety). Here the legal connection to Lev 20:21, concerned with impurity caused by sexual transgression, returns: "If a man takes his brother's wife, she is *impure* (נדה); he has uncovered the *nakedness* of his brother (ערות אחיו). . . ." In this case, she becomes impure *because of wrong sexual action against her.*

[105] Though נידה is a *hapax*, an analogy can be drawn from the feminine noun קימה, from the hollow root קום.

[106] The use of the root נוד meaning 'to wander' occurs in Jeremiah in 4:1; 49:30 (in a compound verbal phrase: נסו נדו; see in Lam 4:15 below), all YHWH as speaker; and in Jer 50:3 (Jeremiah), and 8 (YHWH). Moreover, the root נדד is also employed in the book of Jeremiah to mean 'to flee': 4:25 (Jeremiah); 9:9 (YHWH); 49:5 (YHWH). For a discussion of Jeremiah's use of a Cain and Abel subtext in Jer 2, 14, and Lam 4, see N. C. Lee, "Exposing a Buried Subtext," 87–122.

[107] *Lamentations Rabbah*, ed. Cohen, 109.

[108] Robert Gordis calls the term an example of *talḥin* (where two meanings are intended, one primary and one secondary); he actually recognizes three possible meanings, including "wander" but prefers "unclean" and "object of scorn" as the two most operative; *The Song of Songs and Lamentations*, 123, 155.

Thus while Jeremiah has not denied that Jerusalem has sinned, in this specific context she is a victim of war—raped—and made impure (a נדה). Once again, rather than portray Jerusalem as a prostitute, as YHWH had done in Jer 4:30 and elsewhere, Jeremiah describes her *as a rape victim*, in powerful and empathetic imagery. The admonitions against sexual crimes in Lev 18 and 20 were followed by the warning that if they were not kept, the land will "vomit you out" (18:24–28), a different image employed for the same reality of Jerusalem and her people cast out of the land to become "wanderers." It should be noted that Jeremiah may be indicting Jerusalem's own prophets and priests as "enemies" metaphorically raping the sanctuary, for in vs 10b he *adds*, "*even* (כי) the nations she has seen invade her sanctuary," as though the enemy peoples were not the perpetrators described in the preceding verses, 7c–10a (see Jeremiah's indictments of Jerusalem's own priests and prophets as enemies within the gates of Jerusalem in Lam 4:13).[109]

In the final tricolon of vs 8, Jeremiah says,

> *How* she groans,
> and turns away! (8c)

In vs 9, Jeremiah continues depicting Jerusalem remembering and re-living the trauma:

> Her uncleanness (טמאתה) in her skirts (בשׁוליה),[110]
> she does not think of what comes later (her future offspring);[111]

[109] See N. C. Lee, "Exposing a Buried Subtext," 119–122.

[110] Translated "in her skirts" by E. Tov, *Textual Criticism of the Hebrew Bible* (Minneapolis: Fortress Press, 1992), 259; Babylonian Talmud, *Yoma* 56b–57a (transl. Leo Jung) and *Baba Kamma* 55a (transl. E. W. Kirzner); *Lamentations Rabbah* 43.i, J. Neusner (Atlanta: Scholars Press, 1997), 130; or '36, A. Cohen, (London: Soncino Press, 1939), 109. Numerous commentators implicitly use the line, "her uncleanness was *in her skirts*," to defend the reading of נידה as menstruant and vice versa. As noted above, the impurity of the menstruant does not fit the context. Neither do discussions of menstruants elsewhere refer to a woman's "skirts" (see Lev 12:2, 5; 15:19–33). Interestingly, *no texts* from Lamentations, including this one, are cited in the Babylonian Talmud's volume *Niddah*, dealing with impurities.

[111] Women in contexts of war may face the trauma of becoming pregnant by rape; this perhaps accounts for what may be yet another empathetic line here about Jerusalem, *in context*, not (wanting to) think about her future offspring, a very different reading from the traditional "she took no thought of her future," or Gordis's "Zion is so degraded that 'she does not remember her children'"; *Song of Songs and Lamentations*, 156. Rather, Jeremiah empathetically renders yet another aspect of the *suffering mother* theme (analyzed above). If there is *one thing* Jerusalem is concerned about, it's her children (in Jer 10, Lam 1:16, etc.).

she was brought down[112] astonishingly;[113]
no one is comforting her. (9ab)

In 1:9, the "uncleanness" (טמא) is a result of her being raped. Translators find support for this use of שׁול (skirt) in Jer 13:22 and 26 (cited above):[114] "It is for the greatness of your iniquity that your skirts (שׁוליך) are removed and your heels (עקביך) suffer violence (נחמסו; 13:22)." Yet those texts render *YHWH's speech* against Jerusalem as a prostitute; in Jer 2:25, YHWH had also warned her, "keep your feet from going bare (יחף)."[115] Jer 13 and other texts suggest the humiliation of the stripping off of a person's clothes (also by YHWH in Jb 12:17–19) or sandals (Dt 25:9–10).[116] These actions are also attested in the context of war, as here, where the vanquished victims are plundered.[117] Given these images and context and the fact that an empathetic Jeremiah is speaking who shows propensity for *double meaning*, I propose that בשׁוליה is a wordplay, carrying another layer of meaning, stressing Jerusalem's victimization by attackers:

"Her uncleanness when they plunder/strip her (feet bare) (> שׁלל בשׁוליה)"[118] Reading בשׁוליה as a participle produces only a slight difference in pronunciation: from *bᵉšûle(y)hā* to *bᵉšôlle(y)hā*. The odd

[112] The verb ירד, which can carry a passive sense, at once describes the woman being brought down by the rapist and the fall of the city under siege (BDB reads the occurrence in this verse as passive, 433; cf. Deut 28:52, Ezek 26:11).

[113] Thus D. Hillers, *Lamentations*, 87.

[114] However, the term שׁול is very uncommon in the Hebrew Bible, occurring only 13x (including Is 6:1: the "skirts" or "robes" of YHWH fill the temple; and the "skirts" of the priests in Exod 28:33–34, 39:24–26).

[115] The prophets at times are depicted as purposefully going naked and barefoot as a sign of humiliation (e.g., Is 20:2; Mic 1:8, 11).

[116] Perhaps related to this context is the mourning custom in which the mourner may go with feet or head 'bare' and having been stripped of one's normal clothes in exchange for sackcloth (e.g., Isa 32:11).

[117] See Ezek 16:39; 23:26. For the tearing off of a woman's garments during plundering of war, see the Babylonian lament *balag* 50, cited by F. W. Dobbs-Allsopp, *Weep, O Daughter of Zion*, 48.

[118] This wordplay allows that בשׁוליה may serve as a shortened form of a qal masculine plural participle from the root שׁלל plus feminine direct object suffix with temporal ב preposition. BDB gives meanings of שׁלל to include 'plunder,' 'spoil,' 'draw out,' and an apparently related adjective, שׁולל, to be 'barefoot' (1021; see 2 Chr 28:14–15). In this case, a lamed of the geminate verb would be ellided, reverting to the original biconsonantal root שׁול. The vowel under the first lamed would normally be shortened to a mobile schewa under the influence of the suffix (cf. this participle in Jer 50:10; Ezek 39:10; Zech 2:12), but liquid consonants very frequently cannot hold a mobile schewa and thus the possible omission of the doubling here (see GKC: 20m, 61h, 67a).

Septuagint reading (often literal in Lamentations)[119] of this term may be suggestive of the שׁלל/שׁולל meaning:

> Ἀκαθαρσία αὐτῆς πρὸς ποδῶν αὐτῆς
> ("her uncleanness before/at her feet")[120]

The root שׁלל serves double duty here since it is used for the 'plunder' of women in war (cf. Ju 5:30: "Are they not finding and dividing the spoil [שׁלל], a womb or two for the head warrior?"), and also refers to the plunder of the city and temple treasures.[121]

Jeremiah's compelling and empathetic words in Lam 1:7–9b detailing Jerusalem's suffering both as a city and as a woman evoke, not surprisingly, another voice for the first time in Lamentations: *Jerusalem's poet* breaks in with a *lament to YHWH*: "See!—YHWH—my *suffering/rape* (עניי)! *How* the enemy gloats!" (9c)[122] Here especially, and throughout Lam 1 and 2, an assessment will be made as to whether there is evidence that Jerusalem's speech is really *Jeremiah's* rendering of her speaking persona, or whether she is *another poet* in dialogue with Jeremiah.

Several preliminary points can be made in support of the claim that Lam 1 contains the rhetoric of two different poets in dialogue. First, research on the dirge genre outlined above strongly suggests the *dialogical* nature of the performance of dirges across cultures, i.e., a call and response style that allows for different singers or poets. Indeed, a singer may address someone in mourning, and the mourner

[119] See Bertil Albrektson, *Studies in the Text and Theology of the Book of Lamentations with a Critical Edition of the Peshitta Text* (Lund, 1963).

[120] Ziegler, *Threni*, 469.

[121] A similar double layer of meaning about the invasion/rape of Jerusalem is found in YHWH's speech in Ezek 7:22, using different terminology: חלל rather than שׁלל. After describing Jerusalem's *treasures and idols* as "impure" (נדה) that will be made plunder (שׁלל), YHWH says, "I will turn my face away from them, that they may defile (חללו) my treasured/hidden place (צפוני); the violent shall enter it (באו); they shall defile her (וחללוה; in a sexual sense in Gen 49:4; Lev 19:29; 21:9) . . . their holy places (מקדשׁיהם) shall be defiled" (7:22, 24b). See Julie Galambush on the combined violence against the woman and pillage of city in Ezekiel (*Jerusalem*, 58, 85).

[122] Following the NJPS rendering, the hifil form of גדל by itself can mean a kind of reviling, abusive speech; as NJPS translates similarly in Zeph 2:8, 10 ("gloat," "jeer"), Ezek 35:13 ("spoke arrogantly"), and note especially that it is used in lament psalms regarding the 'enemy' (Ps 35:26: "vaunt themselves over me"; similarly, 38:17; 55:13: in parallel with "revile", חרף; and in Job 19:2–5: "reproaching," parallel to "words that crush," "humiliate," and "abuse").

may respond. It is possible that the Israelite expression of communal dirges allowed for an analogous dialogue of singers/poets.[123] Second, research on the dirge genre also reveals the presence of *lament prayer* as part of the performance of the dirge, thus there is at least the possibility that the different poets performing at a single occasion will each perform a particular genre. In Lam 1, although the two poetic singers use distinctly different genres at the outset, their unfolding dialogue effectively begins to blur the lines in their interest of pursuing certain themes (see below). With these points, I do not intend to reconstruct an original or customary *Sitz im Leben* for the performance of Lamentations texts; it is not necessary. Research shows that dirges in a specific cultural context may be performed in various places (at the scene of death, at the burial, in the home), and this does not seriously affect the basic shape of the genre. What changes the specific content and language of the genre are its *purposes*.

Third, for the prophet to 'impersonate' or present the persona of Jerusalem as a woman of the community lamenting her suffering would suggest either that women had no voice in expressing lament/dirge speech for the community, or it suggests that there was no one, no woman, from the worshipping/singing community available to do this. Is this likely? Not at all, given the long tradition of lament psalms/temple singers, as well as the custom of mourning women who performed precisely in contexts of crisis and death. Moreover, in the aftermath of war, there are usually *more women* left as survivors than men. Obviously there were survivors in Jerusalem, including Jeremiah, and he did not operate in a vacuum. And finally, the consistently empathetic tone of Jeremiah's poetry across Lam 1:1–9b, culminating in his description of Jerusalem's rape, could have elicited a response from a temple singer or mourning woman.

Thus a voice has broken in at Lam 1:9c: "See—YHWH—*my suffering/rape* (עניי)! How the enemy gloats!" While it is obvious that this is a new poetic voice by the abrupt switch to first person speech, her plea (*lament prayer* genre) interrupts Jeremiah's *communal dirge*. Normally a lament plea is preceded by a description, but his previous

[123] Cf. the intrusion of the people's *lament prayer* speech, unannounced, in Jer 14:7–9, following Jeremiah's communal dirge in vss 1–6, followed by YHWH's judgment speech, vs 10, another communal dirge by Jeremiah in 14:17–18, followed by a *lament prayer* by the people to YHWH. Are these speeches simply haphazardly arranged, or do they reflect an oral context of interacting singers?

description of her distress served that function.[124] How else is it evident that she *interrupts* Jeremiah's poem? The use of inclusio (and chiasm) is common in the composition and oral performance of poetry,[125] including Jeremiah's in the book of Jeremiah.[126] After the opening verse of Lam 1, Jeremiah introduced the key refrain "*no one is comforting her*" (vs 2); he uttered it again in vs 9b just before the interruption.[127] While this appears to close the inclusio and make a natural break in his discourse, it is not complete, since an inclusio, as here, can be composed of a *pair* of terms at the beginning and end of a speech (as in Jer 20:7–10).[128] In vs 2, following "no one is comforting her," Jeremiah mentions Jerusalem's "*enemies*." In vs 9, Jeremiah's "no one is comforting her" is followed by *the second poetic singer's mentioning* of her "*enemies*." It is as though the second singer had listened to him and completed his inclusio, but with the primary intention of lamenting to YHWH for help *against* the enemy, not simply describing the enemy's actions. It is less likely that one poet responsible for both voices would interrupt the genre and rhetorical pattern of the first speech, rather than close it off cleanly and begin the second speech from a different point of view. Neither did later editors smooth over this fissure. Rather, an oral context of the poetry is yet reflected in its written form.

The poet expressing a woman's suffering in Jerusalem continues here in Lamentations from where she left it in the book of Jeremiah, beseeching YHWH with *lament prayer* again, after suffering more violence.[129] If she was bold enough to lament to YHWH in Jer 10, after YHWH had ruled out lament prayer, she is doubly bold now, persevering in lamenting to YHWH after surviving the onslaught.

[124] See C. Westermann, *Praise and Lament*, 130.

[125] A. B. Lord witnessed the use of chiasm by oral poets of Yugoslavia (*Singer of Tales*, 42). For examples of inclusio in Yugoslavian poetry, see the repetition of "the white horse" (ibid., II, I:737–50) and the "standardbearers" in the poem of Avdo (Appendix I, 223, 233); ibid., 55.

[126] See Jack R. Lundbom, *Jeremiah: A Study in Ancient Hebrew Rhetoric* (Missoula, Mont.: SBL, 1975).

[127] Jeremiah's only other use of the refrain in Lam 1 is in vs 17 where he uses it to summarize Zion's preceding speech.

[128] In Jer 20:7–10 the pair of terms appearing at the beginning and end of Jeremiah's lament are "deceive" and "overcome"; J. Lundbom, ibid., 45–46.

[129] As was the case in the book of Jeremiah, so too here, there is no introduction of Jerusalem's poet's words, e.g., 'Zion said.' R. Gordis notes such "virtual quotation" is typical in biblical, rabbinic, and Oriental literature, and "the reader is counted upon to recognize the intent of the passage"; *Lamentations*, 123.

Whereas the figures of Jeremiah and Job are daring before YHWH in their claims of innocent suffering, Jerusalem's poet is even bolder because she pleas for YHWH's intervention, while admitting guilt of transgression. She has not claimed innocence, but is claiming forgiveness. Moreover, Jerusalem's poet exhibits a *major role reversal* with Jeremiah. The prophet's voice has been reduced to expressions only of dirge speech and comforting normally handled by the mourning women, while Jerusalem's poet, voicing lament to YHWH, takes on the *prophetic* role of intermediator. It is a role reversal created by the crisis at hand, in which the established leadership (kings, priests, scribes, cult prophets) and the people have failed. One cannot help but wonder who is Jerusalem's Poet.

Her lament evokes from Jeremiah the dynamic of dialogue. As though hearing her, he redirects his speech to say more about the *enemy's* treatment of her.[130]

> His hand the *enemy* has stretched out
> over all her precious things. (Lam 1:10a)

Moreover, her lament to YHWH, as T. Linafelt has noted,[131] seems to lead the previously detached Jeremiah to offer a surprising aside *directly to YHWH* in 10bc:

> Indeed, *you* (YHWH) looked on (as) nations entered *her* sanctuary,[132]
> whom *you* commanded, 'they shall not enter into your assembly!'[133]

To sum up Lam 1:7–10, Jeremiah effects a flurry of double meanings (characteristic of his poetry) with the terms עני (7), נדה/נידה (8), שלל/שול (9), מחמדיה and מקדש (10). The intent of these double meanings was to *enlarge the two key images* of the fate of Jerusalem, *already set forth* in Jer 4 and 10: (1) To the image of *a suffering city* whose

[130] Contra C. Westermann who suggests that vss 10a–11b "exhibit no clear flow of ideas"; *Lamentations*, 131.

[131] T. Linafelt, *Surviving Lamentations*, 80.

[132] S. P. Re'emi notes that Lam 1:10 shows the invasion of the temple, but does not suggest its destruction as yet; *Lamentations*, 87; however, the same poet does render the destruction of the "sanctuary" by YHWH in Lam 2:6f. See the communal lament psalms 74 and 79 for the destruction of the temple, though the dating is not certain; cf. also Ps 44.

[133] Following Gordis's convincing repointing of the 3rd fem. sing. verb to 2nd masc. sing. to make YHWH the subject, with the connotation of 'looking on and regarding the action as proper;' he notes a similar usage of the verb in Lam 3:36; *Song of Songs and Lamentations*, 156. This translation fits the ironic, shocking context of YHWH being aligned with these enemy actions against Jerusalem.

tent is destroyed (Jer 4, 10), Jeremiah *added* in Lam 1 the imagery of the sanctuary's violation, being made "impure," "plundered" of its "precious things," and the city/people becoming a "wanderer," exiled; and (2) to the image of *a woman attacked* with no one helping her (Jer 4), Jeremiah *adds* the image in Lam 1 that she is "raped," made "impure," "plundered" of "her precious things."[134] Then, as happened in Jer 8:18–19, Jeremiah again hears Jerusalem's Poet's lament (in 1:9c), whereas YHWH (as in Jer 4 and 10) again does not answer her lament. In sum, the poet Jeremiah moves from empathetic speech *about* Jerusalem in Lam 1:1–9b that echoed her state of Jer 4 and 10, and now begins directly *echoing her words* of Lam 1:9c and following.

Finally, though Jerusalem's poet had interrupted and closed Jeremiah's inclusio (at vs 9c), now Jeremiah closes off this latest poetic section he began with an inclusio at vs 7 ("*all the precious things*," "*her people*") with the same pair of terms at vss 10–11 ("*all her precious things*," "*all her people*," "*their precious things*"). Jeremiah says in vs 11:

> *All her people* are groaning,
>   searching for bread.
> They give their *precious things* for food
>   to restore life.

Yet, Jeremiah's echoing of Jerusalem's suffering and humiliation evokes another lament plea from her in 11c: "Look YHWH! and see how *despised/worthless* (זוללה) I have become!" She repeats the term Jeremiah used above, to say she feels *despised* (cf. vs 8b). The two poets recorded in the book of Jeremiah independently of one another have begun a mutually encouraging dialogue that was yet foreshadowed in that book. Vs 12 below will reveal several more poignant terms used by *both* poets for their suffering. Their rhetorical activity as it is being described fits the definition of an 'oral poet' each using both formulaic poetry and unique modifications of it in context. The less likely alternative is that the literary art of a single poet, analogous to an author presenting characters in narrative, presents two different personae, first a prophet with dirge speech, then a suffering woman/the city who laments. This latter explanation is

[134] For the overlapping imagery of the plundering of the shrine/treasures and rape (of the city goddess) in a Babylonian lament (*balag* 50), see F. W. Dobbs-Allsopp, *Weep, O Daughter of Zion*, 48, 69.

suggestive of a single author further removed from the original context of destruction who imitates the speeches of figures who experienced it.

....
hurriedly frenetically leafing searching turning
....
...99472.......99396........993170.......99422..... . . .
...dialing.oslo..rome........the hague.....prague.....
...budapest.....bucharest...brussels......vienna.....
...bern..........berlin........bonn..........and all.....
...the baals.and.gods of this world...................
....
not a sound—no connection

oh God in Heaven
is there a fax anywhere
from madrid to moscow
that is not blocked by traders' quotes
assailed by lies of our killers
that could receive the message
from a shelter full of dread
from a deathly-silent classroom

osijek croatia september 17 1991

Borislav Arapović
"Telefax from Croatia"[135]

Jerusalem's Poet in Lamentations 1:12–22

Jerusalem's poet continues speaking from vss 12–15b. Having not received divine attention, she turns to those passing by with the same appeal:

Ah! unto you,[136] all who pass by the way—
Look! and see if there is any *pain* like my *pain* (מכאוב כמכאבי).

[135] Transl. I. Pozajić Jerić; in *Between Despair and Lamentation*, 28–31; the poet depicts his attempt to reach the outside world with graphic descriptions of the destruction of the town of Osijek, but to no avail.

[136] This line poses a difficulty of translation, because it opens with לוא followed by a preposition. Scholars do not agree on a solution. Cross suggests both MT and 4QLam[a] appear corrupt and reconstructs as . . . לוא אלי כל: "Would that on me all who pass by the way gaze and see"; Cross, "Studies," 145. However, instead of reading the לוא as an optative, perhaps it is a remnant Ugaritic asseverative *lamed*—

In Lamentations, Jerusalem's poet tries to gain the attention of passersby and, following traditional theology, attributes her suffering to God. She tells the onlookers about YHWH's anger—the one thing she pleaded against earlier has happened—YHWH has punished her in *anger* (Jer 10:24).[137] She suggests YHWH's anger has been expended in her suffering.

> Look! and see if there is any *pain* like my *pain* (מכאוב כמכאבי),[138]
> with which he afflicted me,
> with which *YHWH* has *grieved* (הוגה < יגה) me[139]
> on the day of his *burning anger*![140] (Lam 1:12)

While it may appear that Jerusalem's poet merely shifts her lament from YHWH to the passersby, *a far greater move* is underway in the social context here. This motif of *dialogue* is also part of the *dirge* genre. Moreover, the motif of *accusation against the murderer*, announced in and to the community, is also part of the dirge, particularly when the death is unnatural (serving as "the voice of public justice," Jahnow).[141] (Indeed, B. Arapović's communal dirge poem above, which ends with a lament prayer, serves as a "voice of public justice" as he also accuses their "killers.")

used to gain the attention of the passers-by; see Daniel Sivan, *A Grammar of the Ugaritic Language* [Leiden: Brill, 1997], 186–87, 190–92. This would parallel D. Zion's emphatic effort to get YHWH's attention in 11c; failing there, she turns to the onlookers. T. J. Meek reads the particle as emphatic and exclamatory, an appeal for sympathy; *Lamentations*, 12.

[137] Jer 10:24: "Correct me, YHWH, but with justice, not with your anger." Cf. the prophet Ezekiel's outcry asking YHWH if *everyone* in Israel was to be destroyed because of divine anger (Ezek 9:8). Ezekiel's objection is not that YHWH is punishing out of anger, but to what extent the punishment will go.

[138] YHWH responds to D. Zion/Jerusalem later in the book of Jeremiah (30:12–17) with a salvation oracle: ". . . Why do you cry out over your *brokenness* (שברך)? Your *pain* (מכאבך) is incurable, because your iniquities are great . . . I will heal your wounds. . . ." That YHWH echoes numerous of Jerusalem's and Jeremiah's terms about her suggests that YHWH's salvation oracles in the book of Jeremiah logically follow sometime after her pleas in the book of Lamentations. Surprisingly, this term for "pain" is not very common among the prophets.

[139] Cf. 4QLam[a] that has הוגירני ("terrified me," hifil of יגר; Cross, "Studies," 145).

[140] These texts' theological struggle about YHWH's anger suggests a larger rhetorical context unfolding here, beyond a form critical recognition alone that the 'day of burning anger' occurs frequently in prophetic oracles of judgment; C. Westermann, *Lamentations*, 133.

[141] As noted earlier, H. Jahnow stated about the dirge genre, "Here *the complaint becomes the accusation* (die Klage zur Anklage), and often the name of the murderer is intoned by the lips of the funeral singer for the first time," *Das hebräische Leichenlied*, 88. See Jerusalem's poet moving toward *naming* the murderer in vss 14–15 below.

Yet Jerusalem's poet, familar with the prophetic communal dirge, concerned as it is with injustices by perpetrators and their punishment, *expands* the genre even further *to include an accusation against YHWH as the perpetrator* of suffering, death and destruction. This shift to such an accusation will become more obvious below as Jerusalem's poet gives a litany of YHWH's destructive actions, culminating in YHWH's killing of her warriors and young men (see vs 14 below). At the same time, the expected distinction between YHWH and the enemy (as in lament) is collapsed: *YHWH is likened to the enemy*. One presumes that Jerusalem's poet, after hearing Jeremiah's graphic dirge-like description of her suffering, has finally shifted to this tact after finding her *lament complaint to YHWH* ineffective. Nevertheless, it must be maintained that this poet is employing both genres, in an overlapping manner: she maintains first person speech (as with lament), but describes YHWH as the perpetrator (as with dirge).

The poet's double expression of "*pain*," along with two more severe verbs describing YHWH's action against her, topped off by "his burning anger," all render not only this individual's expression of suffering, but also *her anger*. She uses the term "*pain*" (מכאוב),[142] not a very common root, but one that appears more often in the book of Jeremiah (4x) than in any other prophetic book.[143] Jeremiah had said, again in a personal lament: "Why is my *pain* (כאבי) unending, my wound incurable (אנוש) . . .?" (Jer 15:18). In a later 'consolation' oracle (the same one where YHWH resists words to Jerusalem of "correction" with "justice"), YHWH says to her, "Why do you cry out over your *brokennness* (שבר)? Your *pain* (מכאבך) is incurable (אנוש) (Jer 30:15); YHWH yet says, "I will heal your wounds . . ." (30:17).

Also, as noted earlier, Jerusalem's poet in Jer 8:18 had said, "My joy has gone; *grief* (יגון) is upon me." Here in Lam 1:12, Jerusalem's poet employs a verbal form of the same root (הוגה) to describe YHWH causing her *grief*.[144]

The analysis of the Jeremiah texts (esp. Jer 4, 8, and 10) and Lam 1 thus far suggests it is misleading to draw the superficial

[142] And again in Lam 1:18.

[143] Baruch also uses the term in his lament (quoted by YHWH in Jer 45:3); and Jeremiah uses the term to describe Babylon's pain in Jer 51:8. Cf. uses in the book of Ezekiel: in 13:22, YHWH accuses false women prophets of causing "*pain*" in the heart of the righteous, though YHWH has not caused such "*pain*"; cf. Ezek 28:24.

[144] In Lam 1:5 also, Jeremiah had said "YHWH has *grieved* (הוגה) her [Zion]" (see above).

conclusion, as M. Biddle does, about the characters in Jer 1–20: that "only God voices any awareness of the ambiguity and conflict involved in the punishment of the chosen people."[145] Though YHWH certainly expresses turmoil and agony over punishing the people (e.g., Jer 12:7–11; 31:18–20), Jeremiah and Jerusalem grieve over this painful ambiguity no less than YHWH! Yet Biddle adds, "in comparison with other voices in this dialogue, God appears to be the complex, 'human,' sensitive character"![146] To the contrary, the Jer 4, 8, and 10 passages show YHWH ignoring Jerusalem's expressions of human suffering and her request to YHWH with its stunning theological challenge about anger and justice.

In Lam 1:13a, Jerusalem's poet next describes the violent action of YHWH's *anger* in more detail:

> From on high he sent *fire*,
> *into my bones* (בעצמתי) he made it sink.[147]

D. Hillers has noted similar imagery used by Jeremiah in his lament of Jer 20:9 to describe the result when he refrains from speaking for YHWH: "there is in my heart like a *fire* burning, contained *in my bones* (בעצמתי)."[148] Jerusalem's poet appears to use Jeremiah's image of YHWH sending fire into the bones, only the image expresses her very different experience—being consumed by YHWH's *anger* rather than being consumed by his *calling*.[149] Moreover, just as Jeremiah took the theme of the destruction of the *sanctuary* of Jer 4 and 10 and made it more explicit, so too here Jerusalem's poet takes her theme of YHWH's *anger* of Jer 10 and describes it in more detail.

The preoccupation with, and growing resentment about, *YHWH's anger* by Jerusalem's poet finds a sympathetic hearing in Jeremiah, who will pick up the theme with gusto at the beginning of chapter 2 of Lamentations (see below). For *18 lines* he will give a litany of

[145] M. Biddle, *Polyphony*, 17. Much of Biddle's view seems to rest on his identification of texts purported to express YHWH's grief.

[146] M. Biddle, *Polyphony*, 17.

[147] D. Hillers also uses the term 'sink'; *Lamentations*, 72. Foll. LXX and 4QLam[a] which agree on a hifil imperfect variant of ירד over against the MT; see Cross, "Studies," 145.

[148] D. Hillers, *Lamentations*, 89; also I. Provan, *Lamentations*, 49.

[149] Contrast the imagery YHWH uses in Ezek 22:17–22 wherein all the inhabitants of Judah will be put into the smelter of YHWH's *anger* to be purified of their dross.

YHWH's destructive actions, *all caused by anger.*[150] Jerusalem's poet continues in Lam 2:21–22: "The young and the old are lying on the ground in the streets . . . in the day of *your anger* you killed them . . .!" Thus, these two poets move into a kind of call and response crescendo, referring to YHWH's anger, until they finally *equate* YHWH *with the enemy* (2:5, 21). By Lam 3:42–43, Jerusalem's poet vociferously summarizes their complaint, entirely in character for the one *whose laments have gone unanswered*:

> *We* (נחנו) *have* transgressed and rebelled—
> *You* (אתה) have *not* forgiven!
> *You have wrapped yourself with anger* and pursued us;
> you have killed, you have not pitied.
> *You have wrapped yourself* with a cloud so that *no prayer* can pass through!

The last lines with double use of "wrapped" (סכתה from סכך, NRSV) likely contain a biting wordplay with סכת, 'to keep silent': 'You are *silent* with anger . . . you *silence* yourself behind a cloud so that no prayer can pass through!'

All of these accusations against YHWH vastly extend the 'accusation' motif found in *both the dirge and the lament* genres. The poets use *two* genres to accuse YHWH. Typical in lament psalms is the accusation/complaint against God, but it is invariably found *alongside* accusations against one's enemies. And though lament psalms often contain harsh complaint against YHWH,[151] they are not so criticizing as the Lamentations text. Prior to Job, the only rhetoric that comes close to this tone are Jeremiah's laments and the people's lament in Jer 14:8–9a. That text marks *the first time* the people speak directly to YHWH in the book of Jeremiah. After a quick

[150] Dobbs-Allsopp notes the focus on the destructive power of the deity against the city also in Mesopotamian lamentations and *balags; Weep, O Daughter of Zion*, 42. One may ask whether the theme of divine anger, formulaic in the biblical prophets and Lamentations, is stressed in Mesopotamian texts, and moreover, is the anger caused by divine displeasure over injustice and idolatry?

[151] Particularly, according to Westermann, in the communal lament psalms (e.g., Pss 44:23: "Why do you sleep?"; 89:46: "How long . . . will you hide yourself?"; *Praise and Lament*, 176–78, 183–84. Perhaps the communal laments more forcefully complain against God because of the greater suffering and the theology of corporate punishment. Jerusalem's poet's lament, then, as an individual sufferer, is even more striking in its severe complaint about YHWH's means of punishing the entire nation. According to Westermann, the *only* individual lament in the Psalter that contains a severe complaint directly against YHWH (in 2nd person) is Ps 22, used by Jesus in the NT: "My God, my God, why have you forsaken me?!"; ibid., 184.

confession, the people in Jer 14 utter a bitter, perhaps sarcastic complaint against YHWH as they begin to face destruction and exile:

Hope of Israel,
Its *savior* in time of trouble,
Why are you being like a *sojourner* in the land?
  like a wayfarer stretching out for the night?
Why are you being like a man confused?[152]
  like a warrior with *no power to save*? (Jer 14:7–9)

The above critique of YHWH's powerlessness, presumably in the face of the invading enemy, is ironically *reversed* in Lam 1 where YHWH is critiqued precisely for *being like a destroying warrior against his own people.*[153]

In Lam 1:13b, Jerusalem's poet continues focusing on YHWH's *enemy-like* actions against her, and though she is alive, her life is threatened:

He [YHWH] *stretched* a net for my feet
  and turned me back.
He made me desolate,
  weak, all the day long.

Like the enemies Jeremiah had described (Lam 1:10) *stretching* (פרשׂ) out their hands against Jerusalem to do her harm, YHWH *stretches* (פרשׂ) out a net. It is a stunning image in light of its normal use by lament psalmists to describe the human enemy's action against them and how YHWH *usually rescues* them from the net.[154]

[152] NRSV.

[153] This is stunning also in light of nearly no description of the outside enemy invaders in Lamentations. C. Westermann notes a similar absence of concrete description of the invading enemy in *Lamentation over the Destruction of Ur* (*Lamentations*, 128). However, what is the theological comparison of the role of the gods in these texts? The city goddess Ningal is primarily portrayed as weeping over her city and making appeals to the higher gods (An and Enlil) for help, to whom also is attributed the destruction. However, Ningal is not presented as *challenging* the enemy-like actions of the god in any way like Jerusalem and Jeremiah do in Lamentations. This is evident from very little lament/complaint speech in LU and a preponderance of dirge/mourning speech. Indeed, while LU contains references to the city mourning, *the city does not speak at all.* Among the ancient Mesopotamian so-called 'city laments,' only in the Nippur Lamentation does the city speak for itself; see F. W. Dobbs-Allsopp, *Weep, O Daughter of Zion*, 77.

[154] Noted by S. P. Re'emi, *Lamentations*, 88. Likewise, YHWH as speaker in Ezekiel also uses the image in predicting how YHWH will capture king Zedekiah in Ez 12:13 and 17:20, noted by D. Hillers, *Lamentations*, 89.

In the next verse (Lam 1:14), the "hand" of YHWH and the "hands" of the enemies work together in yet another image—Jerusalem's poet is yoked into bondage, ironic in light of Jer 2:20 where YHWH said: "For long ago you broke your *yoke* (עלך) . . . you played the whore." The old yoke, symbolic of a marriage covenant with YHWH (2:2) and/or the requirements of the law (5:5), is replaced with a new one, symbolic of servitude under a foreign "master."

The *yoke* (על) of my transgression is fastened,[155]
  lashed tight by *his hand*,[156]
  his *yoke* upon my neck.
It makes my strength falter.
YHWH gives me into *the hands* of
  those I cannot withstand.[157] (Lam 1:14)

Then in Lam 1:15 Jerusalem's poet renders YHWH's killing of her warriors with 'reaping' imagery, a common prophetic formula in other texts voiced by YHWH:[158]

He 'cut down' (סלה) all my mighty ones[159]
  —YHWH in my midst!
He *proclaimed* (קרא) a time against me
  to *crush* (לשבר) my young men. (Lam 1:15)

Jerusalem's poet's rhetoric of "*crushing*" adds specific, graphic imagery of *crushing grapes* at the harvest (like splattering blood) to her earlier

[155] Qumran apparently corrects the corrupt MT verb (נשקד) to נקשר, "is bound"; Cross, "Studies," 146. That a yoke was typically put on the captive is indicated by Cross and suggested by the text of Jer 27:2f. In that narrative, Jeremiah made a "*yoke*" (על) of "bars and straps" for his neck as directed by YHWH, symbolic of coming Babylonian domination and the suppression of Judah's rebellion; in Lam 1:14, however, the poet's exact terminology of YHWH tying on the yoke is different from Jer 27:2f. Perhaps Jerusalem's poet was influenced by Jeremiah's and her people's experience of wearing the yoke. Cf. Jer 30:8 and Lam 3:27 discussed below.

[156] NJPS.

[157] NJPS.

[158] D. Hillers, *Lamentations*, 90. Cf. YHWH's use of the reaping imagery within a dirge song in Jer 9:21: "Human corpses shall fall like dung upon the open field, like sheaves behind the reaper"; Jeremiah's similar imagery used against Babylon in Jer 50:26; the harvesting image used by YHWH in Isa 17:4–6, of reapers and gleaners destroying Ephraim; YHWH renders the reaping image in Mic 4:12–13.

[159] Translators are in wide disagreement on how to translate the verb (סלה) here, thus 'cut down' (as in harvesting sheaves) renders YHWH's action against the warriors, and in parallel with the vintage 'crushing'; see D. Hillers' discussion of this option and in Jer 50:26 (*Lamentations*, 74–75); כל־אבירי, literally "all my bulls," according to Cross, drawing on images "of vintage festival, slaughter, and the celebrations of the rites of holy war"; "Studies," 146.

more general use of "*crushing*" ('destruction') in Jer 4:20 and, especially, to the image of her wound in Jer 10:19 ("Woe is me because of my *crushing* [שִׁברי]! *My wound gushes*" [נחלה מכתי]).[160] She also recalls the "*proclamation*" of the disaster (called for by YHWH in Jer 4:20):

> I hear the alarm of battle,
> *destruction upon destruction*
> (שֶׁבר על שֶׁבר; or, *crushing upon crushing*)
> is *proclaimed* (נִקְרָא). . . . (Jer 4:20; see also 4:5, 16)

Here in Lam 1:15, *Jeremiah* now joins the poetic dialogue and her 'harvesting' imagery, adding yet another verb with third person description of her "*crushing*":

> A winepress—YHWH *trampled* (< דרך)[161]
> Virgin Daughter Judah! (1:15)

By joining in Jerusalem's poetic discourse with communal dirge speech about YHWH's 'harvesting' actions, Jeremiah effectively joins her outcry against YHWH as killer (Lam 1:15). His words also echo *his own mourning speeches* for her in Jer 8:21: "For the *crushing* (שֶׁבר) of the *Daughter of My People I am crushed* (השברתי)"; and in Jer 14:17b–18:[162] "Let my eyes run down with tears day and night . . . with what a great crushing (שֶׁבר) is *Virgin Daughter of My People crushed* (נִשְׁברה), (her) *wound gushes forth* (מאד מכה נחלה)."[163] Jeremiah will later shift from such dirge speech (Lam 1:15) to *his own characteristic mourning speech again* (Lam 2:18f).

Jerusalem's poet resumes speaking in Lam 1:16 as a weeping mother (continuing that theme), only now she mourns not just that her "*children* are gone" (Jer 10:20; Lam 1:5), but adds that they are "devastated":

[160] Thus T. J. Meek's claim that besides in Lam 1:15 "the verb לִשְׁבֹר, to *crush*, is never elsewhere found with animate beings as its object" is incorrect; *The Book of Lamentations*, IB (New York: Abingdon, 1953), 14; see Jer 10:19, and cf. Ezek 6:9 where YHWH is "crushed" because of the people's "wanton heart."

[161] See also the "trampling" of Babylon at the time of harvest described by YHWH in Jer 51:33.

[162] The identification of this text as *Jeremiah's* mourning speech, not YHWH's, follows J. Henderson, "Who Weeps." Henderson follows Holladay's argument (*Jeremiah*, 436–37) that 14:17a really is a summary statement to YHWH's speech preceding it, and that several key terms in the mourning speech are Jeremianic, based on several texts elsewhere.

[163] See note above, chapter 2.

On account of these things I am *weeping.*
My eyes, my eyes, run with tears![164]
Because far away from me is *a comforter,*
restoring my life.[165]
My children are devastated (שוממים),
because *the enemy* overpowers. (Lam 1:16)

Note the double irony of the absence of a divine "comforter" and the irony of who is "the enemy." Note also that Jerusalem's poet uses the common word for "*children,*" בן (as she did in Jer 10:20), unlike Jeremiah's preferred use of the term עולל for "children" (vs 5 above). The word-pair, "*comforter*"/"*enemy*" comprised Jeremiah's earlier inclusio (vss 2 and 9). She had earlier echoed his term "enemy" to close that inclusio; here she employs both terms, *only now in her speech they identify the same 'person'*: YHWH. The earlier inclusio indicated the close of a section and a shift in singers, and so it does here. In the next verse (17), Jeremiah picks up where she leaves off, echoing her use of *both terms* of the inclusio (with "foe" for "enemy"); the word-pair appears in back to back verses. He follows her identification of who is the "no comforter" and "enemy." The dance of poetic dialogue continues.

Zion *stretches out her hands* (פרשׂה ציון בידיה)—
No one is comforting her (אין מנחם לה).
YHWH has commanded against Jacob
those around him (to be) his *foes.* (Lam 1:17ab)

Jeremiah's statement is highly ironic and empathetic—a recognition of her suffering, since the enemies and YHWH have been *stretching their hands* against her (1:10, 14; cf. vs 7).

In his last line in this speech, Jeremiah echoes his earlier wordplay of Jerusalem as a "*wanderer*" (לנידה, vs 8), now with the likesounding נדה ("*impure one,*" MT). As an *oral poet,* he is building on the sound and meaning of his previous term, teasing out the subtextual meaning from before ("impurity"), and bringing it now to central focus:

[164] Cf. "my eyes, my eyes!" (עיני עיני) here to Jerusalem's cry in Jer 4:19 (מעי מעי): "my insides, my insides!" See B. Bakke Kaiser on repetition in Jerusalem's speech; "Poet," 172.

[165] Note Jerusalem's use of נפשׁי with first person possessive ending, used earlier by Jerusalem in Jer 4:19 and 31.

Jerusalem's (or Jerusalem's poet) has become '*an impure one*' (לנדה) among them. (Lam 1:17c) The immediate rhetorical context suggests this meaning of the term. Jerusalem has just been depicted as trampled in a winepress (vs 15) and her warriors cut down and crushed (vs 15); no one comforts her (vss 16, 17); she is abandoned. The imagery suggests she and her people are splattered with blood. Blood defiles those it touches (victims, attackers, and bystanders), rendering them "*impure*"[166] (נדה; cf. the important continuation of this imagery by Jeremiah in Lam 4:13–15 below).[167] The Qumran text (4QLam[a]) has the similar sounding term, נדוה, "one *cast out/banished*," also fitting in this context, describing the resultant treatment of her by those who do not want to come into contact with one defiled with blood and disgraced: "Jerusalem has become *one cast out/banished* (לנדוה) among them." (Lam 1:17c; 4QLam[a])

As before with rape (1:8) and in line with the killing imagery above, Jeremiah implies the impurity is caused by *violence* against her. As Jeremiah finishes his last speech of Lam 1, he closes the rhetorical circle: he has moved from Jerusalem as persona to the person of Jerusalem's poet, a banished outcast (נדה) in vs 17, preoccupied with the days of her suffering/rape and wandering (נידה) in vs 7.

Jerusalem's poet resumes in vs 18 and speaks all the way to the end of the chapter (vs 22). Her focus on YHWH is maintained. She will echo Jeremiah's allusion in the previous verse to YHWH's "commanding" (צוה) neighboring countries to become her enemy. This command is essentially the same "proclaiming" (קרא) of disaster/crushing in Jer 4:20 which YHWH announced, and which she has just recalled herself in vs 15 above: YHWH "proclaimed" a time to crush "*my young men*" (בחורי). It is not surprising, therefore, that she now says something about YHWH's "proclaiming," about this divine *speech*:

[166] Again, any connotation of the meaning of a menstruant does not fit the context.

[167] On that text, see N. Lee, "Exposing a Buried Subtext," 119–22, for Jeremiah's midrashic use of imagery from the Cain and Abel story to indict the prophets and priests of Jerusalem for "shedding innocent blood" and whose garments are now defiled with that blood. Jeremiah's poetic treatment of Jerusalem as נידה and her leaders as being נדה (like Cain because they shed blood) has to do with his general view of empathy toward Jerusalem and defending the people over against the leadership. See discussion on Lam 4 below.

> *Innocent* (צדיק, righteous) is YHWH, *but* I *rebel* against his speech!
> (צדיק הוא יהוה כי פיהו מריתי)
> Hear, now! all (you) peoples, and see *my pain* (מכאבי).
> My virgins (בתולתי) and *my young men* (בחורי) go into captivity. (Lam 1:18)

The translation of Jerusalem's poet's emphatic statement ("*Innocent* is YHWH") is not a straightforward matter in this context, neither is the matter of how to translate the כי in the middle of the line and the term "*rebel*." The traditional reading is "The Lord is in the right, for I have rebelled against his word,"[168] thus a confession. W. Holladay has noted that the formula using the term "righteous" (צדיק) with a subject pronoun appears 9x in the Hebrew Bible, and that 5x it proclaims the righteouness of God ("righteous you are, YHWH," in Ps 119:137, Ezr 9:15, Neh 9:8, Jer 12:1). Only here in Lam 1:18 is the formula for YHWH *not* used with the second person pronoun.[169] That Jerusalem's poet, who has not hesitated to address YHWH in second person before, should refrain from using the standard formula may be suggestive of a different tone behind her speech. Holladay notes the phrase usually carries legal connotations and is used like a "declaration of acquittal" to proclaim someone's innocence. He convincingly argues, however, that when Jeremiah uses the formula in his personal lament in Jer 12:1, he twists its meaning into "*bitter sarcasm*" toward YHWH. Holladay translates:

> *Thou art innocent* (צדיק אתה), O Lord,
> whenever (כי) I lodge a complaint (אריב) with thee;
> yet I would pass judgment upon thee (אך משפטים אדבר אותך). (Jer 12:1)

[168] Most commentators follow the traditional reading: R. Gordis, *Lamentations*, 132; I. Provan, *Lamentations*, 53; C. Westermann, *Lamentations*, 111; D. Hillers, *Lamentations*, 90–91. However, some critics surmise an underlying complaint by Jerusalem within her confession, though they do not garner evidence to support it; thus T. J. Meek who suggests Jerusalem acknowledges the justice of her punishment but is "protesting against its severity," *Book of Lamentations*, 14; also S. P. Re'emi, *Lamentations*, 89–90, who makes the connection with Jeremiah's lament in Jer 12:1f, but concludes that Jerusalem "acknowledges the righteousness of God . . . but without the silent reproach of the prophet," and, there is also "a silent complaint that innocent children have had to suffer for the sins of their parents." In light of the character of the laments by Jeremiah and Jerusalem's poet, the term "silent" to describe them is not apropos.

[169] W. Holladay, "Style, Irony," 50. In Lam 1:18 the הוא is translated as "is": "righteous/innocent is YHWH." Before becoming more argumentative with YHWH, Jeremiah in his first lament (11:20) had addressed YHWH: "YHWH of hosts, *righteous* judge (שפט צדק). . . ."

Or, "let me assert *justice* with you." Holladay notes that most of the translations and commentators soften this abrasive line.[170] I would argue, moreover, in support of Holladay's rendering of Jeremiah's tone, that the כי could be translated as an emphatic "but!" and the אך, not as a restrictive ("yet"), but as an asseverative ("indeed!") particle. Thus, "You are innocent, YHWH, but I will lodge a complaint with you; indeed, I would pass judgment upon you!"

Now here in Lam 1:18, Jerusalem's poet uses the phrase ("YHWH is innocent"). To consider that this poet, too, might use a sarcastic tone,[171] we need only be reminded of her request of YHWH (ignored) in Jer 10:24: "Put me in line, YHWH, but *with justice* (משפט), not anger . . ."; her suffering rape (vss 7–10); her unanswered laments of Lam 1:9c and 11c; and her own intense anger and renewed mourning expressed over YHWH's killing and enemy-like actions in the last five verses.

Her tone is well in line with Jeremiah's complaint, that no matter how she confesses, laments, suffers, or waits for YHWH's help, YHWH will always be pronounced righteous or innocent in the matter. Holladay's insight about how the *tone* of the poet shapes the meaning of the rhetoric fits not only Jeremiah's anguished predicament, but Jerusalem's poet's as well.

YHWH had said in Jer 4:17 that Jerusalem "has *rebelled* (מרה) against me," a common term indicating wrongdoing of some sort, especially in the 'wilderness wandering' narrative.[172] As the above analysis has shown, Jerusalem's poet often echoes YHWH's terms about Jerusalem, but her point of view is more identified with Jeremiah's empathy. Thus, she says, "*Innocent* is YHWH, *but* against his speech I *rebel*!" The clue is in her saying she rebels against *YHWH's mouth or speech*, which the text implies is YHWH's *proclamation* to destroy her and the whole land. It is as though, while admitting sin (vss 14, 22), she nevertheless says, "Against *your decree* I rebel." Her rebellion is against the nature of YHWH's punishment.

[170] Ibid., 49–50. Yet, compare YHWH's complaint in Ezek 33:17, 20 quoting the people who are saying about YHWH: "The way of YHWH is not *just* (יתכן)," in the sense of not "according to regulation" or "standard measure."

[171] In contrast, the traditional translation followed by most commentators implies, in this context a 'docile' Jerusalem: "The Lord is in the right, for I have rebelled against his word."

[172] Cf. also YHWH's frequent use of the term מרה in the book of Ezekiel, usually in the phrase "rebellious house" (e.g., Ezek 2:8; 5:6; 24:3).

Jerusalem's poet, still turned away from an unresponsive YHWH, again beseeches those around her (cf. vs 12):

> Hear, now! all (you) peoples, and see my pain.
> My virgins (בתולתי) and my young men (בחורי) go into captivity. (Lam 1:18b)

After more speech in vs 19 about how her lovers have failed her, Jerusalem's poet turns to YHWH one last time in Lam 1 with yet *another lament*. She intensifies the poetic expression of her suffering, and further emphasizes her "rebelling" phrase by the use of the double root of the verb:

> Look! YHWH, how (כי) distressed I am!
> *My insides* (מעי) churn (חמרמרו).
> *My heart* is in tumult (נהפך) within me.
> Indeed(!) (כי) *I certainly rebel* (מרו מריתי). . . . (Lam 1:20ab)[173]

How does this intensified rebellion/defiance relate to Jerusalem's rebelling against YHWH's decree?[174] (Or is Jerusalem simply more repentant here than earlier?) A clue may be found in Jer 4:19, where she similarly described her inner turmoil:

> *My insides, my insides* (מעי מעי)! I labor in anguish!
> The walls/cities of *my heart*!
> *My heart* is in turmoil (המה);
> I cannot keep silent . . .;
> the whole land is devastated! (Jer 4:19)

In that speech, Jerusalem's inner turmoil was caused by the devastation around her, about which she could not keep silent. Her speech above in Lam 1:20 closely parallels Jer 4:19; in Lam 1:20 her "rebellion" is *to cry out* (not keep silent) because the devastation continues. She describes the devastation in the line immediately following:

> Indeed (!) (כי) *I certainly rebel*—
> in the street the sword bereaves,
> in the house—death! (כמות)[175] (1:20bc)

[173] Reading the second כי as asseverative as does C. L. Seow, but not translating the verb as "bitter"; "A Textual Note on Lamentations 1:20," *CBQ* 47 (1985): 418. The emphatic double root, מרו מריתי, also capitalizes on the alliteration with "churn," חמרמרו.

[174] 'Defiance' is suggested by Gordis in vs 20; *Lamentations*, 133.

[175] Reading with R. Gordis, the *kaph* is asseverative (ibid., 159), as is the כי just above it.

Jerusalem's poet still suffers inner turmoil and is defiant, *because the aftermath and consequences of the horror continue.* Yet why should *not* keeping silent before YHWH be considered 'rebellion'? There are two possible reasons. First, YHWH had ordered Jeremiah and the people *not to lament*, and this lament singer has ignored that decree. Her mere complaint to YHWH constitutes rebellion. Second, to speak out to YHWH about the horrors is implicitly to call YHWH's actions into question (particularly with regard to innocent sufferers, like children), and this is a 'rebellion' against YHWH's decision. Moreover, to lament to YHWH after the horror is to express need for the absent 'comforter' to intervene, and this is a 'rebellion,' because YHWH is withholding comfort.

Jerusalem's poet closes out the end of Lam 1 in vss 21–22 by completing this lament to YHWH—the longest of her speeches so far; amazingly, it includes *confession*, more explicit or certain than in Jer 10. She distinguishes YHWH from the enemies, with an implicit, ironic, motivating reminder, that *YHWH is different.*

> *They hear* how (כי) I groan:[176]
> "there is no one comforting me."
> All my enemies *hear* of my trouble;
> they rejoice that *you* (אתה) have done it. (Lam 1:21ab)

Jerusalem's poet then adds another traditional element of the lament—the call for YHWH's *revenge* against her enemies (see below). Yet in light of everything, it is a stunning and highly ironic request, for two reasons. First, in her earlier speech in Jer 10:24, Jerusalem asked YHWH not to correct her with *anger*, but with justice, but *nevertheless* to "pour out *your wrath*" on her enemies. She asked YHWH that they *not* be treated equally. Now in Lam 1:22 below, Jerusalem asks that they *be treated equally* by YHWH. Note the sardonic mention of YHWH's "*proclaiming*" and, to top it off, *her literal confession* ("my every transgression").

> Make the day come that you *proclaimed* (קראת),
> that they be like I am!

[176] Following MT, thus Albrektson, *Studies in the Text and Theology of the Book of Lamentations with a Critical Edition of the Peshitta Text* (Lund: CWK Gleerup, 1963), 83, not LXX's plural imperative nor the Syriac's singular imperative to YHWH; MT makes sense in the flow of the text where the irony of the enemies 'hearing' is set over against YHWH who may not; 'they hear' also parallels 1:21b.

Let all *their* evil come before your face
and deal with them
just as you dealt with me,
concerning *my every transgression* (פשׁעי).
Because my groans are many,
and *my heart is faint* (לבי דוי). (Lam 1:21c–22)

Her shift back to her suffering with the last two lines draws a large inclusio with her speech of Jer 8:18:

. . . *my heart is faint* (לבי דוי).

Summary of Lamentations 1

Lam 1 has now been thoroughly analyzed in comparison with texts in the book of Jeremiah, particularly Jer 4, 8, and 10, wherein Jerusalem's poet utters speeches. The comparison used an oral poetic/socio-rhetorical approach to trace the poetry of two singers (Jeremiah and Jerusalem's poet) on the basis of five areas: use of genres, imagery/themes, terms, rhetorical technique, and content. Within *each* of those areas, conclusions were drawn as to the poets' use of both formulaic poetry and their unique modification of it in context. The unfolding analysis consistently suggested that these two different 'singers' in Jeremiah were the same two 'singers' in Lamentations, but were, moreover, two different poets. That is, the one who speaks for Jerusalem is more than just a personification by Jeremiah.

There are numerous reasons to posit the presence of two different poets. First, as noted in chapter 2 above, in contrast to the figures that Jeremiah represented in his poetry, quoting their speech, Jerusalem's speech is unintroduced in the book of Jeremiah, like Jeremiah's typically. Second, Jerusalem's poet expressed a unique theological view in Jer 10:24 regarding YHWH's correcting her with justice, not anger, a view not seen in Jeremiah's poetry. In Lam 1:18, Jerusalem's poet was influenced by Jeremiah's lament (Jer 12) to press the case as to YHWH's "justice" or "innocence" with regard to her plea. Third, the interruption of the first singer and completion of his inclusio by Jerusalem's poet at Lam 1:9c reflects a shift in genre. A single poet would not likely interrupt the flow of the rhetoric, would not interrupt the inclusio technique (in the middle of a word pair!) *and* the genre. This strongly suggests an intrusion by a different poet in a dialogical, oral poetic context. Fourth, a developing dialogue is very evident in Lam 1, reflecting one poet 'listening' to the other, and a call and response pattern. The genre of the dirge appears universally in an oral poetic context wherein, it is attested, a dialogue of poets/singers may appear, including one who utters a prayer (lament). Fifth, Jerusalem's poet, while drawing upon the communal dirge genre for incisive effect, is more preoccupied with the *lament* genre and pressing it to its functional limits than is Jeremiah. Even though three times she draws upon key terms from Jeremiah's laments for her own poetry, her laments are structurally more characteristic of lament psalms than they are like Jeremiah's. And sixth, a key characteristic of Jeremiah's poetry is the use of double meaning, which he employs *seven* times in Lam 1 (vss 1, 7–9, 17). On the other hand, I have yet to find an instance of Jerusalem's poet employing double meaning in her lines in Lam 1.

A thorough concordance study of *terms* (and how terms are used within the rhetoric), with careful attention to occurrences in all the other prophetic books and psalms, revealed not only the strongest congruences between Lam 1 and Jer 4, 8, 10, but also surprising and strong congruences with *Jeremiah's laments and mourning speeches* in the book of Jeremiah. Across Lam 1:1–11, in four explicit instances, the first poet used *four different terms* to empathize with Jerusalem that were all used *by Jeremiah in his laments* (Jer 12, 15, and 20). That Jerusalem's poet occasionally draws upon Jeremiah's lament terms suggests she has been influenced by his rhetoric of suffering.[177] As the analysis above suggested, the first poet's explicit rendering of *six* of the same *images*[178] for Jerusalem in Lam 1:1–9b, as in Jer 4, 8, and 10, while using a prophetic communal dirge, is strong textual evidence for the claim that the first poet of Lamentations is the prophet Jeremiah. This poet's proclivity for poetic double meaning matches Jeremiah's style. And finally, this poet's pervasive tone of empathy for Jerusalem and her people in the midst of destruction

[177] In Lam 1:12–22, Jerusalem's poet employs one term and two unique phrases ("fire in my bones" and the ironic, "innocent is YHWH") also emphasized by Jeremiah in his laments (Jer 12, 15 and 20). Thus, in *seven* instances in Lam 1, the poets are tied to terms from Jeremiah's laments, yet develop the imagery of those terms to render Jerusalem's situation. Jeremiah also joins her (Lam 1:15) in developing the imagery of "crushing" they both used before (Jerusalem in Jer 4 and 10, and Jeremiah in his mourning speeches in Jer 8 and 14).

[178] Sitting alone, suffering woman/mother, destruction of tents/sanctuary, children gone, leaders fleeing like animals, city structures mourning.

and suffering in Lam 1:1–9b is one of the strongest reasons for identifying him with Jeremiah.

Finally, while these two poets can be distinguished, they also move toward the same increasing concern: the justice/injustice of YHWH's violent actions against Jerusalem and her inhabitants. Through stunning uses of both the communal dirge genre and the lament genre, the poets *accuse* YHWH as being a killer and an enemy, respectively. Both of these genres, it has been shown, in general and in this text, are seriously concerned with *justice*.

Jerusalem's poet moves Jeremiah from simple empathy toward her to an engagement with her rhetoric, evoking responses from him to her suffering and to YHWH's role, and in effect leads him back to participate, indirectly for now, in the lament genre. One can only infer that the prophet Jeremiah's personal laments had grown silent after the onslaught and trauma.

General Conclusions

The analysis above provides textual evidence that the poet who utters Jerusalem's speeches in Jer 4, 8 and 10 is the same poet who speaks for Jerusalem at length in Lam 1:9c, 11c and following. Further congruences in Lam 2 will extend the evidence. Also, a case is being built for identifying the prophetic poet Jeremiah in that book with the first poet in the book of Lamentations. There is far more congruence than difference between these poets' points of view and specific artistries than has been recognized. As such, the Septuagint's superscription to Lamentations may be viewed in a new light, as making a limited *oral poetic* rather than a sweeping '*authorial*' claim:

> And it came to pass after Israel was carried into captivity
> and Jerusalem was laid waste,
> Jeremiah sat down and wept
> and uttered this dirge (ἐθρήνησεν τὸν θρῆνον τοῦτον)
> over Jerusalem and said:[179]

The superscription points to the *rhetorical* role for Jeremiah in Lamentations, and I would submit, the primary reason for the traditions' relating him to the book.

[179] See *Threni*, J. Ziegler, ed., 467.

Moreover, the empathy, interaction, and rhetorical development apparent between the poets in Lamentations suggests that the book may be regarded as a kind of "extension" of the book of Jeremiah, where Jeremiah's poetic voice still is heard. Why was Lamentations placed separately from Jeremiah in the MT canonical tradition? Perhaps one reason is that, as in the other works in the "Five Scrolls" (*Megilloth*) including Lamentations, YHWH neither speaks or plays a directly active role (yet women do in nearly all of them). Along these lines, it may be said that neither does Jeremiah exercise his typical prophetic role in Lamentations (rendering YHWH's utterances), but nevertheless participates as a survivor in rhetoric with profound theological purposes. Yet even YHWH's *absence* holds its place in Hebrew biblical tradition and liturgy. Ironically, the woman's traditional place, as singers of dirges, does not hold in Lamentations. Jerusalem's poet's laments, however, suggest Lamentations, קינות (dirges), might have been better called, קינות ותפלות (dirges and laments).

CHAPTER FOUR

LAMENTATIONS 2

Listen
to the breathing
of Planet Sarajevo.

Listen
to the Girl crying:
"Death, don't take me along!"

How many times have we
uttered
with tears
our ardent prayers for peace?

Death cares not for the girl's tears,
Death cares not for human prayers . . .

Abdulah Sidran, "Planet Sarajevo"[1]

The analysis will now be applied to Lamentations 2, in the same five areas as before: specific uses of genre, imagery/themes, terminology, rhetorical technique, and content. The question will be considered as to whether the same two poets of Lamentations 1 continue their dialogue, with its particular concerns, into Lamentations 2.

Lamentations 2 begins with איכה ("Alas!", "How!"), suggestive of a communal dirge, just as Jeremiah had opened Lamentations 1. Lamentations 2:1 resumes the description of Jerusalem's distress *precisely* in terms of how the two poets of Lamentations 1 had left the matter: by further relating YHWH's violent actions against Jerusalem, coinciding with the enemy's actions. Moreover, the first poet renders a litany of YHWH's actions against Jerusalem for *the first ten verses*, intensifying the previous picture of destruction of city structures and suggesting mounting pain and anger on the part of the

[1] Transl., D. Dostal, in *Blind Man Sings to his City*, 11–17. Cf. Sidran's poem, "The Sarajevo Prayer," 23–25, in which he pleas with God to remove the "animals" (i.e., soldiers attacking the city) from the world.

Children who survived siege of Sarajevo (N. Lee, 1997)

inhabitants, as well as the poet. The first poet becomes preoccupied with these matters after attending briefly in the first verse to personified Jerusalem.

As will be seen, just as there was a key shift in the rhetoric from communal dirge speech to lament prayer speech (addressed directly to YHWH) in Lamentations 1:20–22, so a similar shift occurs at Lamentations 2:20–22.

Outline of Poetic Singers in Lamentations 2

2:1–10 Jeremiah (communal dirge)
11–12 Jeremiah (mourning speech)
13–19 Jeremiah (direct address to Jerusalem's poet)
20–22 Jerusalem's poet (lament prayer)

While Jerusalem's poet had previously dominated the second half of Lamentations 1, the first poet of Lamentations 2 above (Jeremiah?) dominates most of this chapter. Only in Lam 2:20–22 does Jerusalem's poet re-emerge, with another lament to YHWH, her preferred genre as well in Lam 1. A close reading of Lamentations 2 follows.

Lam 2:1–10: Jeremiah's Communal Dirge

The first poet opens his song with a description of YHWH's rejection of D. Zion. Already he resumes and emphasizes the theme of YHWH's *anger*, an issue of great importance to Jerusalem's poet, as we have already seen, in Lamentations 1 and Jeremiah 10.

How! (איכה) YHWH[2] beclouds[3] *with his anger* (באפו) D. Zion. (Lam 2:1a) The poet summarizes that YHWH is indeed bringing the 'darkening' consequences of divine anger against the city, in spite of the plea in Jer 10:24: "Correct me, YHWH, but with justice not *with your anger* (באפך), lest you diminish me." As noted previously, in Lam 3:43–44 Jerusalem's poet will elaborate on this theme with further complaint:

> You have wrapped yourself *with anger* (באף) and pursued us;
> you have killed, you have not pitied.
> You have wrapped yourself *with a cloud* (בענן) so that no prayer
> can pass through!" (Lam 3:43–44)

The irony of YHWH's action implied by both poets is stunning in light of the usual imagery of clouds in biblical texts to signal YHWH's theophanic power, comforting protection, and guidance of the people.[4] The negative imagery of YHWH draws on motifs of the divine warrior characterized here as a "storm-god."[5]

The first poet of Lam 2 completes the opening statement of YHWH's angry rejection of D. Zion:

[2] MT has עדני ("my Lord," as in Lam 1:14c), but probably a later addition, as multiple other Hebrew manuscripts have יהוה congruent to this term earlier in the book (Lam 1:5, 9c, 11c, 12, 17, etc.).

[3] This is the only occurrence of a verbal form of the root עוב in the Hebrew Bible The customary use is the noun, "cloud" (עב).

[4] Particularly found this way in Exodus (14:19–20; 19:9), Isaiah (19:1), Psalms (18:11–12; 77:17; 104:3), and Job (22:14; 36:29). See S. Re'emi, *Amos & Lamentations*, 92, and I. Provan, *Lamentations*, 59, and his suggestion that the imagery for the "fire" of YHWH's anger (e.g., Lam 2:3) also contrasts to this image for YHWH's positive attributes of leading and protecting Israel (e.g., YHWH's "pillar of fire" in Exod 13:21–22); ibid., 62.

[5] Dobbs-Allsopp, *Weep, O Daughter of Zion*, 62–64.

Alas! YHWH beclouds *with his anger* D. Zion.
[YHWH][6] has cast down from heaven to earth
the (crown of) glory (תפארת) of Israel.
[YHWH] gives no thought to his footstool (הדם־רגליו)
on the day of *his anger*. (Lam 2:1)

The terms "glory" and "footstool" allude to D. Zion's royalty, similar to Jeremiah's use of royal imagery for Jerusalem in Lam 1:1: "Princess" among the provinces. In both places, personified Jerusalem/D. Zion is presented as the once-royal figure, rather than her kings explicitly. The reversal of fortune, or contrast motif, typical of the communal dirge implies the fall of the royal house in Jerusalem and thus a threat to the Davidic throne and its future lineage, a stance not uncommon in prophetic speech (e.g., Jer 22:30). This term for "glory" (תפארה), though not very common in the Hebrew Bible, implies here and in other texts a 'crown' of glory. The term is found most often in prophetic poetry (i.e., 1st Isaiah and Jeremiah), as in Jer 13:18 where YHWH instructs the prophet: "Say to the king and queen mother, 'Take a lowly seat, for the crown (עטרה) of your *glory* (תפארתכם) has come down from your head.'"[7] The Davidic promise and this term "glory" are found, for example, in Ps 89:4, 29–37 where the deity YHWH is confessed to be the "glory" of David's and the people's strength (vs 18; see also below). Of particular relevance is the use of the term in Ps 78:61, where YHWH abandoned to destruction the tent of his dwelling at Shiloh and his "glory" there to the hand of the foe.[8]

In Lam 2:1, the poet says YHWH has cast down the royal "glory" of Jerusalem, but will also relinquish the *sanctuary*, as suggested by "footstool" (הדם־רגליו). This term appears only 6x in the Hebrew Bible but often refers to the ark of the covenant placed in the sanctuary of Zion (Pss 99:5; 132:7; 1 Chr 28.2). Thus in the opening verse, the poet (yet to be identified) has carried forward *three key elements* from Jeremiah's rhetoric in Lam 1: the communal dirge (third-

[6] I have placed the intended subject, YHWH, in brackets, rather than repeat the masculine pronoun (not in the text) with every verb.

[7] NRSV; the editorial note suggests the text refers to king Jehoiachin, one of the kings deposed and exiled during Jeremiah's prophetic activity. Cf. in the communal lament in Lam 5:16: "The crown (עטרה) of our heads has fallen. . . ."

[8] Cf. YHWH's reference to the destruction of Shiloh through Jeremiah's temple sermon in Jer 7:14. Cf. also the restoration of Jerusalem depicted by the poetry of 2d Isaiah, where she becomes "a crown of *glory* in the hand of YHWH" (Isa 62:3).

person) description of distress, the loss of Jerusalem's regal position, and a hint at the fate of the sanctuary. This poet also carries forward Jerusalem's poet's concern for YHWH's acting against the city *in anger.*[9] Whether or not this poet is Jeremiah, or yet a third poet in dialogue, remains to be determined by further analysis of the five rhetorical criteria.

The poet moves from essentially symbolic imagery in vs 1 to more tangible references (land and city structures) in vs 2, yet still using language common to the prophets and psalms.

> YHWH has devoured (בלע),
> without pity, every *pasture-abode of Jacob.*[10] (Lam 2:2a)

YHWH as the subject who "devours" or, literally, "swallows" is rare in the Hebrew Bible, though the term בלע is a common one. Occurring primarily in the prophets and psalms, the term often refers to enemies that threaten to swallow/devour a person. Here there is a *reversal—YHWH* devours, presumably like a lion, the sheep of the "pasture-abode"![11] In the book of Jeremiah, the prophet uses this verb in only one passage, in a later oracle against Babylon to describe king Nebuchadrezzar (Jer 51:34) and the Babylonian god Bel (Jer 51:44), *both devouring Jerusalem.* In vs 34–35, "the inhabitants of Zion say": "King Nebuchadrezzar of Babylon has consumed me (אכלני; Q) . . . he has *devoured/swallowed* me (בלעני; Q) like a monster (כתנין). . . ."[12] The careful, close use of such imagery, terminology, and theological treatment suggests Jeremiah is the poet of both speeches (Jer 51:34 and Lam 2:2).

[9] YHWH's anger is not just a leitmotif of Lam 2, but is a central concern of Jerusalem's poet's speeches in Lamentations 1 and Jeremiah 10; cf. C. Westermann, *Lamentations*, 149, who says of Lamentations 2: "At hardly any other place in the whole of the Old Testament is there so much talk about the wrath of God."

[10] The term for 'pity' is חמל (see below). It is not extremely common in the Hebrew Bible, yet appears most often in prophetic texts (5x in Jeremiah), thus suggesting a customary prophetic usage here in Lam 2:2. Of its eight occurrences in Ezekiel, seven times it appears in a recurring phrase peculiar to that prophet: "my eye will not spare, nor will I have pity" (Ezek 5:11; 7:4, 9; 8:18; 9:5, 10; 16:5); also, Ezek 36:21 refers to YHWH's pity for the dishonoring of the divine holy name. Cf. Job 16:13 for YHWH's treatment of Job. Neither is the term 'pasture-abode' (נוה or נאוה) extremely common, though it occurs most often (15x) in Jeremiah (in feminine and masculine nominal forms).

[11] See YHWH pictured as a lion threatening to devour the sheep of the "pasture-abode" (Jer 25:30, 34–38; 49:19–21; cf. Am 1:2).

[12] See also the suggestive use of the term in the prologue of Job, where the satan/adversary tempts YHWH to "devour/swallow (לבלעו)" Job (2:3; cf. 37:20).

While this term (בלע) is found most often in prophetic literature,[13] only in one instance is YHWH the subject of the verb therein. In Isa 25:7–8, YHWH will "swallow" the shroud or sheet that covers humanity, and will "swallow" death itself forever. In only one instance in the psalms is YHWH the subject of this verb, i.e., Ps 21:10. This particular psalm sheds light on this analysis, however, since it is a *royal* psalm in which YHWH acts *on behalf of the king*: YHWH "will *devour* (יבלעם) [the king's enemies] in his anger (באפו), and fire will consume them" (Ps 21:10). In the Lamentations text, however, the language of royal psalms is echoed, only to be reversed, as any royal status and protection for Jerusalem are overturned. A view typical of prophets in the Hebrew Bible, YHWH is devouring the land of Judah, like an enemy, and rejecting its king(s) (see Lam 4:20).[14]

Moreover, by referring to the "devouring" of the "pasture-abode (נאות) of Jacob," this poet in Lam 2:2a echoes Jerusalem's poet's specific lament to YHWH in Jer 10:25. There she implored YHWH to pour out divine anger upon their enemies who "have *devoured* [אכל, literally, 'eaten'] *Jacob*; they have devoured . . . his *pasture-abode* (נוהו)." Not only did her lament go unanswered, but it too is *reversed* in Lam 2, where *YHWH* is now *equated with* the devouring enemy.[15] *Only in these two texts* (Jer 10:25 [and its citation in Ps 79:7] and Lam 2:2) in the entire Hebrew Bible is there reference to "Jacob's pasture-abode." The stunning reversal of YHWH's expected action is nevertheless congruent with Lam 1, where YHWH acts in concert with, and like, the enemy, as Jerusalem's poet and Jeremiah had already conveyed. The poet of Lam 2:1–2 is focusing in upon that key issue, and by drawing upon verbs common to lament psalms and prophets, he *confirms* Jerusalem's poet's observations, harking back to her earlier speech in Jer 10 concerning 'Jacob's pasture-abode.' Thus the dialogical aspect of Lam 1, which was between Jeremiah and Jerusalem's poet, continues in Lam 2.

The poet of Lam 2:1–2 also shows poetic affinity to the royal Psalm 89, which contains YHWH's eternal promise to David as well as the divine angry rejection of the king and his kingdom. In Lam 2:2b, the poet says,

[13] Twice as often, for example, as in the psalms.
[14] In Lam 2:3, YHWH's *devouring wrath* turns into *consuming fire* against them.
[15] The irony is more apparent in light of Ps 23:2: "The Lord is my shepherd . . . makes me lie down in green pastures" ('in grassy pasture-abodes').

> *In his wrath* (בעברתו), [YHWH] has torn down (הרס)[16]
> the *fortresses* (מבצרי) of Daughter Judah.

Ps 89:39b–40b has,

> You have *dishonored* (חללת) *unto the ground* the [king's] crown . . .
> You have laid in ruins his *fortresses* (מבצריו).

The poet of Lam 2:1 had already referred to the "glory (of the crown)"; continuing here in Lam 2:2c, the poet says,

> [YHWH] has struck (נגע) *unto the ground*,
> *dishonored* (חלל),
> the kingdom and her princes.

It is not surprising that the rhetoric echoes Ps 89 with its analogous content—rejection of the king by YHWH and subsequent battle losses and destructions—to describe Jerusalem and Judah's current situation. Yet, in the Lamentations text, YHWH's eternal promise to uphold David's kingdom appears in much greater jeopardy.

The poet continues the long litany of YHWH's destructive actions against Jerusalem in Lam 2:3, maintaining the dual focus upon YHWH's acting like an *enemy* and divine *anger* from Lam 1 and Jer 10:

> [YHWH] has cut down in his *burning anger* (חרי־אף)[17]
> all the might of Israel.[18]
> [YHWH] has removed his right hand
> in face of the enemy.
> [YHWH] has *burned*[19] in *Jacob* like *a flaming fire*,
> *consuming* all around (אכלה סביב). (Lam 2:3)

YHWH is depicted as a 'divine warrior,' only against his own people.[20] That the prophetic poet of Lam 2:1–3 may be Jeremiah is

[16] The verb "tear down" (הרס) is most often used in *prophetic* rhetoric to describe YHWH's actions.

[17] The term "burning" (חרון from the root חרה) associated with anger is used most often in Jeremiah (9x) among the prophets, and twice in Ezekiel.

[18] The verb (גדע) and object (קרן), "Cut down the horn" (i.e., power) appears in *only two other* places in the Hebrew Bible: in Jer 48:25, where Moab is cut down; and in Ps 75:11, where YHWH cuts down the wicked. The verb is particularly common among the prophets. The noun is especially common in psalms (see 89:18, 25), and it appears again in Lam 2:17, where the same poet says YHWH has exalted the power (קרן) of Jerusalem's foes.

[19] The term for "burn" (בער) is more commonly used in the prophets than in other Hebrew Bible texts.

[20] YHWH as divine warrior shows affinity to the Caananite gods Baal, Anat, and El; Dobbs-Allsopp, *Weep, O Daughter of Zion*, 60–62.

also suggested by his second reference to YHWH's burning anger against "Jacob," echoing Jerusalem's poet in Jer 10:25.[21]

It is formulaic among the prophets to speak of YHWH's wrath or anger that burns like fire; another prophetic formula often appears with it: "and there is no one quenching it" (e.g., Jer 4:4). The prophets, however, are not depicted as proclaiming YHWH's anger without reason; such anger is consistently presented as response to human wrongdoing or injustice. For example, in Isa 9:18–21, 'consuming' or 'eating' is a metaphor for social oppression,[22] as well as for the purging fire of YHWH's concomitant anger:[23]

For wickedness *burned like fire,*
  consuming (תאכל) briers and thorns . . .
In the *wrath* of YHWH of hosts,
  the land was *burned,*
  and the people became like fuel *for the fire.*
No one spared another.
They gorged on the right, yet hungered,
  and they *consumed* (יאכל) on the left, but were not sated.
  They *consumed* (יאכלו) the flesh of their own kindred . . .
For all this his *anger* has not turned away. . . . (Isa 9:18–21)[24]

In Lam 2:4, the poet proceeds, stating explicitly that YHWH's actions are "like an enemy" against Jerusalem's leaders and inhabitants:[25]

[YHWH] has bent his bow (קשתו) *like an enemy,*
  his right hand poised *like a foe;*[26]
[YHWH] has killed all those precious to the eye (מחמדי־עין).[27]

[21] See the citation of this text in Ps 79:6–7. Only two other texts in the Hebrew Bible refer to YHWH's "burning anger" against Jacob; they are both prophetic texts, and they echo the poet of Lamentations: Isa 42:25 speaks of YHWH's punishment of Jacob, and Isa 43:2 speaks of YHWH's rescue/restoration of Jacob.

[22] See Isa 3:14–15 and Ezek 22:25.

[23] E.g., Isa 4:4; 5:5; Jer 21:12, 14; on the use of the term 'burn' to mean 'purge,' see Deut 17:7, 12; 19:13, 19; 21:21; 22:21–24.

[24] Similarly, see Hos 7:4–7. In Jer 5:14, the divine anger over 'false' prophets means YHWH's words become like fire in the mouth of Jeremiah to devour the people who are like wood.

[25] See Michael Emmendörffer, *Der ferne Gott: Eine Untersuchung der alttestamentichen Volksklagelieder vor dem Hintergrund der mesopotamischen Literatur* (Tübingen: J. C. B. Mohr, 1998). I could not peruse this study as I received it as the present book was going to press.

[26] In agreement with R. Gordis, *Song of Songs and Lamentations*, 135.

[27] The turn of speech, 'precious in your eyes,' is found, in slightly different form, only in I Kgs 20:6 (מחמד עיניך) and Ezek 24:16 (מחמד עיניך).

In the *tent* of D. Zion [YHWH] has poured out
his *wrath like fire*. (Lam 2:4)

While the *general* imagery of YHWH as archer against human beings is formulaic in biblical poetry,[28] this *specific* equation of YHWH's actions with the enemy's against Jerusalem is also basic to the rhetoric and theology of Jeremiah's poetry. The term (קֶשֶׁת) is used 5x in the book of Jeremiah to describe the Babylonian archers who are YHWH's instruments against Judah and Jerusalem.[29] The imagery of YHWH's *hand*, stretching the bow and taking aim in collaboration with the enemy in Lam 2:4, also recalls the imagery of Jerusalem's poet in Lam 1:13–14 where YHWH with his hand stretches a net for her feet and lashes the yoke on her neck.[30] Later, in Lam 3:12–13, an individual laments that YHWH with his "bow" (קֶשֶׁת) has fired "arrow(s)" (חֵץ) at him. The complaint or charge that YHWH has "killed" (הרג) people also appears a few times in prophetic texts and psalms, and appears again shortly in the speech of Jerusalem's poet in Lam 2:21 and 3:43.[31]

With the reference to the "*tent* of D. Zion" above, the poet of Lam 2:4 returns to and echoes the same image and concern of Jerusalem's poet about her *tent* in Jeremiah 4 and 10. By referencing the *name* 'Daughter Zion' (the first time since vs 1), the poet invokes this persona represented by Jerusalem's poet. Like Jeremiah in Lam 1, this poet will then move to a lengthy and graphic description of the destruction of the sanctuary (vss 6–7 below).

The poet pauses at vs 5 within this litany of YHWH's destroying verbs to give a summary statement.

YHWH[32] *has become* (היה)—indeed—an *enemy*;[33]
[YHWH] has *devoured* (בלע) Israel.

[28] The image is found in a few psalms (7:13; 18:14; 38:2; 64:7; 144:6), Deut 32:23, and Job (6:4; 20:23–25).

[29] This occurs 3x in Jeremiah's speech and 2x in YHWH's speech. Second Isaiah does not describe the Babylonian archers against Jerusalem, nor depict YHWH in this way; for a different use of the image, see Zech 9:13–14.

[30] Somewhat differently, the image of YHWH as archer appears in Ezek 5:16, where YHWH looses "arrows (חצי) of famine" against Jerusalem.

[31] YHWH is portrayed as a killer (with the term הרג) in prophetic poetry (Am 2:3; 4:10; 9:1, 4; Isa 14:30; 27:1; Hos 6:5), in Psalms (78:31, 34; 135:8, 10; 136:18) and in Exodus (4:23; 13:15; and 22:24).

[32] The MT has replaced YHWH with אדני.

[33] Thus R. Gordis who reads the כ not as "like" but as an asseverative; *Song of Songs and Lamentations*, 162. C. Westermann notes that elsewhere in the Hebrew

[YHWH] has *devoured/destroyed* (בלע) all her palaces.[34]
[YHWH] has laid in ruins (שחת)[35] his fortresses (מבצריו).
[YHWH] has multiplied in D. Judah moaning and mourning (תאניה ואניה). (Lam 2:5)

With this statement, the poet for the first time employs double uses of the same root in very close proximity (here, with *both* בלע and אניה); this technique has been identified as a characteristic of Jeremiah's poetry in the book of Jeremiah and in Lam 1.[36] This technique draws out two different meanings from the same root. Note that the "devouring" of *Israel* parallels his line above in vs 2 ("devouring of *Jacob's* pasture-abode"). Yet the second use of בלע exploits another meaning, to "destroy" city structures, and allows for a smooth shift in imagery. The last phrase ("moaning and mourning," תאניה ואניה) with its double root may have been actually coined by 1st Isaiah, as it appears only there (Isa 29:2) besides here, and also refers to Jerusalem under siege by YHWH. Perhaps the poet here in Lam 2:5, by referring to the "multiplying of moaning and mourning (תאניה ואניה)"[37] in D. Judah, is recalling a like-sounding cognate, 'to groan' (אנח), just heard 5x across Lam 1 (vss 4, 8, 11, 21, and 22). In any event, clear Jeremianic technique suddenly emerges from this poet. We may propose that this last feature, combined with the clear prophetic style (formulaic terminology as well as terms favored by Jeremiah elsewhere) and the continuing of key themes from Jer 4, 10, and Lam 1, all warrant identifying him as Jeremiah.

Jeremiah then proceeds with the litany of YHWH's destroying, now against festivals and cult.

Bible "the theme that God has become an enemy is stated so bluntly and so extensively only in the laments of Job"; *Lamentations*, 151. While Mesopotamian gods are depicted as destroying cities, this specific theme of the "enemy" is used instead to refer to the city goddesses who stand outside the city like an enemy while it is being destroyed by Enlil; Dobbs-Allsopp, *Weep, O Daughter of Zion*, 62–63.

[34] The term 'palace' (ארמון) is not extremely common, but again is found almost exclusively in the Hebrew Bible within biblical prophetic rhetoric in descriptions of military siege.

[35] The verb שחת (to ruin or destroy) is common in the Hebrew Bible and is used most often among the prophets, not infrequently to describe YHWH's destroying actions. It appears again in vss 6 and 8 below.

[36] See W. Holladay, "Style, Irony, and Authenticity," 45–47. Jeremiah's double use of roots was noted in Lam 1:1 above with רבב. Jeremiah's use of double meaning does not appear to make frequent use of Janus parallelism as is found in other biblical texts.

[37] Thus T. Meek, *The Book of Lamentations*, IB, vol. 6 (New York: Abingdon, 1956), 18.

[YHWH] has torn down, like a vine,[38] his booth (שׂכו).[39]
[YHWH] has ruined his *festival* (מועדו).
YHWH has wiped from memory in Zion[40]
festival and Sabbath.
He has spurned in his indignant *anger*
king and priest. (Lam 2:6)

"Booth" suggests the temporary shelter used for the feast of Booths or Tabernacles.[41] Once again, First Isaiah's rhetoric and vision of D. Zion left like a "booth" (כסכה) in a vineyard, or a solitary shelter in a field (after the 8th c. Assyrian attack; Isa 1:8), appears to influence Jeremiah's imagery in Lam 2:6. Is this surprising, that Jeremiah would be inspired by the Isaiah poetic tradition, given the two analogous socio-political contexts the prophets found themselves in? Jeremiah renders YHWH's "booth" in this text as being in Zion. But unlike Isaiah's image, this time she is *not spared*; YHWH tears her down in the Babylonian attack. Jeremiah also picks up the image of the *festival* again. In Lam 1:4, he had conveyed that no one was coming to the *festivals* because of the attack/destruction, but here he carries the thought further—festivals and Sabbaths are even wiped from memory by YHWH. One may see in the artistry of Jeremiah's poetry the incremental development of images.

In Lam 2:6, the severe verb "spurn" (נאץ; "YHWH has spurned in his indignant anger king and priest) is not very common, but found most often in psalms and prophetic texts. Usually it refers to people spurning YHWH (such as David in 2 Sam 12:14 in the matter of Bathsheba and Uriah). In only two instances in the Hebrew Bible besides Lam 2:6 does it refer to YHWH spurning humans, in Deut 32:19 and Jer 14:21 where, in a rare lament, the people plead for YHWH not to spurn them. In Lam 2:6, as in Jeremiah's imagery of Lam 1:4, the destruction of festivals has undue conseqences for the priests. As Jeremiah rendered in Lam 1:4, 5, 6, so now in Lam

[38] LXX: נפן ('vine').

[39] C. Westermann (*Lamentations*, 145) notes a parallel in the *Lamentation over the Destruction of Ur*: "My house . . . like a garden hut, verily on its side has caved in" (ANET, 457:122).

[40] See *JB*. The piel of שכח (to forget) here is the only occurrence of the piel stem in the Hebrew Bible.

[41] See I. Provan for a helpful discussion of the difficult terms and meanings of this line; *Lamentations*, 64–66. Provan cites Isa 1:8 here, but does not explore its rhetorical development in Lam 2.

2:6 (and 9, 10, and 14) he begins singling out social groups in the devastated community.

Jeremiah next describes the loss of permanent *cultic structures*:

> YHWH has rejected (זנח) his altar,
> disowned (נאר) his *sanctuary* (מקדשו);
> [YHWH] has delivered *into the hand of the enemy*
> the *walls* of her palaces.
> Noise was raised in the house of YHWH
> like on a *festival* day. (Lam 2:7)

The term 'reject' (זנח) is uncommon, appearing occasionally in prophetic texts, but primarily in eight lament psalms in which YHWH is asked why he has rejected or cast someone off. Among these laments is Psalm 89 again, where YHWH has "rejected" the king. Moreover, the term "disowned" (נאר) is very rare in the Hebrew Bible, appearing only here and in Ps 89:40 (where YHWH "renounces" [נארתה] the Davidic covenant with the king). In Lam 1:10, Jeremiah had said that enemy nations have invaded Jerusalem's *sanctuary*; here in 2:7a he develops this further: "YHWH has *disowned his sanctuary*." Indeed, "the walls of her palaces" YHWH even "delivers into *the hand of the enemy*" (2:7b). The fall of the city is rendered further as YHWH's doing. In Lam 1:7, Jeremiah had said, "When her people fell into *the hand of the foe*, there was no one helping her." Jerusalem's poet had carried the point further in 1:14: "YHWH gave me *into the hands* of those I could not withstand." In Lam 2:7, Jeremiah states that YHWH has assuredly delivered the city into the hands of the enemy. He ends these lines with the sardonic statement that there is heard "noise in YHWH's house like on a *festival* day." Whereas in Lam 1:4, Jeremiah had rendered the empty city, sans festivals, filled ironically only with groaning and mourning, now Jeremiah renders "YHWH's house" given over to the din, one supposes, of enemy victory. Once again we see Jeremiah's careful artistry in expanding his previous poetic images. This kind of development of imagery reflects a typical composing process of an oral poet who continues to create more poetry on the same themes.

While the descriptions of destruction in the communal dirge by Jeremiah thus far in Lam 2:1–7 continue and extend his imagery from Lam 1, a shift has been apparent (above) in his choice of terminology; he is using more terms that resonate with lament psalms than previously, indicative of the movement from dirge to lament across Lam 1–2, and across the book as a whole. While Jeremiah maintains third-person descriptions, his litany of YHWH's actions inevitably involves him in an underlying, yet growing, *tone of complaint*, typical of lament psalms.[42] This shift has been abetted by the influence of Jerusalem's poet in the dialogue who repeatedly voiced lament, and by Jeremiah's empathetic adoption of her angry expressions about YHWH's enemy-like actions.[43]

Jeremiah continues to make explicit the destroyer's actions:

> YHWH devised (חשב)[44] to *lay in ruins* (להשחית)
> the *wall* (חומת) of D. Zion;[45]
> [YHWH] stretched (נטה) the line,[46]
> he did not withdraw his *destroying* (מבלע) hand. (Lam 2:8ab)

The meaning of the second line is difficult; מבלע is the first *hapax* of any consequence in Lam 2. We have already seen this verbal cognate in two other verses above, in vs 2 with its primary meaning

[42] Thus also C. Westermann, *Lamentations*, 149. Contra S. Re'emi's general reading of Lam 2: "We see no rebellion as in the case of Job; here it is complete surrender and acceptance of God's judgment . . ."; *Amos & Lamentations*, 93. My analysis suggests the opposite: in Lam 2, the poets' complaints prefigure Job's rebellion; see also C. Westermann, *Lamentations*, 151: "Elsewhere in the Old Testament the theme that God has become an enemy is stated so bluntly and so extensively only in the laments of Job." Westermann also notes that this theme appears in *Lamentation over the Destruction of Ur* (line 374); *Lamentations*, 151.

[43] Contra I. Provan's general reading of Lam 2: "In the second poem, the justice of God is again not an issue for the narrator. It is simply assumed that the calamity is sufficiently explained by Zion's 'iniquity,' and that the only proper response comprises prayer and (implicitly) confession of sin, in the hope that her fortunes will be restored" (*Lamentations*, 58). This interpretation, in my view, is reductionistic and overlooks the subtle interplay between these two poets and how the first poet's point of view progresses across the chapters.

[44] The root חשב is common in the Hebrew Bible in both verb and noun forms. It appears most often in prophetic texts (over 50x), including 15x in Jeremiah, more than in any other prophetic book (Jer 18:8, 11; 26:3; 29:11; 36:3; 49:20; 50:45; 51:29 [YHWH as subject]; 11:19; 18:18 [Jeremiah's enemies]; 23:27 ['lying' prophets]; 6:19; 18:12; 48:2; 49:30 [other humans or nations]). YHWH is not the subject of this verb at all in 1st Isaiah or Ezekiel, only once in 2nd Isaiah (55:8–9), and twice in Micah (2:3; 4:12). The root occurs only twice in Ezekiel and half as often in the psalms as in the prophets.

[45] Jeremiah's preoccupation with "*walls*" is due not only to their destruction, but he seems to regard them as symbolic of the persona of Jerusalem/D. Zion; in Lam 2:18, he addresses her as "O *Wall*—D. Zion" (see below).

[46] The image of YHWH using a builder's plumb line to destroy is also found in Am 7:7–8 and 2 Kgs 21:13–15. See I. Provan for a helpful discussion; *Lamentations*, 67–68.

of "devour/swallow" which does not fit the imagery here with YHWH's hand. The secondary meaning of בלע (as in vs 5), to "destroy," works better. In fact, Jeremiah had presented both meanings together in vs 5 and intends the second meaning here in vs 8. In both verses, he places the verb in parallel with "lay in ruins" (שׁחת). As noted above, this habit of drawing double meaning from words within a passage is typical of Jeremiah's poetry. Moreover, in Lam 1 it was several times the case that a *hapax* even signaled Jeremiah's wordplays (e.g., לנידה in 1:8; בשׁוליה in 1:9; מקדשׁה in 1:10). The wordplays in 1:8 and 9 also involved terms that sound alike but are spelled differently (e.g., homonyms like 'plane' and 'plain'). Let us explore whether the *hapax* בלע is not calling attention to something more.

The sentence, YHWH "did not withdraw his hand," in 2:8b recalls a similar thought used by the poet in vs 3: YHWH "*did* withdraw the back of his right hand before the enemy" in order for the enemy to have free reign to destroy Judah/Israel. Vs 8 states that YHWH *did not* at all withdraw his own *destroying* (בלע) hand.[47] This is an extraordinarily ironic statement since "the hand of YHWH" is a symbol of immense importance in Israel's poetic and narrative traditions, referring to YHWH's rescuing the people. A word sounding like בלע is בלה, to "wear out from over-use or old age." The translation of this verb (מבלה), creating a wordplay, would be "YHWH did not withdraw his *fatiguing* hand." The participle's causative sense suggests both the human objects of YHWH's hand are fatigued, but also allows for divine fatigue as well; that is, the divine hand, though fatigued from much destroying action, is still not withdrawn. A suggestive parallel is found in Lam 3:3–4:

> Only against me [YHWH] returns, turning *his hand* all day long.
> [YHWH] has *worn out* (בלה, piel) my flesh and my skin. . . .

While the poetry of Lam 2:1–8 increasingly suggests that Jeremiah is its poet, the final line of Lam 2:8 below makes this claim clear. As shown in the previous chapter, beyond using a formulaic poetic theme common in the ANE that personifies city structures in mourn-

[47] Cf. Lam 1:13–14. In Lam 2:8, YHWH's hand "stretching the line" echoes the imagery of YHWH's hand "spreading a net" against Jerusalem in Lam 1:13.

ing (see Lam 1:4ab),[48] Jeremiah developed a unique poetic image of their *collapsing* (אמל) in mourning. The term אמל is uncommon in the Hebrew Bible, in all but three instances found in prophetic texts (13x).[49] It usually refers to "languishing" *vegetation* of the land, often in parallel with "mourning" (e.g., Isa 24:4, 7; 33:9; Jo 1:10–12; cf. Isa 16:8–10; Hos 4:3). Jeremiah's rendering of it first appeared in Jer 14:2:

> Judah *mourns* (אבלה),
> and *her gates* (שעריה) *collapse* (אמללו),
> they are black (with remorse; קדרו) *upon the ground*,
> a cry of Jerusalem goes up.

Jeremiah's peculiar modification of a recognized *formula* (personified city structures in mourning) reappears now in Lam 2:8c–9a:

> Rampart and wall *mourn* (ויאבל), together they *collapse* (אמללו),
> *her gates* have sunk *onto the ground*.
> [YHWH] has destroyed and crushed (שבר) her bars.[50]

Note in vss 8c–9a the shift away from YHWH as subject for the first time in this long litany. Instead, the personified structures are the acting subjects, yet it is clear they have been acted upon. Indeed, the imagery of *every part* of the city falling down, *brought down to the ground* by YHWH, pervades Jeremiah's poetry in Lam 2:1–10. The movement downward begins from heaven, with YHWH throwing down Jerusalem's "crown" (vs 1), to the kingdom and its rulers brought down *to the ground* (vs 2), to the cutting down of people in the tent (vs 4), to the smashing down of palaces, fortresses, altar (vss 5–7), walls and rampart *into the ground* (vs 9).

Not surprisingly, next Jeremiah shifts attention from city structures collapsed to the ground to *people collapsed in grief*, after a summary statement about their leaders:

[48] Lam 1:4ab reads: "The roads to Zion mourn (אבלות) . . . all her gates (שעריה) are ravaged (שוממין)."

[49] The term's meanings include to "languish," to "wilt," to be "weak," to "wither," to "despair."

[50] "Bars" of the city-gates. I. Provan notes that the verb "sink" likely also suggests personification of the gates, citing its use to describe a person in distress in Ps 69:2, 14; *Lamentations*, 68.

Her king and her princes are among the nations;[51]
  there is no Torah.[52]
Also her prophets find no vision[53] from YHWH. (Lam 2:9bc)

The elders of D. Zion are being silent,[54] sitting *on the ground.*
They throw dust upon their heads[55]
  and have put on sackcloth.
The young women of Jerusalem
  droop their heads *to the ground.*[56] (Lam 2:10)

It is significant that at the end of the litany of violent verbs (in perfect tense/aspect; at vs 9), the aspect in Lam 2:10a *shifts to imperfect* (the *yod*-line in the acrostic signaling an imperfect), suggesting a current, slow-moving picture of survivors emerging, old folks sitting and being silent (incomplete action). After the rapid-fire storm of punctiliar verbs, the survivors now look around in the aftermath. Where perfect verbs and the recent past leave off, imperfect verbs suggest an ongoing present opening into an uncertain future.

Lam 2:11–19: Jeremiah's Mourning Speech and Appeal to Jerusalem's Poet

The lines above bring to a close the first section of Lam 2. From the casting down of the royal crown from heaven to earth to the collapse of her young women in grief on the ground, Jerusalem is undone. Absent are the once-powerful leaders, as well as mothers and children; the only ones left are the vulnerable aged, grimy with war's deprivations and dust of grief, and suffering women, torn by

[51] Jeremiah had said in Lam 1:3: "Judah is exiled . . . *among the nations*."

[52] The term "Torah" or "instruction" appears 11x in the book of Jeremiah, 9x in YHWH's speech, once in Jeremiah's speech (32:23; not poetry), and once in the speech of Jeremiah's persecutors (18:18): "Instruction/Torah shall *not* perish from the priest. . . ."

[53] In the book of Jeremiah, Jeremiah often refers to the other prophets as נביאים, though he is set apart from them. On this matter and for the term "vision," see Jer 14:14 and 23:16; and Ezek 7:13; 12:22–27; 13:16.

[54] I. Provan notes that while it is difficult to determine whether keeping silence was a mourning rite in this instance [it is attested in later Judaism], the elders' silence parallels the absence of words and vision from the other leadership in vs 9 (those who "dispensed wisdom . . . have nothing to say. They are fully occupied with their grieving"); *Lamentations*, 70.

[55] This common mourning practice is attested also in Akkadian and Ugaritic texts; D. Hillers, *Lamentations*, 106.

[56] Cf. Isa 58:5: "to droop the head like a bulrush."

the traumas of loss and rape. Like them, the poet Jeremiah, finally, becomes undone:

> *My eyes* are strained with *weeping* (בדמעות);[57]
> *my insides churn* (חמרמרו מעי);
> my bile is poured out *upon the ground*,[58]
> because of the *breaking/crushing* (שבר)
> of *Daughter of My People* (בת־עמי),
> because *children* (עולל) and infants faint[59]
> *in the streets of the city*. (Lam 2:11)

If there were any doubt before that this poet is Jeremiah, it is diminished by the above rhetoric, filled with the peculiar style and familiar terms of Jeremiah's voice, especially his favored term of endearment, *Daughter of My People*. Jeremiah's personal expressions of weeping (Jer 8:23; 13:17; 14:17) are found in poetry in the book of Jeremiah several times.[60] There he uses not only the common terms "eyes" and "weep," but in both 8:19–23 and 14:17 *five times* he also uses his favored term of endearment for Jerusalem, "Daughter of My People" (בת־עמי), for whom he weeps. Such identification with her suffering is also evident in his words here in Lam 2:11, חמרמרו מעי, "*my insides churn*." Jerusalem's poet had cried the same to YHWH in Lam 1:20, חמרמרו מעי, as in Jer 4:19 she had cried מעי מעי.[61] In both Jer 4:19 and Lam 1:20, her inner turmoil was linked to the need to voice her empathy for those suffering around her, to break the silence and lament to YHWH. Jeremiah is in a similar state in Lam 2:11 and

[57] The root for "weep" (דמע) is not common in the Hebrew Bible, appearing only 23x, including 7x in Jeremiah, 3x in Lamentations, and 6x in psalms. It appears only once in Ezekiel, where YHWH instructs him *not to weep* for the death of his wife.

[58] These phyical manifestations (with "insides" and "bile") refer to the turmoil of emotions; I. Provan, *Lamentations*, 70–71.

[59] Another uncommon verb, עטף, appears only 13x and eight occurrences are in lament psalms.

[60] As noted above, J. Henderson has convincingly identified Jeremiah as speaker in these and other prophetic texts, based primarily upon Jeremiah's use of peculiar terminology ("Who Weeps"). In my discussion of Jeremianic terminology with regard to his rhetoric of "weeping" and his use of "D. My People," I agree with Henderson's findings. The other terms that mark the poetry as Jeremiah's include the phrase, weeping "night and day" (Jer 14:17) or "day and night" (Jer 8:23; Lam 2:18), and especially, "my eyes *run down* (< ירד) with tears" (Jer 13:17; 14:17; Lam 2:18; cf. YHWH's words in Jer 9:17); see J. Henderson (ibid.).

[61] See Isa 16:11, Isa 63:15, and Job 30:27 for different terminology with מעי to indicate suffering or empathy. The highly unusual verb חמרמר ("churn") appears only 6x in the Hebrew Bible.

breaks the silence of those sitting on the ground in grief. He weeps and speaks "because of the *crushing/breaking* (שבר) of *D. of My People.*" We have seen how "crush/break" has been a key word used by all the voices/poets (including Jeremiah) in the larger rhetorical context to describe their suffering; in Jeremiah's speech in Lam 2:11, this Leitwort comes to the fore again (and in vs 13 below).[62]

And for what other reason is Jeremiah finally moved to weep and mourn here in the book of Lamentations? It is for the *same reason* that Jerusalem's poet broke into weeping in Jer 10:20 and Lam 1:16—because he sees the suffering *of the children*—"because infants and babes faint (עטף) in the streets of the city" (Lam 2:11c). Notice Jeremiah's use again, as in Lam 1:5, of the less common term for children (עולל).[63] The term for "faint" (עטף), unusual but characteristically found in lament psalms, immediately suggests here an urgent need that someone must lament to YHWH for the languishing children. Jeremiah says,

> They are saying to their mothers, "Where is bread and drink?"[64]
> as they faint like those *slain* (חלל)
> *in the squares of the city,*
> as their life is poured out onto their mothers' breast.[65] (Lam 2:12)

[62] Besides "crush/break" (שבר) in Lam 2:13; 3:4; 3:47, 48; and 4:10 below, see the following:

YHWH:	"you *crushed/broke* your yoke" (Jer 2:20);
YHWH:	"I bring . . . a great *crushing*" (Jer 4:6);
Jerusalem's poet:	"*crushing upon crushing*" throughout land (Jer 4:20);
YHWH:	"they all *crushed/broke* the yoke" (Jer 5:5; cf. 28:2–12);
YHWH:	"evil from the north and great *crushing*" (Jer 6:1);
YHWH:	"they treated *crushing* of my people carelessly" (Jer 6:14);
YHWH:	"they treated *crushing* of my people carelessly" (Jer 8:11);
Jeremiah:	"for the *crushing* of D. My People I am *crushed*" (Jer 8:21);
Jerusalem's poet:	"woe is me because of my *crushing*" (Jer 10:19);
Jeremiah:	"with *crushing* blow is D. My People *crushed*" (Jer 14:17);
Jeremiah:	"*crushing crush* them" (Jer 17:18);
YHWH:	"I will *crush* this people like a potter's vessel" (Jer 19:11);
YHWH:	"all your lovers are *crushed*" (Jer 22:20);
Jeremiah:	"my heart is *crushed* within me" (Jer 23:9);
YHWH:	"your *crushing* is incurable" (Jer 30:12);
Jerusalem's poet:	"he *crushed* my young men" (Lam 1:15);
Jeremiah:	"[YHWH] has *crushed* her bars" (Lam 2:9).

[63] Also in Jer 9:21, Jeremiah had said, "Death . . . has cut off the *children* (עולל) *from the streets.*"

[64] Literally, 'wine.'

[65] I. Provan notes that while the larger text suggests children are dying, the phrase "life poured out" refers as much to the children's suffering as to their death (e.g., Jb 30:16; 1 Sam 1:15; Ps 102:1); *Lamentations*, 71–72.

The verb "say" is in the imperfect, suggesting the children's ongoing questioning for something to quench their thirst and fill their hunger.[66] With great sensitivity, Jeremiah renders the deeply poignant moment of the mothers holding their dying children and the words spoken between them. His poetry develops the initial concern of Jerusalem as a mother and her suffering children that we saw in Jer 10:20 and again in Lam 1:16.[67]

We may compare a selection from the modern communal dirge over the island of Khíos (1881), where the poet/singer also beseeches God for their suffering children:

> Ah! Have pity on us!
> Allow yourself to grieve for the children,
> those fully innocent, in misery! . . .[68]

In Lam 2:13 below, Jeremiah, who has relinquished his more objective reporting style when overcome with grief, finally turns for the first time to *Jerusalem's poet* and speaks directly to her:

> How can I strengthen you?[69]
> To what can I compare you,
> O Daughter Jerusalem?
> To what can I liken you,[70] that *I may comfort* (ואנחמך) you,
> virgin D. Zion?
> For as great as the sea is your *breaking* (or, *crashing*; שברך);[71]
> Who can *heal* (רפא) you? (Lam 2:13)

We may recall that dialogue among singers/poets (as comforters who address the bereaved and ask questions) is typical of the *dirge* genre, where death and loss are involved.[72] Robert Lowth's statement about Jeremiah's speech here is apropos:

[66] Thus also C. Westermann, *Lamentations*, 145.

[67] This concern for the children by both Jeremiah and Jerusalem's poet will dominate the second half of Lam 2 (also in vss 12, 19, 20, and 22).

[68] Translated from the German translation of the original Greek (researched by Lübke); cited by Jahnow, *Das hebräische Leichenlied*, 178. The communal dirge shifts to lament prayer at the end.

[69] The translation follows R. Gordis who derives the verb from עדד, meaning to "strengthen" or "fortify"; this verb is in chiastic parallel with "comfort"; *Lamentations*, 165.

[70] LXX has "who will *save* you (מי יושיע לך) or comfort you?"

[71] Jeremiah uses a *talḥin*, a rhetorical device that is a wordplay with primary and secondary meaning ("breaking" as in both "destruction" and in the image of "breaking" waves); thus R. Gordis, *Lamentations*, 165.

[72] The dialogical element is also found in the Mesopotamian communal dirges, like the Lamentation over the Destruction of Ur, where one poetic voice addresses

> The Prophet, indeed, has so copiously, so tenderly, and poetically bewailed the misfortunes of his country, that he seems completely to have fulfilled the office and duty of a mourner.[73]

Jeremiah's concern to "comfort" 'D. Zion' at this poignant moment answers the repeated cry by Jerusalem's poet across Lam 1 that there is "*no one comforting her*" (vss 2, 9, 16, 17, and 21).[74] Jeremiah's empathetic identification with her suffering and need for a "healer" may relate to his own need for "healing" reflected in his personal laments. In Jer 15:18, he says, "Why is my pain unceasing, my wound incurable, refusing to be *healed* (הרפע)?" In Jer 17:14, he says, "*Heal me*, YHWH, and *I will be healed*; save me and I will be saved. . . ."

The theme of healing is an important one in the poetry of the book of Jeremiah, the term (רפע) appearing 16x (only 3x in 1st Isaiah, 6x in Ezekiel, 4x in 2nd Isaiah). Jeremiah's question above ("Who can heal you?") is part of that larger rhetorical context. Certainly the poetic imagery of YHWH capable of "healing" the people is *formulaic* among some of the prophets and psalms.[75] Some prophets also refer to the leaders as responsible for correcting and, specifically, "healing" the people with regard to their sin.

Jeremiah's rendering of this theme regarding the leaders is unique. It begins with YHWH's speech on the matter in Jer 6:13–14: *as physicians*,[76] prophets and priests "have treated (*healed*, > רפא) the 'crushing' (brokenness/wound) of my people as 'not serious,'[77] saying 'Peace, peace (i.e., wholeness, health),' when there is no peace" (vs 14).[78]

another poet representing the city goddess; F. W. Dobbs-Allsopp, *Weep, O Daughter of Zion*, 33.

[73] Lowth's comment is within his discussion of the importance of prophetic uses of the dirge; *Lectures on the Sacred Poetry of the Hebrews*, 137–38.

[74] On YHWH's response to the complaints in Lamentations, see Patricia Tull, *Remember the Former Things: The Recollection of Previous Texts in Second Isaiah*, SBLDS 161 (Atlanta: Scholars Press, 1997).

[75] See Isa 6:10; 19:22; 30:26; Hos 6:1; 7:1, 11:3, 14:5; Ps 6:1–2; 41:5; 60:3–4; 103:3; 107:17–20.

[76] Different from Jeremiah's emphasis of this theme with the image of the "physician" is Ezekiel's who uses the image of the shepherds who should "heal" an injured sheep. In Ezek 34:4, Ezekiel, speaking for YHWH, blames the leaders in general, who like "shepherds" should have strengthened the weak, *healed* (> רפא) the sick, bound up the injured sheep, etc; Zech 11:16 also uses the imagery of a "shepherd" who didn't "heal" those injured.

[77] Literally, "light" (> קלה), suggestive, perhaps, of a surface wound. This rhetoric is re-stated by Jeremiah in 8:11.

[78] YHWH had said in vs 13: "Everyone is greedy for unjust gain (NRSV; אבוצע בצע); from prophet to priest, everyone deals falsely."

One of the few instances where the people's speech is rendered in Jeremiah follows then in 8:14–15. Expecting to die, they say ironically, "YHWH our God has ended us, made us drink poisoned water, for we have sinned against YHWH. (We) look for health, but there is no good, for a time of *healing*,[79] but instead—terror!"[80] The implication is that the priests and prophets, 'sick' themselves, have not done their job in assessing the people's true (sinful) condition or in administering the proper remedy. Then in Jer 8:22, in a speech where we have already seen that Jeremiah uses his term of endearment for the people (Daughter of My People) four times, he also says,

> Is there no balm in Gilead?
> Is there no *physician* (*healer* or *healing*, רפא) there?
> Why then is the *healing of the wound* (ארכה) of *Daughter of My People* not apparent? (Jer 8:22)[81]

Jeremiah then goes into extreme weeping over her death (Jer 8:23). Indeed, his sudden weeping, noted above, in Lam 2:12 over the dying children in the streets of Jerusalem is also a lamentation over the *absence of a physician* to help (YHWH), or who could have prevented the deaths. By Lam 4:13–14, the entrusted physicians, priests and prophets, appear, but instead of bringing help and healing, they emerge covered with the blood of the slain (see below)!

Indeed, in light of this larger context, immediately after Jeremiah's statement in Lam 2:13c, "Who will *heal* you?"[82] he says,

[79] MT has מרפה, which appears to be a variant spelling of מרפע ('healing'). This speech by the people reappears in a lament to YHWH in Jer 14:19 (where "healing" twice is spelled מרפע).

[80] See especially Jer 19:10–11 where the terms "heal" and the other important term "crush/break" appear together. YHWH tells Jeremiah, because the people are "broken" (שׁבר) by their own wrongdoing/sin and will not turn away from it, "You shall *break* (שׁברת) a vessel before the eyes of the people walking with you, and you shall say to them, 'YHWH . . . says, "Just so will I *break* (אשׁבר) this people and this city, as the potter *breaks* the pot which is no longer able to be mended ("healed," להרפה, variant spelling of להרפא)." Cf. Isaiah's use of the image of the people's "crushing" like that of a potter's vessel in 30:14, though without the image of mending or healing.

[81] See Jeremiah's speech against Egypt in Jer 46:11: "Go up to *Gilead* and *take balm* Virgin Daughter Egypt! In vain (לשׁוא) you have increased *healing* remedies (רפאות); there is *no healing* for you" (cf. Ezek 30:21 where YHWH "breaks" the arm of Pharaoh [and it is not "healed"] to limit his power). In Jer 51:8–9, Jeremiah speaks against Babylon: "Suddenly Babylon falls and is *broken*" (תשׁבר) . . . *take balm* for her wound, perhaps she will be *healed* (תרפע). We *healed* (רפאנו) Babylon but she was not *healed* (נרפתה). . . ."

[82] Jerusalem's subsequent "healing" by YHWH is anounced in a salvation oracle

Your prophets' visions for you have been empty and vapid;
They have not unveiled/exiled (> גלה) your iniquity
in order to restore your fortunes.
Their visions for you were utterances empty and evicting[83]
(שוא ומדוחים). (Lam 2:14)

The above statement had been taken by some scholars as argument that the prophet Jeremiah could not have 'written' Lamentations, because it is critical of the prophets. But in fact, it is an important part of the evidence *supporting* Jeremiah as prophetic poet, because critique of the prophets is in fact widespread in the book of Jeremiah (e.g., Jer 2:8; 6:13–14; 8:10–11; 14:13–16; 23:9–40; 27:14–28:17). Two of the terms used in Lam 2:14 to describe the prophets (תפל, מדוח > נדח) are used as well in judgment speeches in the book of Jeremiah against the prophets.[84]

Next, in Lam 2:15–16, Jeremiah gives standard prophetic and psalmic speech describing the ridiculing actions of enemies and onlookers, "*all those passing by the way/road*" (כל־עברי דרך) who witness Jerusalem's downfall (vs 15a; cf. Jer 18:16; 51:43; Ezek 27:35–36; Pss 13:4; 79:4).[85] With this he echoes Jerusalem's poet's exact words in Lam 1:12: "*all you passing by the way/road.*" In Lam 2:15b, Jeremiah

in Jer 30:12–17. See also in Jer 33:6–8 where YHWH tells Jeremiah of the coming divine *healing* and restoration of Judah and Israel. Also in Isa 57:18–19. See a development from this theology in the sacrificial, mediating suffering of the servant, wounded for the sins of others, by whose own suffering "healing" is then brought to them (Isa 53:5).

[83] For support of the idea of being banished, see LXX. I. Provan draws out the the verse's nuances of interpretation, as referring to the prophets' *past* failure to expose iniquity and prevent exile, or *present* failure to expose iniquity and thereby restore fortunes; *Lamentations*, 73.

[84] In a long passage against the prophets in Jer 23:9–40, the term תפל appears to describe them; the term is used this way only in that text, in Lam 2:14, and in Ezek 13:10–15 and 22:28 (of 9x total in the Hebrew Bible). Ezekiel, however, speaking for YHWH, uniquely uses the term תפל to mean "whitewash" (yet derived from טפל) to describe the other prophets' speech. It is within this passage on "whitewashing" that Ezekiel quotes the prophets saying "Peace" ("when there is no peace"; 13:10), whereas Jeremiah's concern is with their saying 'Peace' when they fail to 'heal.' The root נדח (suggesting to "banish," "expel," "evict") appears often (19x) in the book of Jeremiah (usually in prose), but in the poetry of 23:12, YHWH says the prophets will be "expelled." This imagery suggests punishment of the prophets congruent with the way in which the prophets' oracles caused the "evicting" of the people in Lam 2:14; Ezekiel, however, does not use the term נדח to describe the expelling of the prophets. In Jer 30:17, in the salvation oracle to D. Zion, YHWH will "restore her health" and "heal" her, because 'they have called you an *outcast*' (נדחה). . . ."

[85] Also D. Hillers, *Lamentations*, 107; and I. Provan, *Lamentations*, 74–75.

quotes the passersby: "Is this the city that was called, 'Perfection of Beauty' (כלילת יפי), Joy of All the Earth'?" The first epithet is not peculiar to Jeremiah's speech, but is also found in Ezekiel's, and apparently belonged to more widespread usage (see Ezek 16:14; 27:3; 28:12; and also Ps 50:2).[86] YHWH describes Jerusalem's beauty in Ezek 16:14: "Your name (fame) has spread among the nations because of your *beauty* (ביפיך), for it was *perfect* (כליל) because of my splendor that I set upon you." In Ezek 27: 3–4, YHWH tells Ezekiel to raise a dirge over Tyre: "O Tyre, you have said, I am '*Perfection of Beauty*' (כלילת יפי) . . . your builders *made perfect your beauty*."[87] While the preponderance of poetic/rhetorical evidence in Lamentations supports Jeremiah as the poet of Lam 2:1–15, it still must be asked why this phrase used in the book of Ezekiel appears here. Was Jeremiah familiar with Ezekiel's rhetoric? The second epithet above, "Joy of all the Earth" (משוש לכל־הארץ), is found in just one other place in the Hebrew Bible, in Ps 48:1. YHWH is praised on Mount Zion, "Joy of all the Earth" (משוש כל־הארץ). The likeliest explanation for these epithets in Lam 2:15 is that they were commonly heard in temple songs by Jerusalemites[88] (and the implied audience for this poetry would be Jerusalemite survivors after 587), even though Jeremiah's poetic construct is to put the phrases into the mouths of invading strangers. In Lam 2:16 their speech grows more viscious, with hissing and gnashing of teeth, and saying, "We have *swallowed* (בלענו) her!"—a term much at play in the early lines of Lam 2 (see above).

Jeremiah continues with more actions by YHWH; it is a summary statement much like the one in Lam 2:5 above.

> YHWH has done what he intended (זמם);[89]
> [YHWH] accomplished by violence (בצע) *his word* (אמרתו)
> that he commanded in days of old;

[86] Noted by D. Hillers, *Lamentations*, 101.

[87] Continuing in this vein, in Ezek 28:12, YHWH tells Ezekiel to raise a dirge over the king of Tyre in which he is called "Perfection of Beauty."

[88] Thus also C. Westermann, *Lamentations*, 156.

[89] Among all the prophets, only Jeremiah and Zechariah use the root זמם to describe YHWH's actions; it is a term similar to חשב, to 'devise,' used in Lam 2:8, where YHWH "devises to lay in ruins the wall of D. Zion" (see next verse, Lam 2:18, where Jeremiah speaks to "the wall of D. Zion"). Jeremiah says about YHWH in Jer 23:20: "the anger of YHWH will not turn back until [YHWH] has done and until [YHWH] has established the *intention* of his mind" (and repeated in Jer 30:24); in YHWH's speech (again) in Jer 4:28, regarding desolating the land of Judah: "I have spoken, I have *intended* . . ."; see also Zech 1:6; 8:14–15.

> [YHWH] has *torn down* (הרס) without pity.[90]
> [YHWH] has caused the enemy to rejoice over you;
> [YHWH] has exalted the might of your foes. (Lam 2:17)

The first four cola are reminiscent of YHWH's calling a young Jeremiah in Jer 1:9b–10:

> Look!—I have put *my words* (דברי) in your mouth.
> See!—I appoint you today over the nations and the kingdoms,
> to pluck up (לנתוש) and to pull down (לנתוץ),[91]
> to destroy (להאביד) and to *tear down* (להרוס),
> to build and to plant.[92]

However, to the statement of YHWH's destroying verbs in his calling, Jeremiah adds in Lam 2:17 not only that YHWH has torn down without pity, but also that YHWH has "*accomplished his word by violence* (בצע)."[93] This root has the connotation of "unjust gain" (by violence) in Jer 22:17; it is what YHWH accuses the king of Jerusalem of doing.[94]

There is no question that within the next verse (18bc) Jeremiah shifts to a direct address of Jerusalem's poet again, moving beyond comforting to exhorting her to *lament* to YHWH. Translation of the beginning of vs 18, however, is greatly debated by scholars. Most would emend the first verb, "cry out" (צעק), to a feminine imperative,[95] lacking in the text, since it is followed by another imperative in 18b and a jussive in 18c. The next term, however, which appears to be "their heart" (לבם), makes no sense following such an

[90] Jeremiah said YHWH "swallowed without pity" in Lam 2:2 above.

[91] Recall in Jer 4:26, Jeremiah had used another of these destroying verbs in his description of the undoing of creation by YHWH: "I *look* upon the *earth*, and *behold!*—'*waste and void*' . . . I *look* and *behold*! the *garden-land* a desert! and all its cities are *pulled down* (> נתץ)."

[92] The above statement is cited or referred to seven times elsewhere in the book of Jeremiah (18:7–9; 24:6; 31:28, 40; 42:10; 45:4; 50:15). Cf. Ezek 36:35, 36.

[93] While this use of the verb with YHWH as subject is not unique to Jeremiah, it does not appear at all in Ezekiel; yet it does appear this way in several prophetic texts: Am 9:1; Isa 38:12; 57:17; it also appears in Job's speech in 27:8; and in 6:9 Job wishes that YHWH would *violently end his life* (> בצע).

[94] YHWH says to the king: "For are not your eyes and your heart even upon *accomplishing your gain by violence* (בצעך), and upon shedding innocent blood, and upon oppression and upon crushing?"

[95] Thus NRSV. R. Gordis proposes the verb is not צעק, but a rarer יצק, meaning to "pour out" (*Lamentations*, 166). He thus translates "pour out your heart to the Lord"; however, his numerous emendations and the fact that the forms of the two verbs don't sound that much alike make this proposal less convincing.

imperative.[96] I propose the following reconstruction, which fits the rhetorical context. First, every verse in Lam 2 (except 19) consists of a three-line stanza. Within the whole chapter, the pausal accent (*'atnach*) that typically divides a verse *never occurs* in the middle of one of these lines, *except in 18a*. This exceptional indicator of how the line was recited suggests that the second half of 18a through 18c belong together, and the first half of 18a (its thought) belongs with 17c, thus:[97]

> [YHWH] has caused the enemy to rejoice over you;
> [YHWH] has exalted (הרים) the might of your foes.
> He cries out toward the high place (לבם), "El (אל), my Lord!"
> (2:17c–18aα)

Vss 15–17c had stressed the enemies exulting vocally over Jerusalem (cf. 1:7c), enabled by YHWH. The "he" of 18a" refers to that enemy who now (mockingly?) "cries out"[98] toward a high place (< במה),[99] saying "El-YHWH!".[100] This would be highly ironic since this enemy, by defeating Jerusalem, has also presumably defeated her god. Jeremiah's rhetoric is acerbic, given the larger context, in that YHWH has refused to hear the laments of Jerusalem and Judah. The term "cry out" is typically used for someone praying to YHWH for help. One would expect the preposition "to" (אל) with the verb (and most translators read thus here), yet the verb appears at times without it (e.g., Gen 27:34; Isa 33:7; 65:14; Jer 22:20).

Having called attention to this vocal action of the enemy, Jeremiah turns to beseech *Jerusalem's poet to lament* to YHWH (18aβ–19)[101] in

[96] The MT suggests, "Their heart cries out to my Lord" (thus NJPS), yet there is no immediate antecedent for "their" (unless, unlikely, the "children" six verses earlier in vs 12). There is a "they" referred to in vss 15, 16, and 17 (the enemies and passersby), which may provide a key to unraveling this difficult line.

[97] Note the *'atnach* as well at the end of 17b.

[98] This explains the third masculine singular verb.

[99] I read the term לבם as the directive preposition ל plus an apocopated form of the singular noun במה ("high place") that may have reverted to its biconsonantal root in the poetry (cf. the singular use in Jer 48:35).

[100] Instead of YHWH, the text has אדני.

[101] While H. Jahnow had stressed that the dirge genre in Lamentations is modified from its more 'secular' usage to a theological one, she nevertheless did not draw a complete dichotomy between secular and profane uses, noting that prayer was a part of the dirge in various Christian and Muslim cultures (see Introduction of this study, and Jahnow, 98–101, 171, 178). Her analysis suggests S. Paul Re'emi's conclusion about genre in Lam 2 is misleading: "This song has nothing in common with a secular dirge, for it speaks about the acts of Yahweh" (*Amos & Lamentations*, 92).

a kind of competition for YHWH's ear; she has been silent since the end of Lam 1.[102]

> O *Wall* (חומת)—D. Zion!
> Let *tears run down* like a torrent, *day and night*;
> Do not give yourself to numbness (פוגת);[103]
> Do not let the 'daughter' of your eyes[104] cease.[105] (Lam 2:18aβ–c)

As noted above, the combination of terms ("tears," "run down," "day and night") are peculiar to Jeremiah's poetry, and his calling Jerusalem's poet to lament to YHWH with tears follows his own weeping in Lam 2:11. While at the outset of Lamentations Jeremiah empathetically identified with the city of Jerusalem, now he seems to regard the '*wall*' of Jerusalem as symbolic of its persona.[106] This is understandable for Jeremiah in light of how YHWH had used the same image *to characterize him* in calling him to his prophetic task:

> See!—now I make you today a city fortressed,
> an iron pillar, and a bronze *wall* against the whole land. . . . (Jer 1:18)

Within Jerusalem YHWH had made Jeremiah a resistent and 'iron-clad' *wall* against which the people would fight, for YHWH's words were intended to "tear down" their kingdom (Jer 1:10). Meanwhile, *outside* the invading enemy pushed against the walls of the city to conquer it. The man Jeremiah is under the "crush." From such a position, the prophet had uttered a nearly blasphemous *lament* against YHWH for failing him (Jer 15:20–21), and he was reminded by YHWH again of his calling (vs 19):

> If you return, I will take you back . . .
> If you utter what is precious, not worthless,
>   you will be as my mouth.

[102] Jeremiah's exhortation flies in the face of YHWH's commands in the book of Jeremiah *not to offer lament prayers*, as there would be no divine hearing (see discussion above).

[103] From פוג, to "be numb," "grow cold"; contra NRSV ("give yourself no rest").

[104] This may be a reference to tears; a similar expression in Ethiopic means the 'pupil' of the eye (BDB: 123). I. Provan notes the expression used in Ps 17:8; *Lamentations*, 76.

[105] Cf. much of the same terminology (discussed above) in Lam 3:49 below; see also Jer 14:17.

[106] See R. Gordis who also regards the phrase (חומת בת־ציון) as "virtually an appositional genitive" (*Lamentations*, 167). Contra I. Provan, *Lamentations*, 76, who regards the term "wall" as referring to YHWH.

I will make you to this people
a fortified *wall* of bronze (חומת נחשת).
They will fight against you,
but they will not prevail over you.
For I am with you to save you . . .
I will snatch you from the hand of the wicked. . . . (Jer 15:19–21)

When Jeremiah addresses Jerusalem's poet in Lam 2:18 as "O Wall—D. Zion," he uses an image of the city that YHWH had used to describe him. Jeremiah encourages Jerusalem's poet to be *a "wall!"* before YHWH—to cry out in the night in lament to YHWH, even like a watchman whose voice rings out from the wall of the city:[107]

Stand up (קומי), cry out (רני) in the night!
—*at the head* of every watch.[108]
Pour out[109] your heart like water,[110]
in front of[111] the face of YHWH![112]

[107] Perhaps the imagery he suggests is that she cries out from the wall, over against her enemy who is crying out from the 'high place,' both appealing to YHWH.

[108] I.e., at the "beginning" (ראש); note the parallel with "head" (ראש) of every street in 19c.

[109] The term "pour out" appears 7x in Lamentations and is a *leitwort* particularly in Lam 4.

[110] This imagery ("heart like water") occurs in lines 346 and 348 of the *Lamentation over the Destruction of Ur*; S. Kramer, 61.

[111] The unusual preposition "in front of" or "opposite" (נכח; seen 20x in Hebrew Bible) is found in Jeremiah's lament to YHWH in Jer 17:16. The *only other* similar use of the term in the Hebrew Bible by a prophet is Ezek 46:9 where he describes the people coming 'before' YHWH for appointed festivals.

[112] What appears at first to be a 'call to mourn' is actually a 'call to lament'; see C. Westermann who notes that a 'call to mourn' is typical of the communal dirge genre,; *Lamentations*, 157. The growing emphasis upon *lament prayer* across Lam 1 and 2 through the above dialogue is a serious contrast to *LU* (see also C. Westermann's discussion, *Lamentations*, 148, 157). In *LU*, the predominance of its 435 lines are given over to mourning/dirge speech, while fewer (approx. 68) contain "laments" (lines 62–64, 80–85, 145–159, 209, 250, 293, 310–318, 374–384, 405–414, 425–435). At line 40, the poet first exhorts the city *to mourn* (though translated by the word "lament"):

O city, a bitter lament set up as thy lament;
Thy lament which is bitter—O city, set up as thy lament.
His righteous city which has been destroyed . . .
His Ur which has been destroyed—bitter is its lament. . . . (*LU* 40)

This is the most striking *divergence* of the book of Lamentations from *LU* and points to how labeling all such classical Mesopotamian texts simply as "city-laments" is form-critically unclear. On the other hand, a much stronger parallel to D. Zion in biblical Lamentations is found in numerous *balag* laments where the city goddesses more often beseech a superior god on the city's behalf. Thus, recent scholars (Gwaltney,

Lift up your hands to him[113]
for the lives of your *children* (עולליך),[114]
fainting for hunger at the head of every street! (Lam 2:19)

In Jer 6:17, YHWH had said "I caused sentinels (צֹפִים) to *stand up* (הקמתי) over you;[115] did they pay attention to the sound of the *shofar*? They said, 'We will not pay attention.'" One is reminded of Jerusalem's poet in Jer 4 and 10, *hearing* the sound of the *shofar*,[116] being alarmed, and even then lamenting to YHWH. Just prior to Jeremiah's calling in Jer 1:18, that he was being made like a fortified city and a *wall* against the people, YHWH had commanded him, "*Stand up* (קמת) and tell them everything I command you." Here Jeremiah exhorts Jerusalem's poet to *stand up* and *lament* again to YHWH, because, again, of the suffering *children, fainting in the streets* (also in Lam 2:11 and 12).

Lam 2:20–22: Jerusalem's Poet Laments to YHWH

After being silent for the first 19 verses of Lam 2, Jerusalem's poet answers Jeremiah's challenge and speaks out again—as a mother on behalf of her children:

Look YHWH! and see!
To whom have you thus *dealt* (עוללת)?
Should women eat their offspring?![117]
The *children* (עללי) of their upbringing (טפחים)?!
Or should priest and prophet be killed (יהרג)
in the sanctuary of YHWH?! (Lam 2:20)

Jerusalem's poet opens her lament with the same words of address she used in Lam 1:9c and 11c: "Look" (ראה) and "See" (הביטה).

Frymer-Kensky, Hillers, Dobbs-Allsopp) suggest a *basic parallel* between the "weeping goddess" in Mesopotamian lamentations and Daughter Zion in biblical Lamentations, yet it must be made clear that the commonality there is in these figures' *lamenting with prayer*, not primarily in their mourning. Indeed, in *LU*, Ningal the city goddess has probably more in common with the male poet Jeremiah in biblical Lamentations, as they both express mourning, weeping, and communal dirge speech.

[113] See Lam 3:41 below for a new singer's use of this statement to Jeremiah and Jerusalem's poet.

[114] Note the consistent preferred use by Jeremiah of this term for "children."

[115] Cf. Lam 4:17 below.

[116] See Jer 4:5, 19, 21.

[117] See this topic in Lam 4:10.

Note the wordplay (unprecedented in her speech thus far in Lam 1–2) with עלל (children) in vs 18 and עולל ("you dealt") in vs 19; both terms have appeared separately throughout the speeches. The implication is that YHWH's actions have meant the suffering of the children. Jerusalem's poet's viewpoint is different from Jeremiah's with regard to the priests and prophets; in vs 14 he had critiqued the prophets' wrongdoing; here she notes the outrage of their deaths in the sanctuary. She continues.

> Young and old lie *on the ground in the streets.*
> My young men and women fall by the sword.[118]
> *You have killed* them on the day of *your anger*!
> You have *slaughtered* (טבחת) *without pity* (לא חמלת)! (Lam 2:21)

Jerusalem's poet continues Jeremiah's pathos and anger about *those dying in the streets.* She goes on to make explicit YHWH's responsibility in the action: "You have killed them." And she returns to her original concern (from Jer 10 and Lam 1) about the danger of *YHWH's anger*, now tragically gone forward. Note the incisive wordplay that YHWH "slaughters" (טבח; vs 21) the very children she has "reared" (טפח; vs 20 and 22), and "without pity"! Her last line adds to this angry, bitter complaint of the lament.

> *You proclaimed* like on a *feast* (מועד) day
>   my terror all around (מגורי מסביב).[119]
> And on the day of *the anger of YHWH*,
>   no one escaped or survived,
> those whom *I brought up* (טפחתי) and proliferated (רביתי),[120]
>   the enemy has annihilated (כלם). (Lam 2:22)

These words hearken back to YHWH's "*proclaiming*" against Jerusalem in Jer 4 and Lam 1:15 ("YHWH *proclaimed a feast day* [a "harvest" festival] against me to crush my young men" and her, as in a winepress), and in Lam 2:7 (where the din of the celebrating enemy is heard in the house of YHWH like on a *festival*). The phrase "*terror all around*" was certainly coined by Jeremiah in the book of Jeremiah

[118] Cf. her reference to them in Lam 1:18.

[119] R. Gordis notes that this phrase is another example of *talḥin* (wordplay with two intended meanings) in which the root גור at once refers to "neighbors" who sojourn around Jerusalem, as well as the "terrors" surrounding her; *Lamentations*, 169.

[120] Note the same use of this verb in Lam 2:5 where, in contrast, Jeremiah says YHWH is "multiplying" or proliferating "moaning and mourning" in the land of Judah.

(see 6:25; 20:3, 10; and in YHWH's speech in Jer 46:5 and 49:29). Jerusalem's poet again stresses that *YHWH's anger* is a cause of the suffering, and that YHWH *as enemy* has killed the *children* she reared. On this note, Lam 2 comes to a close.

Conclusion

Genre

Two poets appear in Lam 2 as in Lam 1. While the two poets in Lam 1 carried on an indirect dialogue, in Lam 2 two poets engage one another directly. While the first poet is not immediately identified as Jeremiah, he begins and continues where the prophet left off in Lam 1. As in Lam 1, he begins with with a communal dirge, but now gives a long litany of verbs describing YHWH's destroying actions like an enemy against Jerusalem and Judah. The other poet, identified here as in Jer 4, 10, and Lam 1 as Jerusalem's poet, does not speak until vss 20–22; as before, in Lam 2 Jerusalem's poet speaks another lament to YHWH. A new feature of Lam 2 is that the first poet directly addresses Jerusalem's poet (at vs 13) and encourages her to voice that lament (at vs 18). Thus in terms of genre, the first poet in Lam 2 (who is identified as Jeremiah by his peculiar style), though he continues using the communal dirge genre, evidences a subtle shift toward the lament genre as his descriptions of YHWH's actions increasingly have the tone of complaint, and he directly encourages Jerusalem's poet to lament.

Images/Themes

Among the images/themes employed and developed by the two poets of Lam 2 that also appeared in Lam 1, Jer 4, 10, and other key texts in Jeremiah are those depicting Jerusalem as a royal figure, the suffering mother, the fate of children, destruction of the tent/sanctuary as well as the altar, festivals and Sabbaths; the swallowing/eating of Jacob's pasture-abode, city structures mourning, and YHWH's anger consuming like fire.

Terminology

Jeremiah's terminology in Lam 2 is drawn from formulaic language commonly found in prophetic rhetoric, and from his own phraseology attested in the book of Jeremiah, but also increasingly from the psalms. This is indicative of a shift in rhetorical/theological attitude *toward* lament speech typical of the psalms. He uses his own peculiar cluster of terms that describe "weeping" (vs 11; from various places in the book of Jeremiah) where he himself breaks down into mourning speech for the first time in Lam 1–2. Above all, his favored term of endearment for Jerusalem, "Daughter of My People," clinches his identification as the first poet of Lam 2.

In Lam 2, Jeremiah develops the rhetoric around the terms "crushing" and "healing," which are pervasively used in the rhetorical context across Jer 4, 10, and Lam 1. Two 'new' features appear in Jeremiah's poetry in Lam 2: he identifies with Jerusalem's poet through the image of the "wall" (he now calls her "O Wall—D. Zion"), congruent with YHWH's identification of Jeremiah as a "wall" in his call narrative. Also, Jeremiah critiques the prophets (vs 14) and will continue this emphasis in Lam 4.

Rhetorical Techniques

Jeremiah continues to use and develop double roots (vs 5) and double meanings (vs 8) characteristic of his style. A completely new feature, not found in the book of Jeremiah or Lam 1, is Jeremiah's direct address of Jerusalem's poet in vs 13. While dialogue and address is common in the popular dirge genre, this interchange is striking within the larger rhetorical context, especially since YHWH never responds to Jerusalem's poet's pleas in these texts. Jeremiah's key concern in addressing her is to "comfort" her where there has been "no one comforting her" (thus answering the refrain they both raised in Lam 1). Not only is he performing the role of comforting a mourner in the dirge context; as a prophet he is also filling the gap where one expects a divine oracle of salvation offering comfort that has yet to materialize. Another completely new aspect of his speech is that, in addressing Jerusalem's poet, he also exhorts her to raise another lament to YHWH, an appeal to YHWH for her dying children (thus developing that concern). Jeremiah thus opts to participate in the lament genre as required by the moment, moving away from the communal dirge genre.

Content

Overall, Lam 2 is preoccupied with the following matters of content already presented in Jer 4, 10, and Lam 1: YHWH destroys like an enemy; and YHWH's anger causes the destruction. A 'new' emerging focus, foreshadowed in the book of Jeremiah, is how YHWH's anger and destroying actions have resulted in the suffering and deaths of Jerusalem's children. A third focus is upon the need for lament prayer to YHWH about the children's suffering.[121]

In sum, Lam 1 and 2 belong together as a rhetorical piece, suggestive of oral performance of two poets in the crisis of a particular context, continuous with much in the poetry of the book of Jeremiah and their utterances there.

[121] Thus Westermann concludes, "One finds such a sharp and intense juxtaposition of these two features [YHWH's anger and summons to lament] nowhere else in the Old Testament" (*Lamentations*, 159).

CHAPTER FIVE

LAMENTATIONS 3–5

millions of steps . . .
steadily slowly monotonously
over the sands of the desert
for forty years israel
out of egypt we out of canaan
with no burning bush
with no cloud
with no promise
with no God
no tablets of stone . . .
we are treading from age
to age . . .
under the curse of the tower
of babel
farther and farther from canaan
all in different directions
and they wonder at us and point at us
marching
into the red sea

Borislav Arapović, "Over the Sands of the Desert"[1]

This chapter will treat Lamentations 3–5 in light of the previous findings in Lamentations 1 and 2 in relation to poetry of the Jeremiah texts, including Jeremiah 4, 8, and 10. Lamentations 3–5 will be considered as part of the synchronic flow of the book thus far and in terms of the five areas dealt with above (genre, images/themes,

[1] Transl., I. Jerić, In *From Despair to Lamentation*, 14–15. Again, Arapović wrote this poem before the wars broke out in Croatia and Bosnia. Note, in his perspective here, his people's identification with an exile of the Canaanites. The contrast and complete reversal of Exodus motifs suggests despair. It is a worse "2nd Exodus" than depicted by 2nd Isaiah. Indeed, this is not a lament prayer to God, but is a kind of communal dirge, and in socio-political context strikes one as prophetic of anguish that was soon to come. It is also reminiscent of Jeremiah's rendering of the reversal of creation/Genesis motifs in Jer 4, suggestive of the coming fate of Judah.

terminology, rhetorical technique, and content). Using these criteria, I will argue that there are four distinct poetic singers in Lamentations 3 (a man [גבר],[2] a respondent, Jerusalem's poet, and Jeremiah). In Lamentations 4, Jeremiah and Jerusalem's poet are the two sole poets again (though the latter speaks for the people), and in Lamentations 5 there is a new singer.

Excursus: Cracking the Acrostic Code?

I shall pause here to take up an element the import of which scholars have attempted to decipher—the acrostic pattern in each of the Lamentations chapters. My approach is not to automatically assume that the acrostic was added later by a redactor (though this may turn out to be the case), but first to allow for the possibility that it might have been part of oral performance. Various poetic elements that appear restrictive to us (e.g., metrical requirements, chiasms) apparently were not a problem to those poets accustomed to their use. After considering David Noel Freedman's ongoing treatment of the metrical element in acrostic poems in Lamentations and the Hebrew Bible,[3] I turned to consider just what were the *themes* being driven home by the various other acrostic poems (i.e., Ps 9, 10, 25, 33, 34, 37, 38, 94, 111, 112, 119, 145 and part of Prov 31).

Even a brief survey of these poems shows that they all are either heavily invested in the idea of '*retributive justice*' or are confessional laments (Ps 25, 38) (except for Prov 31 which is not explicit on this point, though no doubt would fall in line.) In these texts the favored term is צדיק ("righteous") to describe YHWH and his righteous followers. YHWH rescues and protects the righteous, but the unrighteous suffer—i.e., all who suffer are evil and being punished by YHWH. (This sheds further light on Jerusalem's poet's ironic/sarcastic use of the term in Lam 2, and on Jeremiah's in his personal lament. Her use of the term *in context* may be less a criticism of YHWH's righteousness as she might understand it than a criticism of the *retributive justice school's understanding* of YHWH's righteousness.) For example, Ps 33 repeatedly emphasizes YHWH is righteous,

[2] In Lam 3:1 the singer/poet identifies himself as a גבר or (strong) "man."

[3] Subsequent to his earlier treatment, "Acrostic Poems in the Hebrew Bible: Alphabetic and Otherwise" (1997).

YHWH loves righteousness and justice (vs 5), as well as emphasizes that the proper attitude of the righteous is to praise YHWH (vs 1) and to "fear" YHWH (vss 8, 18; formulaic in wisdom literature). See also these same themes and the ever-recurring "righteous" in the acrostic Ps 34:7, 11, 15, 17, including emphasis that YHWH hears the cry of the righteous when they are hurting, but is against evildoers no matter what. Similar retributive themes appear in the acrostic Ps 37:12, 16, 17, 21, 25, 28, 29, 30, 32, 39; also in the acrostic Ps 94:1, 2, 10, 13, 15, 21, 23; in the acrostic Ps 111:5, 7, 10; in the acrostic Ps 112:1, 2, 3, 4, 5, 6, 8, 9; in the long acrostic on the "righteous ordinances" of the law, Ps 119:7, 40, 62, 69, 74, 75, 79, 106, 119, 120, 121, 122, 123, 137, 138, 142, 144, 160, 164, 172; and in the acrostic Ps 145:17, 19, 20. The point is that in all of these songs the overall "order" being hammered home by each letter (or each line of 22 when there is no alphabetic element) is retributive justice. Most of these psalms are a type of wisdom psalm. Though it is beyond the scope of this study to pursue whether this style of composition/singing (or scribal art?) could have been part of the Jerusalem context in which the singers of Lamentations resided, I shall pose a possible scenario in which this acrostic pattern is being used in a rhetorical battle, at some stage along the way, between two groups of singers with very different theological outlooks. I shall do this by another look at the specific Lamentations texts.

As noted Lam 1 opens with a communal dirge; Jeremiah (or someone re-singing his song) begins with a typical איכה. This single formulaic word for the communal dirge is pivotal for the introduction of the acrostic form not simply because it begins with the first letter of the alphabet, but because *this dirge genre* prophets used not only to critique injustice and idolatry, but also to forewarn of the 'retributive justice' of YHWH's punishment. According to this way of thinking, in Lam 1 the punishment was now unfolding in the destruction of Jerusalem. At this point, we may say that if Lam 1 fairly well preserves a song by Jeremiah, then he may be opting to employ an acrostic form as he is familiar with its use by psalm singers to convey a theology of retributive justice. This is plausible. But it appears this purpose of the acrostic *does not hold up* across the book as the singers engage the context. Already in Lam 1, the outcry of Jerusalem's poet nine lines into Jeremiah's song may be not only her negative reaction to the content he is conveying, but also to the *form*. Yet her own speeches in the second half of Lam 1 also 'participate' in the acrostic, but for a different purpose, as she uses the lament genre to complain against YHWH's actions (and deconstructs "righteous" rhetoric, noted above). Soon after, the first two singers employ the acrostic to give long lists of YHWH's destroying actions (as the man will in chapter 3), but as has been noted, to critique YHWH; the effect is an implicit critique of retributive justice that either condones such punishing or interprets events this way.

It is beyond the scope here, but to reconsider the lines of Lamentations using this scenario may throw open some new insights. For example, in Lam 2 Jeremiah has completed a long litany of YHWH's destroying actions (using the acrostic), and then moves in vs 15 (the ס-line) to describe those who ridicule and "wag their heads at Daughter Jerusalem," but just as he must move next to the ע-letter, instead he jumps to פ! And with it he describes "all your enemies who open their *mouths* (פה) against you," "ah! this is the day we longed for; at last we have seen it!" Is this reversal of letters Jeremiah's foil against the gloating group who love retributive justice? The NRSV indicates their speech ends there in vs 16, but perhaps vs 17 (now the ע-line) is *not Jeremiah's* but still his quoting their ridiculing speech: "YHWH has done what he purposed; he has carried out his threat . . . he has made the enemy rejoice over you. . . ." Precisely at this point, Jeremiah calls for Jerusalem's poet to cry out to YHWH, precisely what the retributive justice crowd believes is futile for one so damned. Thus, it is possible that the singers in Lamentations (thus far Jeremiah and Jerusalem's poet) use the acrostic form to 'throw' an answer back to the 'retributive justice' (wisdom) group.[4] This becomes more apparent in Lam 3 below where more people start joining the dialogue.

Lamentations 3

In terms of genre, scholars have noted that the *individual lament* dominates Lamentations 3, and they have often separated this chapter

[4] Some may argue that the acrostic 'layer' comes later, reflecting a later debate on these matters. This is possible, though I prefer to think it is part of the singers' dialogue I have been discussing. In either case, the acrostic may also reflect a later re-singing of these songs in such a way that the basic components from Jeremiah and Jerusalem's poet were re-configured by different singers adding the alphabetic element. Or some may prefer to see this reconfiguration as carried out by scribes cognizant of a prior oral context; cf. Robert C. Culley's discussion on the matter

(along with the communal lament of Lamentations 5) from Lamentations 1, 2 and 4 (each of which opens with the communal dirge).[5] When Lamentations is read synchronically, however, the movement toward lament by the two poets in Lamentations 1 and 2 has already been evident (Lam 1:9c, 11c, 20–22).[6] In this larger movement, Jerusalem's poet tends to co-opt the description of distress from the dirge for use in her laments to detail the enemy's actions. What has been striking about such speech in Lam 1–2, and now here in Lam 3, is the heavy use of *accusations* against YHWH, heretofore unprecedented in the Hebrew Bible.

That the singer/poet who opens Lam 3 (vss 1–24 and 52–66) would also construct a lengthy description of YHWH's actions *against him* is entirely continuous with the flow of rhetoric by Jeremiah and Jerusalem's poet in Lam 1 and 2.[7] Such extreme complaint suggests that this male singer[8] has listened to and is responding to the first two poets. In this dialogue, his first person description of his suffering is similar to Jerusalem's poet's first person description of her distress in Lam 1. One might claim certain *generic* reasons for identifying this man opening Lam 3 as Jeremiah, one of the two poets responsible for Lam 1–2. First, Jeremiah also briefly relinquished third person dirge-description and slipped into *first person* mourning speech in Lamentations 2:11 as a witness to the suffering around him; the first person lament that opens Lam 3, thus, would not be out of character for Jeremiah. Second, this lament in 3:1–24 would also follow upon the heels of Jeremiah exhorting Jerusalem's poet (2:18–19) to lament herself (2:20–22). And finally, Jeremiah especially employed individual lament more than any other prophet, as evidenced in the book of Jeremiah.[9]

of composition and form of text as we have it; "Orality and Writtenness in the Prophetic Texts," 45–64.

[5] For a summary of scholarship, see C. Westermann, *Lamentations*, 24–85, 160–193.

[6] Note especially Jeremiah's direct appeal to Jerusalem's poet to lament to YHWH in 2:18–19.

[7] Lam 3, unlike chapters 1 and 2, differs in the intensity of its use of the acrostic in that there are three *aleph*-lines, three *bet*-lines, and so on for 66 verses in the chapter. Whereas, in chapters 1, 2, and 4, only the first line of the verse has the acrostic letter.

[8] See D. Hillers' discussion of scholarly views on identification of the poet/man of Lam 3; Hillers does not identify him with Jeremiah, but he is "Everyman"; *Lamentations*, 119–23.

[9] See individual laments by Jeremiah (i.e., lament prayer, not mourning or dirge speech) in Jer 4:10; 6:10–11; 11:18–20; 12:1–4; 15:10, 15–18; 17:14–18; 18:18–23;

However, in the method I am using, generic reasons *alone* are insufficient to identify the singer/poet of Lam 3:1–24 as Jeremiah. Only additional evidence in a paralleled use of images/themes, peculiar terminology, rhetorical technique, and content, like that compiled above in Lam 1 and 2, would be sufficient to identify the poet in Lam 3:1–24 as Jeremiah. A preliminary analysis does not suggest this. The singer's images, themes and terms, rather, are simply typical of many *lament psalms*; neither are they especially congruent with those elements in Jeremiah's personal laments in the book of Jeremiah. Thus, I shall designate the first singer of Lam 3 as *a new poet*, citing evidence as it unfolds. There are four poetic singers in Lam 3, as set forth below.

Outline of Poetic Singers

Lamentations 3:

vv 1–24	1st new poetic singer (lament)
vv 25–41	2nd new poetic singer (response)
vv 42–45	Jerusalem's poet (lament)
vv 46–51	Jeremiah (lament)
vv 52–66	1st poetic singer (completion of lament)

Lamentations 3:1–24: A New Poetic Singer Utters a Lament

Lam 3:1–24 appears to be an *unanswered* individual lament,[10] just as the laments of Jerusalem's poet have been (Jer 10:23–25; Lam 1:9c, 11c, 20–22). Beginning in 3:1, the new singer continues the litany of YHWH's destructive actions, only now the actions are specifically against this man himself. The image of YHWH's "hand" against him echoes Jeremiah's description of YHWH's destroying "hand" against D. Zion at the beginning of Lam 2 (vss 1, 3–4). These continuities suggest a singer joining the dialogue of Jeremiah and Jerusalem's poet and their radical use of the lament genre.

20:7–18. For an analysis, see Kathleen M. O'Connor, *The Confessions of Jeremiah: Their Interpretation and Role in Chapters 1–25*, SBLDS 94 (Atlanta: Scholars Press, 1988).

[10] Unanswered to the extent that the lamenter does not indicate YHWH's intervention to transform the situation, often seen in lament psalms. He does indicate some personal transformation, a shift to hope, at vss 21–24.

I am the man (אני הגבר) who has seen suffering (עני)
by the rod of his [YHWH's] wrath. (3:1)

The singer's use of the independent pronoun "I" (אנכי or אני) is common in lament psalms.[11] His admission that he has *seen* the suffering may be a direct response to the speech of Jerusalem's poet just before (2:20), where she pleaded unsuccessfully with YHWH to "see" her suffering. As such, this singer's point of view *identifies* with Jerusalem's poet and complements Jeremiah's compassion toward her.

The singer continues the accusation begun by Jerusalem's poet previously and piles up verbs (across eight verses) to describe YHWH's destroying actions against him:

He [YHWH] has driven me and made me walk
in darkness (חשך), with no light (לא־אור).
Indeed, against me [YHWH] repeatedly turned
his *hand* all the day long.
[YHWH] caused my flesh and skin to waste away,
crushed (שבר) my bones.
[YHWH] has built (a siege) against me,
enveloping (me with) bitter poison and weariness.[12]
[YHWH] made me sit in dark places (מחשכים)
like the dead of long ago.
[YHWH] has walled me in (גדר), and I cannot depart;
he has weighed me down with bronze chains.
Even though I cry out (אזעק), and call for help (אשוע),
[YHWH] has *shut out my prayer.*
[YHWH] has walled up (גדר) my pathways with stone,
and made my paths crooked. (Lam 3:2–9)

By and large, the images/themes and terminology of these lines are typically found in lament psalms. The imagery of darkness and/or light (vss 2, 6) often appears in lament psalms (e.g., Pss 18:29; 35:6; 74:20; 107:10, 14; 139:11–12; 143:3), where YHWH is usually the bringer of light, not darkness; however, compare Pss 88:6, 12, 18;

[11] It is also common in prophetic call narratives (by Moses in Exod 3:11, 13; 4:10; Isaiah in 6:1–8; Amos in 7:14; Jeremiah in 1:6, 7, 11, 13; and Ezekiel in 1:1), yet nowhere is Jeremiah referred to as a גבר.

[12] The term for "weariness" is the unusual noun תלאה, used numerous times to describe Israel's fatiguing hardship in Egypt (e.g., Exod 18:8; Nu 20:14); the noun does not appear in the book of Jeremiah, but the *verb* is used three times in Jeremiah's individual laments: in Jer 6:11 ("I am fatigued with holding in [the wrath of YHWH]"); in Jer 20:9; and by YHWH to describe Jeremiah in Jer 12:5.

105:28; and 107:10, 14, where YHWH brings darkness against rebellious people. "Dark places" (מחשכים) appears in Ps 143:3: "he makes me sit in dark places like the dead of long ago"; this line must be a lament song *formula*, as the singer uses it in Lam 3:6. The closest parallel to this use of the dark/light imagery by Jeremiah is in Jer 13:16–17, where Jeremiah warns the people, "Give glory to YHWH your God before he brings darkness (יחשך) . . . when you look for light (אור), but he makes it the shadow of death. . . ."[13] In Lam 3:2, the poet sings of the darkness into which YHWH has brought him.

As noted above, the metaphor of YHWH's *hand* against all Israel and Jerusalem was rendered by Jeremiah in Lam 2:3 and 8. In Lam 3:3, the singer indicates being the recipient against whom YHWH turns his hand "all the day long." As noted above, this use of YHWH's hand *against him* in a lament is highly ironic, given the usual expectation of the lamenter that YHWH's hand will *save him* from his enemies. While the expression, "all the day long," is used twice by Jeremiah in one of his laments (Jer 20:7–8), it is also common in lament psalms (Pss 25:5; 38:6; 44:22; 56:2–3; 86:3; 102:9).

In Lam 3:4, YHWH *crushes* the man's bones. In addition to the prevalent use of "*crush*" (שבר) by Jeremiah and Jerusalem's poet, this more elaborate image appears in the lament of Ps 51:10 ("the bones you [YHWH] have *crushed*"), a metaphor for YHWH's punishing of sin. In Lam 3:5, "YHWH has built a siege against me" is suggestive of the invading army's siege against the people of Jerusalem as well as Jeremiah's being like a fortress or wall against them. Compare and contrast Ps 31:22: "Blessed be YHWH, for he has wondrously shown his covenant loyalty to me, when I was a city besieged." The poet of Lam 3:5 laments that YHWH *causes* the siege. Continuing this imagery of vs 5, in vs 7 YHWH has "walled" the man in so he cannot leave and weighed him down with "bronze" (נחשת) chains. This is analogous to D. Zion's being weighed down by the yoke of her transgressions in Lam 1:14 and *in contrast* to Jeremiah being like a "wall of bronze" (נחשת) *against* the people (Jer 1:18; 15:20).

The verbs in vs 8, to "cry out," to "call for help" (זעק, שוע), are prevalent in lament appeals to YHWH.[14] This poet's complaint that

[13] See also the absence of light in Jeremiah's rendering of the undoing of creation in Jer 4:23–26.

[14] E.g., Pss 28:2; 31:23; 77:2; 107:6, 28.

YHWH has "shut out" his prayer is congruent with the larger rhetorical context of the book of Jeremiah wherein YHWH refuses to hear prayer (Jer 7:16; 11:11, 14; 14:11; cf. 15:1). Likewise, in Lam 3:44 below, Jerusalem's poet's also complains that YHWH will not accept prayer.

The first singer/poet of Lam 3 continues his list of YHWH's actions against him in vss 10–18, drawing upon lament terms and imagery normally reserved for the enemy.

> [YHWH] is a bear lying in wait for me,[15]
> a lion in a hiding place.[16]
> Turning me away from my path, [YHWH] tore me in pieces;
> he set me up for ravaging.
> [YHWH] bent his bow and stationed me
> as a target for the arrow.[17]
> [YHWH] shot into my vitals
> the arrows of his quiver.[18]
> I have become a laughingstock of all my people,[19]
> (the object of) their taunt-songs all the day long.[20]
> [YHWH] has satisfied me with bitter herbs,[21]
> and sated me with wormwood.[22]
> [YHWH] has made my teeth grind on gravel,[23]
> and pressed me into the dust.

[15] Cf. the use of the verb for the enemy "lying in wait" in Lam 4:19; also in Pss 10:9 and 59:4.

[16] Cf. the use of "lion" to describe enemy actions in lament psalms (7:3; 10:9; 17:12; 22:14, 22).

[17] While a lament psalmist occasionally depicts YHWH as shooting him or another with arrows (7:13; 38:2; 64:7; 144:6), just as often it is the psalmist's human enemy doing so (11:2; 57:5; 64:4; 120:4).

[18] NRSV.

[19] The noun "laughingstock" (שׂחק) is unusual in the Hebrew Bible, appearing only in the books of Jeremiah (4x), Ecclesiastes (4x), Proverbs (2x), and Job (3x). That it appears in one of Jeremiah's individual laments (Jer 20:7) could be suggestive of him as singer here in Lam 3:14, though insufficient evidence by itself.

[20] נגינה, translated "taunt-songs" here, is found primarily in lament psalms, where it often appears in headings that designate a kind of music or instrument (4:1; 6:1; 54:1; 55:1; 61:1; 67:1; 69:13; 76:1; 77:7); it appears as well in Lam 3:63 and 5:14.

[21] This form of the noun "bitter herbs" (מרורים) is unusual in the Hebrew Bible, but elsewhere only refers to the substance eaten in the Passover meal (Exod 12:8; Nu 9:11).

[22] "Wormwood" (לענה) is very uncommon in the Hebrew Bible, appearing only 7x elsewhere (include Lam 3:19). Cf. YHWH's speech in Jer 9:14: "I am making this people eat *wormwood*, and making them drink poisonous water (מי־ראשׁ)" and in Jer 23:15, where YHWH's same sentence refers not to the whole people, but explicitly to "the prophets."

[23] NRSV.

My soul is bereft of peace;[24]
  I have forgotten good things.
So I say, "My endurance has perished,
  and my hope from YHWH."[25] (3:10–18)

By vs 18, the poet has reached a moment of despair and for the first time *names* YHWH, not only as the subject of all the previous verbs against him, but also as *no source* of present hope.

Then, as with lament psalms, the singer abruptly shifts to an imperative, directed to YHWH who has just been named.[26]

Remember my 'suffering and wandering' (זכר־עניי ומרודי),
  the wormwood and gall!
Do remember![27] For my soul is sinking down upon me.[28] (3:19–20)

The singer repeats Jeremiah's exact phrase "suffering and wandering" from Lam 1:7 (where Jeremiah described Jerusalem's suffering she "remembered"), only now this poet implores YHWH, "Remember *my* 'suffering and wandering'!" While his use of this phrase, on the surface, appears to suggest that this poet might in fact be Jeremiah, there is little other evidence in the poet's speech to suggest it. Rather, his repetition of the phrase suggests that he has overheard the previous rhetoric between Jeremiah and Jerusalem's poet and now enters their pathos-filled dialogue, as if to say, "I *also* have experienced 'suffering and wandering'" in the destruction of the city.[29]

[24] NRSV.

[25] See the similar use of the term "hope" (תוחלת) in the lament psalm, 39:8.

[26] Contra NRSV for Lam 3:19: "*The thought of* my affliction and my homelessness is wormwood and gall!" Many commentators read (as NRSV) the initial זכר as a noun; not only does this reading neglect the pointing of the term as an imperative, it also neglects the necessity in the lament passage for an imperative to YHWH, as well as leaves this verse *without a verb* at all, whereas every line (3:1–18) thus far has had at least one verb, sometimes two or three. Evidence for this precise vowel pointing of this same root as an imperative, also connected by a *maqqēf* to the direct object, is found in the lament psalm, Ps 25:7: זכר־לי ("remember me"). The same imperative use of זכר appears in Lam 5:1.

[27] He intensifies the imperative "remember" in vs 20 by using the infinitive absolute plus imperfect of זכר.

[28] The verb form of שׁוח is rare in the Hebrew Bible, appearing elsewhere only in Prov 2:18 and in lament psalms (42:6; 43:5; 44:26) also with the "soul" sinking down.

[29] William Lanahan suggests that the man uttering this lament is a soldier, reflected in his references to being held prisoner, hunger, fatigue, ambush, siege, and being wounded; "The Speaking Voice in Lamentations," 45–47. Lanahan's proposal is supported by use of the term גבר for the man, and by the phenomenon of warriors' lament songs (of defeat) in oral traditional cultures.

While a typical transition does not then follow indicating YHWH's intervention or answer to the poet's lament, there is nevertheless a shift in his speech to *hope* with the next lines. This shift in itself may implicitly suggest that YHWH has stirred hope within the man.[30]

> This I bring back to mind,[31]
>   and so I am hoping:
> YHWH's acts of covenantal love (חסד)—[32]
>   indeed, they have not ended;
>   indeed, his mercies have not finished.
> They are made new every morning—
>   great is your faithfulness!
> "My lot is YHWH," says my soul;
>   "therefore, I am hoping in him." (3:21–24)

Significantly, nearly every biblical lament psalm appeals to the "*covenantal love*" (חסד) of YHWH as an immediate cause for divine intervening help.[33] Indeed, the phrase or lyric, "covenantal love in the morning," appears as a *formula* in lament psalms; however, the term חסד not found in Jeremiah's personal laments.[34] This singer's recollection of YHWH's covenantal love helps bring its present reality into his awareness; he moves to praise speech and another direct address of YHWH in vs 23. The singer has moved, or been moved, from profound hopelessness (vs 18) to hope (vs 24), following his direct lament to YHWH, even though there is no indication of

[30] In discussion with Marija Koprivnjak of Bosnia regarding the move to hope in these lines, she suggests that while a lament prayer may go unanswered in the larger sense, the lamenter at the same time may experience moments of hope and grace within the reality of traumatic suffering.

[31] Or, "reconsider" or "remember".

[32] Cf. Katharine Sakenfeld, *The Meaning of Hesed in the Hebrew Bible* (Atlanta: Scholars Press, 1978). W. Brueggemann notes that there is no indication why the man "remembers" here, but could not have done so had he not "available a stylized rhetoric about the God of fidelity" that "overrides the moment of despair"; *Theology of the Old Testament*, 221–22.

[33] The term חסד ("covenantal love") appears in the following lament psalms: Ps 5:7; 6:4; 13:5; 17:7; 25:6–7, 10; 26:3; 31:8, 17, 21; 36:5, 7, 10; 40:10–11; 42:8; 44:26; 51:1; 57:4, 11; 59:11, 17–18; 61:8; 62:13; 63:4; 69:14, 17; 77:9; 85:8, 11; 86:5, 13, 15; 88:12; 89:2–3, 15, 25, 29, 34, 50; 90:14; 94:18; 106:1, 7, 45; 107:1, 8, 15, 21, 31, 43; 108:5; 109:21, 26; 119:41, 64, 76, 88, 124, 149, 159; 130:7; and 143:8, 12.

[34] Lament Ps 77:9 asks, "Has [YHWH's] covenantal love ceased (אפס) forever?" Moreover, with reference to "the morning," see Ps 59:17: "I will sing until morning of your covenantal love"; Ps 90:14: "Satisfy us in the morning with your covenantal love"; and Ps 143:8: "Let me hear of your covenantal love in the morning. . . ."

YHWH's intervention to alleviate physical suffering. Overall, the singer's specific terms and phrases in Lam 3:1–24 are very typical of lament psalms (albeit extending the complaint). While such language *does not preclude* Jeremiah from being the singer, neither does it give much indisputable evidence *for* his peculiar poetry here.

Lamentations 3:25–51: Antiphonal Exchange: Second New Poetic Singer, Jerusalem's Poet & Jeremiah

The singer pauses after his "avowal of confidence" in YHWH's mercy (vss 22–23), and one expects him next to raise a typical "plea" to YHWH;[35] yet precisely here a second poet/singer intrudes. This new singer breaks into the first singer's lament in midstream, admonishing him (vss 25–41). This is evident from the shift in tone, content, and genre from first-person lament prayer to a third-person sapiential, theological discourse.[36] Reminiscent of the friends' discourse in Job, the interrupting admonisher defends YHWH's actions, critiques the singer's complaints, and advocates his *silence* instead of lament.[37] This advocacy *of silence* is the main reason for identifying a new singer here, and it is also the reason why this new singer cannot be Jeremiah, since the prophet has advocated lament and its complaint, not silence. After bitter complaint and inner turmoil, the singer of Lam 3:1–24 finally reached a place of calm in trusting YHWH again. But at precisely that moment of quiet the new singer rushes in to say in effect, "Good, good, good . . . for one to keep silent, bear the punishment for his sin, and simply wait on YHWH." Thus, where YHWH has not significantly intervened on behalf of the first singer, this second singer steps in with ready anwers:

Good is YHWH to the one waiting for him,
  to the soul seeking him—
Good (to the one)
  who hopes *silently* for the saving of YHWH—
Good to the man (גבר)
  who bears the *yoke* in his youth.
  who sits alone *silently*,

[35] C. Westermann, *Lamentations*, 170, 173, yet cf. 176.

[36] Shifts in singers are not explicitly indicated in the text of Lamentations, but must be inferred.

[37] Cf. C. Westermann who judges that vs 25 belongs with the speech of the previous lamenter, but that there is an "expansion" in vss 26–41 representing a different viewpoint in which "lamentation is disallowed"; *Lamentations*, 168, 179–80.

since [YHWH] has laid (it) upon him;
who puts his mouth in the dust,
perhaps there is hope;
who puts forward his cheek to the one who strikes him;
and be satisfied with insult. (3:25–30)

While the first singer had emphasized YHWH's destroying anger and covenantal love, he also strikingly omitted explicit confession of sin on his part, though he likely assumed it. Yet the second singer, perhaps intent upon making the man's lament a *confessional* lament, now emphasizes that his suffering *is punishment for his sin* (vs 39). His suffering parallels Jerusalem's poet in so far as she also had to bear the "yoke" (1:14; i.e., punishment of servitude) imposed by YHWH. The second singer continues with a long defense of YHWH.[38]

For the Lord will not reject forever;
For even though [YHWH] has caused grief, he has shown mercy,
according to the greatness of his covenantal love.
For [YHWH] has not caused suffering,
nor grieved the children (בני) of humanity
out of his own heart.
To crush (דכא) under his feet
all the captives of the land,
to turn aside the justice (משפט) of a man (גבר)
is against the desire of the Most High.[39]
To twist a human with his dispute—
the Lord does not look upon with approval.[40]
Who has said this and "it was"?[41]
the Lord has not commanded (it).
Not from the mouth of the Most High has it issued
to bring suffering to a good man.[42]
Why does a living human, a man, complain[43]
about the punishment of his sin?[44]

[38] While R. Gordis analyzes Lam 3 as though it were the work of a single poet, he notes that in vss 31–38 the poet's standpoint is very similar to that of Eliphaz (Job 5:6, 7); *Lamentations*, 175.

[39] "Elyon." Following R. Gordis on translating נגד פני עליון (literally, "over against the face of") in vs 35; ibid., 181.

[40] Following the sense of R. Gordis's translation; ibid.

[41] Perhaps a reference to YHWH's speech in Gen 1 and its generative power.

[42] Following Erlich's slight emendation of הרעות to הרע את; cited by Gordis, ibid., 183.

[43] This verb for "complain" is very rare in the Hebrew Bible, appearing only here and in Nu 11:1 to refer to the people's complaining during the wilderness wandering.

[44] Gordis, ibid., 184.

Let us search and examine our ways,[45]
  and let us return to YHWH.
Let us lift our hearts, and not our hands,[46]
  to El in heaven. (3:31–41)

This poet's speech in vss 34–38 is unclear,[47] perhaps because it strives to resolve simply the difficult issues of YHWH's transcendent power and immanent help, divine justice and mercy, human sin and divine punishment.[48] Nevertheless, the poet's reference in the last two verses to "us" directs everyone in the dialogue to lift a presumably silent, yet *confessional* lament prayer to YHWH. Silent confession would break the overall flow of severe complaints by these previous poets across Lamentations 1–3. Thus, it is hardly surprising that one of them will respond to this new singer, disagreeing with his/her point of view.

Indeed, Jerusalem's poet now rejoins the dialogue (at the נ-line), speaking for the first time in Lam 3. The shift to a different singer is indicated by the shift in genre, tone, and content again, from defense of YHWH to accusing lament against YHWH. She ignores the previous singer's advice to keep silent and utters more angry speech—understandable for one whose laments have gone unanswered. She turns the previous singer's meek cohortative, "let us," into an emphatic, confessional "we" and an accusing "you" against YHWH:

We (נחנו) have transgressed and *rebelled*;
You (אתה) have *not* forgiven.
You have wrapped/silenced yourself *with anger* and pursued us;
  you have killed; you have not pitied!
You have wrapped/silenced yourself *with a cloud*
  so that *no prayer* can pass through!"[49]

[45] Similarly, see Ps 139:1, 23.

[46] LXX read אל and rendered ἐπί ("upon"), but likely the Hebrew intended "not" (cf. Joel 2:13); following Gordis, ibid., 185.

[47] The commentaries have difficulty determining its meaning(s).

[48] See I. Provan for an especially helpful discussion of the ambiguity of these lines; *Lamentations*, 97–100.

[49] As noted above, the lines with double use of "wrapped" (or "overshadowed," סכתה from סכך) likely contain a biting wordplay with סכת, 'to keep silent': 'You are *silent* with anger . . . you *silence* yourself behind a cloud so that no prayer can pass through!' The root סכך also produces the noun מסך, a "covering" or "screen," and the noun סכה, a "thicket" or "booth" (for the harvest festival). Cf. the earlier speech of the individual lamenter in Lam 3:8: ". . . [YHWH] shuts out my prayer."

You make us dirt and refuse[50]
in the midst of the peoples. (3:42–45)

Jerusalem's poet continues her complaint that YHWH's anger has prevented divine forgiveness of the people and divine help, vociferously heightened by the assonance of her three-fold ס-line. Her use of cloud imagery is an ironic and negative critique of YHWH's use of transcendent power, in contrast to the usual theophanic imagery of the psalms[51] and perhaps a sardonic rejoinder to the previous poet's defense of Elyon, the "Most High." She also echoes and extends Jeremiah's use of cloud imagery in Lam 2:1 in connection with YHWH's anger.[52]

While at first glance in the next lines (vss 46–47), the identification of the poet may not be clear—one wonders if Jerusalem's poet has left any room for the previous advocate of confession to retort. But when that inverted פ—line is uttered—it must be Jeremiah! He used nearly the exact same speech at the 2:16 פ-line!

All our enemies have opened
their mouths against us.
Panic and pitfall (פחד ופחת) have come upon us,[53]
the crashing and *crushing* (השאת והשבר).[54] (3:46–47)

Only now he slightly shifts the phrase from "your enemies" to "our enemies." This phrase (cf. vs 46) is used numerous times by Jerusalem's poet and Jeremiah in Lam 1, and to a lesser extent in Lam 2. Second, evidence that Jeremiah is the singer of 3:46–47 is also found in vs 47. The two word-pairs, the pun (paronomasia) "panic and

[50] "Refuse" translates the noun מאוס in the phrase סחי ומאוס; I have changed the order of the terms in English translation to avoid misconstrual of "refuse" as a verb. Note the alliteration of the "s" sound across vss 42b–45, perhaps suggestive of the poet's angry tone. Cf. Jer 33:23–26 for YHWH's oracle of future restoration, reversing the "rejection" (> מאס) of "my people" among the nations.

[51] See especially Ps 18:12 where, in a theophany, YHWH (= "Elyon," vs 14) "has made darkness around him his hiding place and his canopy/covering (סכתו) thick clouds dark with water."

[52] Jerusalem's poet also uses the noun "*refuse*" (מאס) similarly to Jeremiah in Jer 6:30 where he says the people are being refined and are "*refuse* (נמאס) silver, for YHWH has *refused/rejected* (מאס) them." Also see Jer 4:30 where YHWH says to the prostitute Jerusalem, "your lovers *refuse* you." Cf. the people's lament in Lam 5:22, their final words: "You have utterly *refused/rejected* us; you are exceedingly wrathful."

[53] NRSV.

[54] Translating שאת as "crashing" from the root שאה, likely as a synonym to שאון ("din, crash, uproar" sometimes in reference to battle; BDB: 981).

pitfall" (ופחת פחד) and the alliterative "crashing and crushing" (השאת והשבר) are more typical of prophetic poetry. The biblical word-trio "panic, pitfall, and trap" appears elsewhere only in Isaiah 24:17 *and* in Jeremiah's oracle against Moab in Jer 48:43: "*Panic, pitfall, and trap* are upon you, O inhabitants of Moab!"[55] Moreover, Jeremiah uses a very similar alliterative word-pair with שׁבר to describe Moab in Jer 48:3: "Desolation and *destruction/crushing*!" (שׁד ושׁבר). As has been noted, the term "*crushing*" is a leitwort in the poetic rhetoric of the books of Jeremiah and Lamentations and is specifically used by Jeremiah to describe the "*crushing of Daughter of My People*" in Jer 8:11, 21; 14:17; Lam 2:13 and 4:10.[56] That this precise phrase, "*crushing of Daughter of My People*" (note Jeremiah's peculiar appellative for Jerusalem) then appears in the very next verse (3:48) strongly suggests that Jeremiah is the poet of vss 46–48.[57]

My eyes run down[58] with streams of water,[59]
 because of the *crushing of Daughter of My People.*
My eyes spill forth and *will not cease,*
 without *numbing,*
 until YHWH looks down from heaven and sees.
My eyes afflict my soul,
 from (seeing) all the daughters of my city. (3:48–51)

[55] Cf. also the subsequent line in Isa 24:18 that is repeated, though not verbatim, in Jer 48:44, suggesting once again that Jeremiah's poetry is influenced by Isaiah's artistry.

[56] Cf. Lam 2:13, where Jeremiah uses the term שׁבר to convey two meanings, to refer at once to Zion's "crushing/crashing" like the sea.

[57] It is interesting to speculate regarding the acrostic here between vss 46–48 (all beginning with the "p" letter, פ) and vss 49–51 (all beginning with the ע) in terms of it being part of an oral performance of poetic singers in dialogue. Since Jeremiah is the singer of all six of these lines, it is possible that he inverted these letters of the alphabet. This same inversion also occurred in Lam 2:16–17 *and* 4:16 where he is also the singer; yet at Lam 1:16, Jerusalem's poet is the singer, and there the expected alphabetic order appears. Though 3:46–48 begin with the פ-letter and confirm Jerusalem's poet's observations about the people's suffering, the next three ע-lines (two of which begin with "my eyes," עיני) convey Jeremiah's intense weeping. Is it possible that the poetic singer is in full control of the imagery and acrostic pattern here? One may note the presence of acrostic psalms in the Hebrew Bible, presumably composed and sung by oral poets/singers. See an example of an inversion of the ע and פ letters in some abecediaries in the Kuntillet 'Ajrud inscription, *ABD*, vol. IV, David N. Freedman, ed. (New York: Doubleday, 1992), 107.

[58] See similarly Lam 2:18b.

[59] See similarly Ps 119:136.

As has been previously discussed (see chapter 4), the key terms "eyes," "run down," and "Daughter of My People" are characteristic of Jeremiah's poetry. The passage above closely parallels his first person speech with weeping in Lam 2:11 and his directing Jerusalem's poet to lament and weep in Lam 2:18–19. In the latter, Jeremiah appealed to Jerusalem's poet to weep and not grow "numb," as he says of himself in 3:49 above. Also in 2:18 Jeremiah tells Jerusalem's poet to let her tears run down like a "torrent" or "wady," and here in 3:48, his own tears run down like "streams of water." Thus, given the similarities in terminology, style, and genre of the above verses to his other speeches, Jeremiah is likely the poet of 3:46–51.

Lamentations 3:52–66: First Singer in Lamentations 3 Returns

The rhetoric that follows in Lam 3:52–66 is not distinctively Jeremianic but contains typical lament psalms terminology and elements. In these lines, the first singer reappears to finish his interrupted lament begun in vss 1–24. In vss 52–66, he describes his human enemy (vss 52–54, 61–63), refers to his previous calling upon YHWH for help and YHWH's hearing (vss 55–57), remembers YHWH's former seeing and saving action (vss 58–60), and offers an imperative plea regarding his enemies (vss 64–66). Thus, the first singer of Lam 3 continues his individual lament, after the interruption of other voices, only now he moves beyond his previous accusation of YHWH and trust in YHWH to more direct appeals for vengeance/justice against the human enemy. In this last matter, his lament is not unlike those of Jerusalem's poet in Lam 1:22 and Lam 2:22.

One may be tempted to identify the singer of Lam 3:52–66 as Jeremiah by *literally* interpreting a few key lines and terms. That is, the singer refers to his being thrown into a pit (בור), something which the narrative of the book of Jeremiah conveys happened to the prophet (Jer 38:6). However, other characters in the Hebrew Bible also suffered such a fate (Joseph in Gen 37:20, Absalom in 2 Sam 18:17, even the group of men at Mizpeh in Jer 41:7). More importantly, it is not unusual for lament psalmists to refer to such an experience of being thrown into a "pit" (e.g., Pss 28:1, 30:3, 40:3, 88:5–7, 143:7; cf. Jer 18:20, 22 [שׁוחה]; Isa 24:22, Zech 9:11).

On the other hand, Jeremiah's own laments also contain several of the same terms found in Lam 3:58–63: in Jer 11:19–20 ("my cause," ריבי; "vengeance," נקמה; "plot plots" or "plan plans," חשבו

מחשבות); in Jer 15:10, 15 ("strife/dispute," ריב; "vengeance," הנקם; "insult," חרפה); in Jer 18:18 ("plot plots," נחשבה . . . מחשבות); and in Jer 20:8, 10, 12 ("insult," חרפה; "vengeance," נקמה; "my cause," ריבי). But again, these particular terms are also typically found in many lament psalms (e.g., ריב in Pss 18:44, 35:1, 43:1, 55:10, 119:154; נקמה in Pss 18:48, 79:10, 94:1; חשב in Pss 10:2, 35:4, 36:5, 41:8, 56:6, 140:3; חרפה in Pss 22:7, 31:12, 109:25, 44:14, 39:8, 69:20–21, 71:13, 74:22, 79:12, 89:51, and 119:22). Thus these terms cannot be said to be characteristically Jeremianic; they alone are indeterminate for identifying him as the singer of Lam 3:52–66.

Conclusion: Lamentations 3

Unlike Lam 1 and 2, Lam 3 contains four different poetic singers. The first singer (vss 1–24) is a new one and his words also close the chapter (vss 52–66). His self-identification as a "man" precludes him being Jerusalem's poet (in Lam 1–2), who is female. That this is a new singer and not Jeremiah is evident in his lack of terminology, imagery, and style characteristic of Jeremiah's poetry in Lam 1–2 and the book of Jeremiah. Indeed, the singer of Lam 3:1–24 draws primarily upon stock lament psalm terminology, though he does participate in its radical intensification to accuse YHWH, as Jeremiah and Jerusalem's poet have done. Thus, he continues the severe complaint against YHWH begun by Jerusalem's poet in the first two chapters. His subsequent brief appeal to YHWH in 3:19, however, gives way to something heretofore unseen in Lamentations—reference to YHWH's *positive* attributes. Still using the lament genre, he remembers YHWH's covenantal love and mercy, and is thereby able to move from despair to hope and even praise (vss 21–24).

Another new poetic singer enters the dialogue in vss 25–41, responding directly to the first singer about "hope" (vs 26). This singer, however, instead of accusing, *defends* YHWH. Moreover, he/she critiques any "complaining" against YHWH (vs 39) and advocates keeping silent before YHWH's punishment. YHWH will be "good" to the one who *silently* hopes for YHWH's help. This theological perspective is diametrically opposed to the attitude of the previous singer who came to a hopeful state precisely by lamenting. The second singer's perspective, however, advocates further confession (vss 40–41).

Jerusalem's poet, on the other hand, interrupts this second singer at vs 43 with an angry confession and immediately utters another complaint against YHWH: "You have not forgiven!" Moreover, she states that YHWH refuses to hear prayer. Her final line (vs 45) accuses YHWH of mistreating the people. At this point, Jeremiah rejoins the dialogue with more description of the enemies' treatment of the people; he then resumes weeping in order to gain YHWH's attention (vss 46–51). The chapter closes with the first singer's conclusion of his individual lament.

It may be said that Lam 3 begins to restore more of the traditional elements of the lament genre to the dialogue, that is, remembrance of YHWH's positive attributes and vow of confidence. Jeremiah and Jerusalem's poet, however, maintain their previous perspectives of urgent complaining against YHWH and of trying to gain a divine hearing and response.

Since Lam 4 will be seen to have much in common with Jeremiah's communal dirges in Lam 1 and 2, and since Lam 5 is a rather straightforward communal lament, the following section will treat these last two chapters more briefly.

Lamentations 4

> Perhaps the war has been won, at last,
> both on the battlefield and "on the table,"
> but not in the growling stomachs of
> those who leave their babies in cradles,
> run out before 6 a.m., half-asleep
> looking for a store which has milk or bread.
> They stand in line for hours
> hoping to get something before the babies awake . . .
>
> Biljana Obradović, "Swells"[60]

> We watch farmers waiting on the road for truckers
> to stop, let them buy some gas to go to their fields,
> get into the combines and get the wheat,
> golden . . . sell it so that Serbs can have enough flour for the winter.
> The sanctions have killed many, but we will survive!

[60] In *Frozen Embraces*, 168.

> . . . My childhood friend, Nena, newly married, with a son
> says she was lucky she had milk in her breasts.
> Her son Dušan . . . would have died . . .
> My best friend, Jovan, lived through the winter
> on bread and lard, he didn't have a job,
> his father doesn't have a pension, skinnier now,
> he still receives humanitarian aid, a loaf of bread a day. . . .
>
> Biljana Obradović, "Box of Matches for a Pension"[61]

Just as Jeremiah alternates between communal dirge and first person expressions of mourning in the book of Jeremiah, so too in Lamentations he shifts away from first person mourning speech (Lam 3:48–51) back to communal dirge to begin Lam 4 (vss 1–16). His is not the only voice in this chapter, however. Once again a voice speaking for "the people" arises using "we" language in 4:17–20. Previously, across Lam 3:40–47, three voices—an unidentified individual, Jerusalem's poet, and Jeremiah—were all presented as speaking *for* the people. Thus, one may ask whether the poet in Lam 4:17–20 is one of those previous three, or another new poet. The analysis below will present evidence that it is *Jerusalem's poet* again, continuing her speech from Lam 3:42–45 on her people's behalf.[62] The following is an outline of poetic singers in Lam 4.

Outline of Poetic Singers

Lamentations 4

vss 1–16	Jeremiah
vss 17–20	Jerusalem's poet
vss 21–22	Jeremiah

[61] Ibid., 64–67. Severe hunger and starvation depicted in Lam 4 is the consequence of being under a military siege. In these poems by Obradović, people suffer hunger and starvation due to an embargo, the economic siege placed upon Serbia by outside countries to limit the power of its then-dictator.

[62] That Jeremiah's voice arguably can be identified as the more objective, third person communal dirge singer in Lam 4 contrasts him to this other voice's point of view as belonging to the people. Neither is a case made that this latter voice should be identified with the sapiential voice who advocated silence in Lam 3:25–41.

Lamentations 4:1–16: Jeremiah's Communal Dirge

The first 16 verses of Lam 4 may be regarded as Jeremiah's poetic voice for the following reasons pertaining to the key areas of genre, content, imagery, technique, and terminology (see further details below). First, the chapter marks a return to the communal dirge genre, with which Jeremiah also opened Lam 1 and 2. Second, the poetry returns to the content of Jeremiah's earlier preoccupation, children dying in the streets (Lam 2). Third, this poetry, like Jeremiah's in Lam 1, 2, and 3, resumes the use of double meaning (already four instances in Lam 4:1–2). Fourth, this poetry draws less upon lament formulas and more upon *prophetic* speech traditions (4:1–2, 6, 9, 11, 13, 21–22). Fifth, the poetry resumes use of Jeremiah's favored term of endearment, "Daughter of My People" (4:3, 6, 10).

Jeremiah opens the communal dirge of Lam 4, as in chapters 1 and 2, with "Alas!" ("How!", איכה). As in Lam 1:1–2, 6–8 and 2:1, Jeremiah uses the contrast motif of the dirge to render the former glory of the people and their present miserable state (4:1–3). Just as Jeremiah had said YHWH "beclouded" D. Zion in Lam 2:1, in Lam 4:1 he says the "gold" has "grown dim." In 4:1b–2, he amplifies the "gold" metaphor to further elaborate on the deaths of the *children* of Zion:

The "sacred stones" (אבני) tumble down/are poured out (שפך)
  at the head of every street; (1b)
The precious sons (בני) of Zion,[63]
  worth their weight in fine gold.[64] (2a)

In returning to emphasize the fate of the children, Jeremiah employs the term "sons" (בני) instead of "children" (עולל) in order to create a wordplay with "sacred stones" (אבני), both tumbling to their demise. Note his previous references to such deaths of children, and the "pouring out" (שפך)[65] of their lives in "the squares" or "streets" of the city in Lam 2:11 and 12.[66] "Worth their weight" renders the

[63] See YHWH's use of the term "precious" in the book of Jeremiah (15:19 and 20:5), including reference to Ephraim as a "precious son" (31:20).

[64] NRSV.

[65] See Jeremiah's use of this term "pour out" also in other imagery in Lam 2:4, 11 and 19.

[66] YHWH tells Jeremiah to "pour out" his wrath upon the "children in the streets/squares" in Jer 6:11; see also Jer 9:20.

verb, to "weigh" (סלא).[67] Yet it can also be spelled סלה (as in Job 28:16, 19). With his proclivity for double meaning, Jeremiah likely intends the ironic hearing of the homonym (סלה), with its opposite meaning, to "make light of" or "toss aside"[68]—that is, the sons of Zion, precious as gold, are nevertheless "tossed aside" in the streets, paralleling "they are poured out/tumble down." Moreover, they are tossed aside/rejected (סלה), instead of being 'forgiven' (סלח; called for by Jerusalem's poet just prior in Lam 3:42). This rhetorical interplay reflects the process of the inspired oral poet in the context, hearing earlier speeches and imaginatively composing and performing new speeches in dialogue. Next he adds another simile:

> *How* (איכה) they are *planned* (נחשבו)
> to become vessels of sherd (לנבלי־חרשׂ)—
> the work of a *potter's* (יוצר) hands! (2b)

Jeremiah likely draws upon several prior prophetic traditions and speeches to create double meaning and imagery here. The phrase "vessels of sherd" appears only here in the Hebrew Bible The very unusual term "vessels" (נבלי)[69] sounds like the word for "corpse" (נבלה). Isaiah (5:25) had said of YHWH's smiting Jerusalem, "their *corpses* (נבלתם) were like refuse *in the streets*." Perhaps that poetic phrase of Isaiah, along with the reference to YHWH making the people "refuse" in Lam 3:45, reminds Jeremiah of the analogous image he was shown by YHWH of the slain people as discarded "vessels of sherd."[70] According to Jer 18, YHWH had Jeremiah go down to the

[67] This spelling of the verb (to "weigh") is a *hapax*. Both spellings appear as a *pu!al*.

[68] See the use of this term (סלה) by Jerusalem's poet in Lam 1:15, where her mighty warriors are "tossed aside" after being cut down/harvested by YHWH.

[69] נבל ("vessel") occurs in Isa 30:14 (with חרשׂ), Jer 13:12 and 48:12.

[70] Jeremiah's turn of phrase may include another ironic wordplay within "vessels of sherd" (חרשׂ) if the close-sounding חרשׁ, meaning "speechlessness" or "muteness," is heard, especially in light of the concern of Lam 3 about how to speak or keep silent before YHWH. That is, in Lam 4:1–2 the sons of Zion tumble down (lie dead in the streets), like "corpses of speechlessness"/vessels of sherd. This meaning would relate to Second Isaiah's use of the potter/pottery metaphors for divine maker/people (Isa 45:9, 11), where YHWH says the sherd (חרשׂ) should not speak back or question the Potter: "Woe to you who strive with your Potter, the potsherd with the sherd-Shaper of '*adâmâh*'; does the clay say to its Potter, 'What are you making (תעשׂה)?' or 'Your work has no handles'?" . . . Thus says YHWH, Holy One of Israel and its Potter: "Will you question me about my children ("sons," בני), or command me about the work of my hands?" Also cf. YHWH's ironic use of the term "corpse" (נבלה) for the "detestable" idols (שקוציהם) of other gods (Jer 16:18) which the people make, but which *are unable to speak* (Jer 10:5).

potter's house where the potter was at work, reshaping pieces on the wheel or breaking them for discard. YHWH has Jeremiah tell the people, "See, I am a potter shaping (יוצר) evil against you and *planning* a plan (חשׁב . . . מחשׁבה) against you" (18:11). In the narrative of Jer 19:1–13, YHWH had Jeremiah buy a potter's *sherd* (יוצר חרשׂ) flask and go to the *Potsherd* (החרסות) Gate of Jerusalem. After a judgment speech against the people, that "their dead bodies" (נבלתם) will become food to birds and animals, Jeremiah breaks the flask into sherds and says on YHWH's behalf: "Accordingly I will break this people and this city as I break the potter's jar (כלי היוצר) which cannot again be mended . . ." (vs 11).

The poet's use of the term of endearment for Jerusalem, *Daughter of My People*, in the next verse (3), as well as in vss 6 and 10, further identifies him as Jeremiah. Moreover, vs 4 also serves to identify Jeremiah, as he continues emphasizing his earlier concern for the *children's* suffering, and expands the image from Lam 2:11–12 of the thirst and hunger of "children" (עולל) and "infants" (יונק) fainting in the city squares. He adds,

> The tongue of the infant (יונק) clings
> to the roof of its mouth for thirst.
> The children (עוללים) ask for bread;
> no one is dispersing it to them. (Lam 4:4b)

With vs 6, Jeremiah refers to the iniquity and punishment of *Daughter of My People* in terms of another city "overturned":

> The chastisement of *Daughter of My People* has become greater
> than the punishment of Sodom;
> The one overturned (ההפוכה) in a moment,
> though no hands attacked her.[71] (Lam 4:6)

Beyond reference to the city of Sodom in Genesis, it was primarily *the prophets* who referred to the proverbial sin and fate of Sodom in their rhetoric (Am 4:11; Isa 1:9–10; 3:9; 13:19; Je 23:14; 49:18; 50:40; Ezek 16:46–56; Zeph 2:9). Four of these speeches also use the term "overturn" (הפך), including YHWH's judgment speeches in Jer 49:18 and 50:40.[72] This evidence further supports a prophetic voice here in Lam 4:6.

[71] Cf. Jeremiah's reference to "cities overthrown" (הפך) by YHWH, in his lament in Jer 20:16. Cf. the "overturning" of Sodom in Deut 29:22; see also Deut 32:32.
[72] Also Am 4:11 and Isa 13:19.

The poet's imagery, terminology, and wordplay in Lam 4:9 are *almost exact* with Jeremiah's rhetoric in Jer 14:18.

Better off are those *stabbed* by the *sword* (חללי־חרב)
than those *stabbed* by *hunger* (חללי־רעב),
who are drained,[73] wounded[74]
for lack of produce from the *field*. (Lam 4:9)

If I go out into *the field*,
look! those *stabbed* by the *sword* (חללי־חרב);[75]
And if I enter the city,
look! the sicknesses of *hunger* (תחלואי רעב [> חלא]).[76] (Jer 14:18)

Together, these lyrics of the poet Jeremiah can be paraphrased, "Better are those who die *immediately* by the sword *in the field* than those who die *slowly* of hunger in the city, deprived of the produce *of the field*." Thus deprived, mothers even "boil their children" for food, in the "*crushing of Daughter of My People*" (Lam 4:10). With vs 10, Jeremiah brings this section of the communal dirge to a close with its graphic and morbid images.

While Jeremiah has noted the people's "iniquity" as one cause of their suffering and destruction, with vs 11 he gives a summary statement of the divine cause behind it, using familiar imagery:

YHWH has spent his *hot rage*;
[YHWH] has poured out his *burning anger*;
[YHWH] kindled a *fire* in Zion
that consumed her foundations. (Lam 4:11)

BLAMING THE LEADERS

You lied to us. Told us there was a future.
My generation, others to come, believed in you,
trusted every word you said, all promises
of peace, brotherhood, of unity, oneness,
and now we have nothing to live for—
now we cannot get married, bear children,

[73] "Drain" or "flow" is from the root זוב, highly ironic here in light of its famous use in the phrase, "a land *flowing* with milk and honey" (see Jer 11:5).

[74] D. Hillers notes the parallel use of the terms "stabbed" (חלל) and "wounded" (קדר) in Jer 51:4; *Lamentations*, 141.

[75] See YHWH's wordplay with "sword" (חרב) and "drought" (חרב) in Jer 50:35–38.

[76] See also רעב and חרב closely paired together in the poetry of Jer 5:12. Prose texts in the book of Jeremiah often pair רעב and חרב (e.g., Jer 11:22; 14:12, 15–16; 16:4; 21:7, 9), though without the precise poetic wordplay with the verb חלל as in Jer 14 and Lam 4. Cf. Ezek 5:16–17; 6:11–12.

now we have to defend our ethnicity
that we suddenly seem to possess . . .
When today you desire our bodies to kill others,
fight those that once, only a few minutes ago,
were us? They were us and we them.

Biljana Obradović, "Another Lost Generation"[77]

While Jeremiah had referred to the failure of Jerusalem's prophets to warn of her people's wrongdoings and thus help avert disaster (Lam 2:14), in 4:12–16 he moves to a more penetrating explanation of why YHWH has allowed the devastation of Jerusalem. As the Babylonians, the enemies from without, burst through the city gates, the real enemies are already residing within:

The kings of the earth did not believe,[78]
  nor all the inhabitants of the world,
  that foe or enemy could enter
    the gates of Jerusalem. (12)
It is for the sins of her prophets,
  the iniquities of her priests,
  who poured out in her midst,
    blood of the righteous. (13)
They *wander* (נעו)[79] blindly in the streets,
    defiled (נגאלו) with blood;
    no one can touch their clothes. (14)

Jeremiah's imagery of the prophets and priests shedding righteous blood, thus "defiling" themselves (נגאלו), echoes his earlier imagery of D. Zion "defiled/made impure" (נדה; Lam 1:17) with blood, though that was *because* she had been crushed by YHWH (as in a winepress; Lam 1:15). Here in Lam 4:14, YHWH's representatives (priests and prophets) are accused of shedding blood. Jeremiah has inverted the blood image by focusing upon the perpetrators who supposedly were to represent YHWH.[80] He expands upon this imagery with priests and prophets:

[77] *Frozen Embraces*, 54. Below Jeremiah will suggest that the leadership of Judah has divided the people and brought their destruction.

[78] A poet from former Yugoslavia, Iva Šarčević, writes of those neighboring European countries who could not believe war had come again to his country; "Believe", in *Prayers Unheard: A Collection of Poems from the Former Yugoslavia*, ed. Eleanor Cave (Huddersfield, England: E. Cave, 1996).

[79] The root is נוע.

[80] Cf. the imagery by 2nd Isaiah of YHWH's blood-soaked, defiled (גאל) clothing after returning from battle in Isa 63:3.

"Turn aside! Unclean!" people call at them;
"Away! Away! Do not touch!"
Indeed, they flee—even *wander as fugitives* (נצו גם־נעו)!
Among the nations, it is said, "They no longer sojourn." (15)

With a stunning rhetorical stroke, Jeremiah casts the priests and prophets *as Cain*, of whom it was said, "You will be *a fugitive and a wanderer* (נע ונד) on the earth" (Gen 4:12). In this haunting scene, after complicity in shedding blood, the priests and prophets in Lamentations are sentenced to "flee—even *wander as fugitives*" (נצו גם־נעו). The rhetorical technique appearing in both texts is called a *farrago*, wherein, according to J. Sasson, "two usually alliterative words combine to give a meaning other than their constituent parts" (e.g., תהו ובהו in Gen 1:2).[81] In Lam 4:15, Jeremiah exploits the Gen 4 farrago to create a new one, yet intentionally retains the original meaning while piling on a surplus meaning for this context. I have argued elsewhere that a subtext with a Cain and Abel oral tradition may be traced within poetic texts in the book of Jeremiah, a subtext which emerges again here in Lam 4.[82]

With the next line (vs 16), Jeremiah carries forward the parallels: just as with Cain who lamented to YHWH, "From your *face* I will be hidden," (Gen 4:14), and "Cain went away from the *face* of YHWH" (4:16), so now with priests and prophets before YHWH:

The face of YHWH scatters them;
[YHWH] will no longer look upon them;
They [the people, the nations] do not lift up *the faces* of the priests;[83]
they show no grace to the elders.[84] (16)

[81] Jack Sasson, "Time . . . to Begin," in *"Sha'arei Talmon": Studies in the Bible, Qumran, and the Ancient Near East Presented to Shemaryahu Talmon*, eds. M. Fishbane and E. Tov (Winona Lake, Ind.: Eisenbrauns, 1992), 188. NRSV apparently sees the connection with Cain and Abel in Lam 4:15, for it translates this phrase as "fugitives and wanderers," as though it were exactly the same as that in Gen 4:12 and 14. The translation in this study attempts to capture the ring of the familiar phrase as well as its aggadic/poetic modification.

[82] Nancy C. Lee, "Exposing a Buried Subtext."

[83] The verb is נשׂא (meaning to "honor/accept/forgive"); see Isa 3:3, and Gen 32:20 (where the expression refers to Jacob's hope that Esau will "accept," even "forgive" him); see a similar expression in Jer 52:31 explaining king Jehoiachin's being honored in Babylon ("his head lifted").

[84] This translation of vs 16b is a slight correction of my translation in "Exposing a Buried Subtext," 121. See the translation in the Stone edition of the Tanach (1998).

Unlike the biblical story of Cain's treatment by YHWH, including a measure of divine protection in his "wandering" life, the book of Lamentations keeps silent on YHWH's further response to the priests (and prophets) who go into exile.

Lamentations 4:17–20: Jerusalem's Poet Responds for the People

In vs 17 another poet answers Jeremiah's aggadic imagery, giving the people's point of view. It is evident that this poet "hears" and carries on the Cain and Abel imagery begun by Jeremiah by *identifying the people with Abel* in need of rescue. The genre is still the dirge, appropriate for describing their death.[85]

Still our eyes grew weak (looking)
  for our help—*Abel* (הבל) *futility*!—[86]
in our watchpost, we watched
  for a nation not saving.
They dogged our steps,[87]
  so we could not go in our squares.
Our end drew near, our days were finished,
  for our end had come.
Our pursuers (רדפינו) were swifter
  than the eagles in the heavens;
Upon the mountains they chased us;[88]
  in the wilderness they lay in wait for us. (4:17–19)

The key evidence that this poet initially renders the Cain and Abel subtext is in the wordplay with the appellative/noun הבל (Abel/futility), which creates a Janus parallelism in vs 17. The pivot term הבל at once suggests the name "Abel" in light of the previous aggadic

[85] The voice of the people continues in Lam 5, where the survivors utilize the *lament* genre.

[86] הבל appears here with pausal lengthening with the *'atnah* as it does in Gen 4:2 where the character Abel is first introduced; in that text the appellative appears syntactically as part of a double accusative. NRSV's translation here in 4:17 is questionable as it renders the stative noun הבל as though it were an adverb modifying how the people watched ("Our eyes failed, ever watching *vainly* [הבל] for help"). Yet the term הבל is never used elsewhere as an adverb in the Hebrew Bible. Moreover, the term also is exclamatory in its identification of Abel and in its emphatic double meaning; cf. C. Westermann who translates הבל ("in vain!") as an exclamation; *Lamentations*, 195.

[87] NRSV.

[88] See the study cited (N. Lee, "Exposing a Buried Subtext") and its reference to the *Midrash Haggadol*'s account: "When Abel . . . began to shepherd the flock, Cain *chased after* him [רדף אחריו] from *mountain* to valley and from valley to *mountain*. . . ."

imagery; it reiterates (at the end of the colon) the person whose "eyes" are the subject in the first colon, whose eyes grow weak with death as he waits for help from his mortal wound.[89] Yet, as the pivot word in the Janus parallelism, הבל also begins the thought of the second cola: "futility" is in the watchpost, as the people look for help from political allies not forthcoming.[90] Thus the pivot term הבל also serves a double grammatical function: it serves as an object at the end of the first colon and a subject at the beginning of the second colon.

Lam 4 is the only chapter of Lamentations that does not contain a "plea" to YHWH for help;[91] indeed, the larger text suggests that all pleas have gone unanswered, and no help is forthcoming. This poet's preoccupation with an *unanswered plea for help* as the enemies "pursue" (רדף) them, in 4:18–19, makes it at least plausible that *Jerusalem's poet* has once again picked up the dialogue. In Lam 3:43, Jerusalem's poet spoke of the people being "pursued" unto death while YHWH refused to answer their pleas.[92]

Lamentations 4:21–22: Jeremiah's Oracle

In Lam 4, Jeremiah shifts the focus from Jerusalem to neighboring Edom (vss 21–22). With typical prophetic and Jeremianic imagery/terminology (also found in his oracle against Edom in Jer 49:7–22; "cup" of judgment, "uncover," "punish," "like an eagle," "like Sodom

[89] Similar to the Cain and Abel theme in Jeremiah's rhetoric in Lam 4 is the destructive theme of "brother against brother" that appears in Marija Koprivnak's poem about the destruction of Mostar in Bosnia. In this selection, she addresses the persona of Mostar:

> Who cares now for the words of your great poet, Aleks Santić,
> whose birthplace was until recently the meeting place
> of God's people of all nations,
> and which is now being looted by lawless men?
> Your son Aleks wrote, in truth, that we are all brothers,
> three nations—three branches—of one tree.
> See—within you brother has risen up against brother . . .

Transl. Janet Berković and Ružica Papen, in *Ratni blagoslovi*, 28–31. The poet goes on to console Mostar, with a quote from Lam 3:16–26.

[90] Numerous Jeremiah texts also call the false gods or idols of other nations by the same term (הבל; Jer 8:19; 10:3, 8, 15; 14:22; 16:19; 51:18).

[91] C. Westermann, *Lamentations*, 199.

[92] Finally, in Lam 4:20, Jerusalem's poet indirectly quotes the people's speech referring to their king who has been taken captive.

and Gomorrah"), Jeremiah warns Edom of its future judgment (4:21, 22b). Within the last line (and in the last acrostic element of the book), Jeremiah addresses D. Zion directly, beginning with the last Hebrew letter of the alphabet, ת, with the Hebrew word תם—"finished."

> Finished (תם) is your punishment, D. Zion;
> [YHWH] will not keep on exiling you. (22)

Thus, while the book of Lamentations contains no response from YHWH to the numerous laments, it does contain a brief consolation oracle in 4:22, finally, from the prophet Jeremiah. The end of suffering will come.

Lamentations 5: A New Poet Sings a Communal Lament

while still trembling on the edge of time
and in the depth of space
we heard the throb of our name
and the flow of the atoms
of our genes—gehennas

already on euphrates
at the tower of babel
you lined us up
into first ranks

we planted a tree amid cindered rafters
and on its top we stuck
glagolitic writing
and we have been waiting with no response
for eons on end

are we really the ones you will use
to put out the flame of the bush?

where is your abode
why are you not among us too
since you are everywhere
and if you are also with us
why do we not see that we are not alone?

Boris Arapović, croatian psalm 137[93]

[93] Trans. I. Jerić, In *Between Despair and Lamentation*, 19.

While Jeremiah closes Lam 4 with words of comfort about what YHWH will do, the poetic singer of Lam 5 moves to a direct plea/lament to YHWH again. Lam 5 is a communal lament from the people's point of view who are left behind in the aftermath of devastated Jerusalem and Judah. The singer of Lam 5 carries the insistence upon lament in the book to its fullest form thus far (including confession).[94]

While at first glance one might conclude that such a lament singer must be Jerusalem's Poet uttering a last song, there are two reasons why it is unlikely that this is the same singer. The overall content and 'pace' of the lament is suggestive of people left in the land in the aftermath of war, resigned to moving slowly through the detailed, everyday hardships in their lives. Thus, the song seems to reflect a later time than the first four songs. Also, the emphatic alphabetic acrostic of the first four songs falls away, leaving only a 22—verse acrostic, which is different in style, yet still familar to the singer (or later scribe?). Also, this is the only song in Lamentations that is not dialogic, suggesting a different performance context.

However, this singer does speak to a key theme emphasized in the other songs, perhaps being aware of them. The singer ends the entire song with a question about YHWH's anger as reason for their abandonment. However, there is a notable shift in this singer's description of distress, compared to Jeremiah and Jerusalem's poet. This singer refrains from the long, severe accusations against YHWH voiced earlier. Yet neither does the poet include lines describing YHWH's characteristic saving actions customarily included in a lament to motivate YHWH to act in the present. This absent element suggests a tone of resignation (perhaps defiance) toward YHWH who does not elicit the poet's praise of former divine saving action.

While this singer is not Jerusalem's poet, there are clues that the lament singer may be one of the women. Certain details in the song are suggestive of a woman's point of view. For example, in Lam 5:2–16, the poet speaks of the people's losses, yet in first-person speech, of "our" losses—of inheritance, homes, and family members, and orphans and widows left behind (vss 2–3). The perspective hints at a woman's perspective, lamenting the state of things as a survivor

[94] Dobbs-Allsopp notes that while communal lament is not absent from Mesopotamian lamentations, neither is it very common; *Weep, O Daughter of Zion*, 37.

after war. Note the mention of the occupation of their destroyed homes by "strangers," the foreign invaders (vs. 2).

In vs 4, a female perspective may also be reflected, since women typically collected water (e.g., Gen 24:11–20; Exod 2:16; John 4:6–7; a similar argument might be made for the activity of securing "bread," vss 6 and 9). The singer speaks of how women are raped (vs 11). She notes how "young men are compelled to grind" with the mill-stone (vs 13), an ironic reversal of affairs, since this was normally an occupation of women and slaves (see especially Exod 11:5; Ju 9:53; 2 Sam 11:21; Isa 47:2; Matt 24:41).[95] In vs 12–14 she refers in *third* person to the actions of "princes," "elders," "young men," "boys," "old men," and "young men who have left their music" (14b); yet in the very next line (vs 15a) where one would expect the counterpart description of women's activity, she gives a statement in *first* person plural: "the joy of *our* hearts has ceased; *our* dancing has been turned to mourning,"[96] activities often ascribed to women singers. In vs 17, she says "our hearts are *faint/weak* (דוה)."[97] Jerusalem's poet used the same term in Lam 1:13, and in 1:22 ("my heart is faint/weak").[98] Finally, the poet in the second half of 5:17 says "our eyes have grown dim"; this echoes Jerusalem's poet's image of the people's eyes growing weak in 4:17 above. In sum, numerous lines of Lam 5 carry subtleties of a female point of view, at times echoing terminology used by Jerusalem's poet in her songs.

In 5:19, the singer affirms YHWH's sovereignty.

> But you, YHWH, will reign forever,
> your throne from generation to generation. (19)

She then moves to typical "why" questions of the complaint, and her tone becomes sardonic as she contrasts YHWH's *everlasting* reign with YHWH's *perpetual* forgetting of the people:

[95] See "mill" in *HarperCollins Bible Dictionary*, rev. ed., ed. Paul J. Achtemeier (HarperSanFrancisco, 1996), 684–85.

[96] Dobbs-Allsopp notes the use of virtually this same phrase in several Mesopotamian lamentations over cities where "song and singing are turned into weeping and lamentation"; *Weep, O Daughter of Zion*, 41.

[97] A rare term also used to describe the unwell feeling/state of menstruation (Lev 12:2; 15:33; 20:18; perhaps also Isa 30:22) or illness in general (Ps 41:4; Job 6:7; Dt 7:15; 28:60).

[98] See Isaiah's similar use with the "heart" in Isa 1:5.

> Why do you forget us on and on?
> Why do you forsake us for such a length of days? (20)

She then offers typical imperative pleas:

> Restore us to yourself, YHWH,
>   that we may be restored.
> Renew our days as of old . . . (21)[99]

However, while Lam 4 ended with Jeremiah's assurance that YHWH will no longer punish D. Zion or keep her people in exile, this singer's final line in Lam 5:22 ends on an ambiguous note with no typical avowal of confidence that YHWH will choose to restore them. Indeed, she implies that YHWH's anger is still standing in the way.

> . . . renew our days as before.
>   For even if (כי אם) you had utterly rejected us (מאס מאסתנו),
>   you have already raged (קצפת) sufficiently against us (עד־מאד).[100] (21b–22)

The singer uses the term "reject" (מאס), which Jerusalem's poet used in 3:45 ("you have made us dirt and *refuse*," מאוס. In sum, the *individual* lament of Jerusalem's poet from the book of *Jeremiah* (10:24) has grown into *the people's* lament by the end of Lamentations.

[99] She echoes the lamenter in Lam 3:23, who remembered that YHWH has the power to make things "*new*."

[100] Following the Stone edition translation of the Tanach (1998). I am grateful to Larry Mattera for calling my attention to this more nuanced translation. Commentators differ on how to render this final important line of Lamentations (see Hillers, *Lamentations*, for a discussion of the options, 160–61). Hillers suggests four possible translations of כי אם: (1) "for if," introducing a conditional cause followed by a consequence (the Stone translation above fits this option); (2) "unless," as expressing a possibility that is *uncertain* or in doubt; (3) translated as a question; and (4) "but instead," as an adversative (ibid.).

CHAPTER SIX

CONCLUSION

"My anguish, my anguish . . . I cannot keep silent."
Jerusalem's Poet[1]

"Pour out your heart like water before the face of YHWH!"
Jeremiah[2]

"But Zion said, 'The Lord has forsaken me,
my Lord has forgotten me.'

'Can a woman forget her nursing child,
or show no compassion for the child of her womb?
Even these may forget,
yet I will not forget you.
See, I have inscribed you on the palms of my hands;
your walls are continually before me.
Your builders outdo your destroyers,
and those who laid you in waste
go away from you.
Lift up your eyes all around and see;
they all gather, they come to you.'"

2nd Isaiah for YHWH

This study opened with three women poets' personification of their cities—Sarajevo and Vukovar. We have seen how from ancient Ur, to Jerusalem, to contemporary South Slavic lands, poets and prophets often personify their towns to render their community's suffering. What does this long cross-cultural tradition of the poets have to say to the comfortable in modern nations? It reminds us of something important we are missing and at risk of losing—for where the city or village is felt to be a *persona*, a living entity, there is genuine community. That when any part of it is injured, the whole body really does suffer and calls for compassionate attention, intervention, and healing. The recent tragedy in New York and Afghanistan attests to

[1] Jer 4:19.
[2] Lam 2:19.

this reality, and likewise the larger risk, that desperate suffering in the world in the end will affect the whole human family. This study has used a methodology rooted in the study of folklore, specifically oral poetry, to analyze the biblical book of Lamentations. There, one poet, identified as Jeremiah based on his formulaic and individual style, described a personified Jerusalem and comforted her as she mourned the deaths of her inhabitants. Jerusalem's poet, whose poems and individual style in the context were identified as 'inscribed' in the book of Jeremiah, sang a response.

When ancient Hebrew prophets borrowed from the popular dirge genre to warn a (personified) city of coming destruction, or to mourn over its destruction, they were participating in the practices of a traditional oral culture. In this study, an oral poetic methodology has also allowed for comparisons of Lamentations to contemporary lament literature (especially from the former Yugoslavia). Integrated to this, a socio-rhetorical approach has considered how poetry works in context in Lamentations, suggestive for contemporary social contexts.

Avenues for Further Investigation

Beyond the artistry of the poetic singers of Lamentations, they raise some themes which might be highlighted here and brought into conversation with social contexts. First, Jerusalem's poet had adapted the individual lament prayer (typically found in biblical psalms) and employed it as a first-person lament to the deity on behalf of the city in crisis, calling for justice. Where does this phenomenon occur elsewhere, whether in ancient Mesopotamia,[3] other cultures, or even in contemporary contexts? We have seen how lament genres have been historically neglected by western or industrial society, media, religious liturgies, even scholarship, though they have played a constructive role in the popular life of traditional communities. Analogous to the way oral poetry can powerfully infuse literary poetry, the rhetoric of lament provides a powerful vehicle to give voice to a community being oppressed or suffering in crisis. Lament may serve not only as a voice of the faithful to appeal to God, but as an appeal

[3] In Mesopotamian lamentations the city goddess *primarily mourns* over her city (more than lamenting to the deity), and she is less a parallel to Jerusalem's poet than to *Jeremiah* who mourns over Jerusalem.

for social justice. When communities are in trouble, mechanisms are needed for the expression and hearing of lament and mourning (communal dirge forms) to prevent worsening crisis. One such effort is seen in the women's group, Women in Black, formed in Israel, Belgrade, and elsewhere, that seeks to unite women and all people of different ethnoreligious backgrounds to protest political policies that lead to violence and war.

Second, in Lamentations, Jerusalem's poet and Jeremiah, by their songs, helped the community process grief after the devastation. How might the genre be employed in contemporary contexts?[4] When so often the victim becomes the victimizer, the persecuted the persecutor, how might traditional religious communities incorporate into their liturgies a 'singing' of lament that constructively helps process hurt and grief toward healing and wholeness? Surely African-American church traditions have discovered an important key here to the constructive role of lament in sorrow songs and spirituals that continue to serve their communities in modified dynamic forms in the present day.

Third, a role of poetry/song in Lamentations in the aftermath of destruction of Jerusalem was to provide the survivors an arena for disagreeing voices to process the cause of what happened, to deal with what was both a social tragedy and a theological crisis. Related to this, we may ask to what extent the oral poetic, composing process by temple singers in ancient Israel allowed them to introduce new theological questions or developments. That is, apart from singers who simply sang the traditional, formulaic repertoire, were there lyricists who in their individual modifications of songs pushed the community to consider new theological possibilities about YHWH and themselves? The view that one's nation and city could be *arbitrarily* destroyed by one's deity was a view typically held in the ANE.[5] While Israel must have been influenced by this thinking, it appears that only in Israel was such a destruction interpreted as divine punishment for wrongdoing.[6] Jerusalem's poet, in the midst of crisis,

[4] David Steele has used the lament genre in Bosnia to help people and communities process grief and deal with injustice. How has the model worked and how might it be instructive for other contexts?

[5] Dobbs-Allsopp (*Weep, O Daughter of Zion*, 45) citing Albrektson (*History and the Gods*, 24–41).

[6] This point is brought out by Dobbs-Allsopp in his discussion of the element in

nuanced this belief by making a stunning theological challenge: "Correct (punish) me, YHWH, but with justice, and *not with your anger*, lest you belittle me" (Jer 10:24). Held in tension were the prophetic and retributive justice theologies on the one hand that injustice and idolatry brought on social collapse with insistence on the other hand that the suffering of innocent ones itself was unjust. In this regard, Jerusalem's poet and Jeremiah complain against God not only about innocent suffering but also that the 'punishment' is too severe. Thus Lamentations implicitly begins moving away from one aspect of traditional prophetic theology: the belief in retributive justice (held to by Deuteronomy, some Wisdom literature, such as Proverbs and some Psalms). That is, no longer will a simple understanding that God rewards the righteous and punishes the evil hold up in light of a major crisis, as the likely later dialogue in the book of Job attests. Yet Lamentations still holds in tension that there can be both individual innocence and corporate guilt. However, the book does nuance corporate guilt in the end by laying more blame upon the political and religious leaders of its capital city.

And this leads to a fourth theme emerging from Lamentations. Just who are these singers? They are a woman lament singer and a single outsider prophet who represent *the people*, whose rhetoric and song lyrics rooted in sound theology, responding to their life-threatening crisis, have eventually found their way into the community's *liturgical repertoire*. In that context, the socio-politico-religious leadership in Jerusalem had apparently come to hold an ideology that since Judah was God's 'chosen people,' no injustice practiced within itself would put that covenant in danger, no enemy could ever enter Jerusalem and defeat it, since Jerusalem was God's chosen city, and God was always, no matter what, on Israel's side (sometimes called the 'inviolability of Zion motif, or royal-Zionist ideology). In spite of it's internal debate about divine retribution, Lamentations insists upon giving the prophetic voice its say (a self-critique of its own nation).[7] In spite

Mesopotamian lamentations of the 'assignment of responsibility' for destruction (citing Gwaltney, 208–9); ibid., 52–53.

[7] In the final analysis, Lamentations says little about the invading enemy and does not scapegoat them. Indeed, in numerous texts, the invading Babylonians are YHWH's instrument of punishment (e.g., Jer 27:1–11; 34:1–3); thus the deity does not aim to favor one nation over another (cf. Isa 19:24).

of an ideological rhetoric of religious 'chosenness',[8] social collapse will be a consequence of injustice, and such a theology speaks to nations and communities everywhere.

Fifth, related to the socio-political role of traditional poetry or songs, it has been shown that women have been the primary performers of dirges across cultures and through history. In contexts where traditional dirges are still performed, to what extent has this genre been co-opted to serve destructive socio-political ends, for example in contexts of ethnic conflict, fueling endless cycles of violence by its call for vengeance in reaction to the deaths of members of its community? The Palestinian-Israeli conflict comes to mind. But, using Jahnow's category, what constitutes a "call for public justice"? Is it only for 'our people' or is it blind to ethnicity and race? What if a dirge singer sang for the death of someone in another ethnic group, and the injustice of it, thus *critiquing* interethnic violence? How shall religious traditions participate in this arena?

Sixth, an oral poetic method allows us to move beyond, or better, add to our knowledge of the *formulaic* aspects of prophetic poetry in the Hebrew Bible bequeathed by form and rhetorical criticism. With this method we may look at the poetry traditionally acribed to the different prophets and ask also what is *peculiar* about Isaiah's poetry in comparison to Jeremiah's? Using the criteria set forth here (of analyzing a prophet's uses of genre, images/themes, terminology, rhetorical technique, and content), we may gain a greater appreciation of the contributions of the *individual* Hebrew prophets.

South Slavic Voices: Dzevad Karahasan and Pontanima of Sarajevo

Dissident voices from this region have sought to critique destructive leadership and to reconstruct their cities and communities. In addition to all the poetic singers cited here, two additional voices will suffice to bring this study to a close. The first is Bosnian writer and

[8] This self-critical element in Israel aimed to prevent the dangerous identification (equation) of the people and its leadership *with God*. YHWH stands over against an independent Israel. One may especially credit biblical prophets for maintaining this separation, even in what was a theocracy.

literature professor, Dzevad Karahasan, writing about the destruction of his city, Sarajevo, and Bosnia.[9]

> I come from a destroyed country.... I used to take seriously diverse formalisms, structuralisms, constructivisms, deconstructivisms, and numerous other isms that my schooling forced me to confront. I took them seriously, believing that literature creates "pure" forms; that it has no connection with immediate reality.... I have become convinced that I was wrong, because literature ... is also greatly responsible for people's actions in immediate reality.... That is why sages and rulers have strived to control literature and to create an unnatural relationship wherein literature would serve the purposes of politics....
>
> I come from a destroyed country.... Misuse of the literary craft is responsible for that. The first form of misuse [is] ... art for art's sake ... that literary work has no content ... is a "pure form" ... that does not point to anything beyond itself ... completely free from any ethical questions.... [This] is responsible ... [for] contributing ... to the spread of general indifference in an indifferent world. For, let us not fool ourselves: the world is written first—the holy books say that it was created in words—and all that happens in it, happens in language first.... The second misuse of the literary craft is not so indirect; ... as "heroic" literature ... it actually respects all the rules except the fundamental one—that a craft must not be used for evil.... The hero's destiny ... does not reside in his character, but in the group he belongs to.... This motivational technique sanctifies the collectivity.... The political community appears as God and belonging to the political community looks like destiny.... The martyr's role ... as a series of individual decisions and acts [with] the appearance of free will is really a charade. This is how we arrived at a literature that presents the collective as divine....
>
> [The] misuse of my craft can only be described as a sin.... Because of that literature ... the cities burn now, children become invalids, everything human is being destroyed, abased, and annulled.... [L]eaders of the Serb nationalistic parties who have destroyed Yugoslavia ... have been profoundly influenced by writers and professors of literature.... I am not interested in their personal guilt ..., but in the culpability of my craft, the craft I cannot practice anymore, before answering some questions.

Finally, the traditional symbolism of the bridge in Bosnia is cultural, rhetorical, and spiritual. Thus the rebuilding from the ravages of

[9] Dzevad Karahasan, *Sarajevo, Exodus of a City*, transl. Slobodan Drakulić (New York: Kodansha Intercommunal, 1994), 67–86; Karahasan gives a long list of destructive literary works, especially heroic epic poetry, that flamed the war and genocide in Bosnia.

Members of Pontanima singers

war is not only being carried out with stones and mortar, but with *words*, constructive speech, with poetry and music lyrics that reconstitute something of a lost world while creating a new one. Such is the effort of the interethnic, interfaith Bosnian singing group *Pontanima* ("Spiritual Bridge") that has toured that country, Croatia, Italy, Austria, and the U.S.[10]

From Sarajevo, these singers who survived the war form a group whose performances try to facilitate healing through music. From the Serbian Orthodox, Croatian Roman Catholic, Bosniak Muslim, and Jewish communities in Sarajevo, the group's members perform sacred songs from every religious heritage; the singers exemplify acceptance of their own diversity, an acceptance once common in

[10] Founded by Fr. Ivo Marković, at the Franciscan monastery in Sarajevo. Another member of the group is Josip Katavić. He directed a number of these same singers and others in the community when they performed Mozart's Requiem during the war inside the ruins of the National Library in Sarajevo, performing with Jose Carreras.

the region before the war. In a sense, not unlike the suffering singers of biblical Lamentations, they gather together amidst the rubble and try to make sense of what happened. More than five years after the destruction, they find their songs are a spiritual bridge for transformation, from anguish to healing, from lament, eventually to praise. One of the most poignant songs these survivors of the destruction sing is "Mashpil Geim." They performed it and other powerful songs as they toured the U.S. last year, including at Elmhurst College. The song is a Bosnian Jewish lament based on the Hebrew lament prayer genre, in which the singers' voices in effect blend with the ancient Israelites', and with the few Jews left in Sarajevo after WWII, as they cry out to God for help and wait for a response from the God who rescues.[11] The lead singer, Dragana, was a Muslim woman who rendered it so powerfully that its beauty still rings in our memories, vibrates a world of meaning, reaches the truth of the universality that God (Allah) hears all human lament and suffering, when the true "Israel", to which the Bible points, becomes all humanity. I am reluctant to reduce the song to writing, but perhaps "the singer persists and the performance goes on,"[12] indeed, that the wounded cities and communities shall be healed, those silenced intruments and "pianos in shattered chambers" mended, made whole, mourning turned to singing.

He brings low the arrogant and raises the meek,
  frees the bound, rescues the humble,
  helps the needy, and answers his people when they cry to him.

Praise belongs to the supreme God, ever blessed be he.
Moses and the children of Israel chanted to you
  in song with great exultation,
and all proclaimed:
  "Who is like you, Lord, among the mighty,
  Who is like you, glorious in holiness,
    inspiring in praises, working wonders?"
All together they praised you;
they proclaimed your kingly power, saying,
  "The Lord shall reign for ever and ever."

[11] "Mashpil Geim" by Semjo Vinaver (1956), on the compact disc *Tanja Mira* (Mystery of Peace) by the Pontanima Choir (Sarajevo: the Franciscan Seminary, 1999).

[12] Thanks to John Miles Foley for giving us this great line.

Rock of Israel, rise up to the aid of Israel,
and fulfill your promised word to deliver Judah and Israel.
  "Our Redeemer, the Lord of hosts is his name,
  The Holy One of Israel."
Blessed are you, Lord who has redeemed Israel.

BIBLIOGRAPHY

Albrektson, Bertil. *Studies in the Text and Theology of the Book of Lamentations with a Critical Edition of the Peshitta Text.* Lund: CWK Gleerup, 1963.

Albright, W. F. "Some Oriental Glosses on the Homeric Problem." *American Journal of Archaeology* 54 (1950): 162–76.

Alexiou, Margaret. *The Ritual Lament in Greek Tradition.* Cambridge: Cambridge University Press, 1974.

Althann, Robert. *A Philological Analysis of Jeremiah 4–6 in the Light of Northwest Semitic.* Biblica et Orientalia 38. Rome: Biblical Institute Press, 1983.

Arant, Patricia. "Aspects of Oral Styles: Russian Traditional Oral Lament," *Canadian-American Slavic Studies* 15 (1981): 42–51.

Arapović, Borislav. *Iz noćnog dnevnika* [From the Diary of the Night]. Zagreb: Grafički zavod hrvatske, 1989.

———. *From Despair to Lamentation*, ed. Nancy C. Lee. Transl. Ivana Pozajić Jerić. Elmhurst: Elmhurst College, 2002.

———. "Telefax from Croatia" ["Telefaks iz Hrvatske"]. In *From Despair to Lamentation*, ed. Nancy C. Lee. Transl. Ivana Pozajić Jerić. Elmhurst: Elmhurst College, 2002.

Auerbach, Susan. "From Singing to Lamenting: Women's Musical Role in a Greek Village," in E. Koskoff, ed., *Women and Music in Cross-Cultural Perspective*, 25–43. Urbana, IL: University of Illinois, 1989.

Bail, Ulrike and Elke Seifert. Introduction: "Zur Person Hedwig Janhows." In *Feministische Hermeneutik und Erstes Testament*, u.a. Hedwig Jahnow. Stuttgart, Berlin, Köln: Verlag W. Kohlhammer, 1994.

Bailey, Wilma Ann. "The Sorrow Songs: Laments From Ancient Israel and the African-American Diaspora." Forthcoming in *Semeia.*

Baillet, M., J. T. Milik, and R. de Vaux. "Les 'Petites Grottes' De Qumrân." Vol. 3. *Discoveries in the Judaean Desert.* Oxford: Clarendon Press, 1962.

Balentine, Samuel. *The Hidden God: the Hiding of the Face of God in the Old Testament.* Oxford: Oxford University Press, 1983.

———. *Prayer in the Hebrew Bible: the Drama of Divine-Human Dialogue.* Minneapolis: Fortress Press, 1993.

Bauman, Richard and Charles L. Briggs. "Poetics and Performance as Critical Perspectives on Language and Social Life." *Annual Review of Anthropology* 19 (1990): 59–88.

Beal, Timothy K. "The System and the Speaking Subject in the Hebrew Bible: Reading for Divine Abjection." *Biblical Interpretation* 2, 2 (1994): 171–89.

Ben-Amos, Dan. *Folklore Genres.* Austin: Univ. of Texas Press, 1976.

———. "The Seven Strands of *Tradition*: Varieties in Its Meaning in American Folklore Studies." *Journal of Folklore Research* 21 (1984): 97–131.

Berger, Peter L. and Thomas Luckmann. *The Social Construction of Reality.* Garden City, N.Y.: Doubleday, 1966.

Biblija: Stari i Novi Zavjet [Croatian Bible]. Zagreb: Kršćanska Sadašnjost, 1994.

Birkeland, H. *Zum hebräischen Traditionswesen: Die Komposition der prophetischen Bhcher des Alten Testaments.* Oslo, 1938.

Biddle, Mark. "The City of Chaos and the New Jerusalem: Isaiah 24–27 in Context." *Perspectives in Religious Studies* 22 (1995): 5–12.

———. *Polyphony and Symphony in Prophetic Literature: Rereading Jeremiah 7–20.* Macon, Ga.: Mercer University Press, 1996.

———. "Lady Zion's Alter Egos: Isaiah 47.1–15 and 57.6–13 as Structural Counterparts." In *New Visions of Isaiah*, ed. Roy F. Melugin, Marvin A. Sweeney. Journal for the Study of the Old Testament Supplement 214. Sheffield: JSOT Press, 1996.

Brueggemann, Walter. "Jeremiah's Use of Rhetorical Questions." *Journal of Biblical Literature* 92 (1973): 358–74.

———. *The Prophetic Imagination.* Philadelphia: Fortress Press, 1978.

———. "The Costly Loss of Lament." *JSOT* 36 (1986): 57–71.

———. *Israel's Praise: Doxology Against Idolatry and Ideology.* Philadelphia: Fortress Press, 1988a.

———. *To Pluck Up, To Tear Down. Jeremiah.* International Theological Commentary. Grand Rapids: Eerdmans, 1988b.

———. *Finally Comes the Poet: Daring Speech for Proclamation.* Minneapolis: Fortress Press, 1989.

———. *A Commentary on Jeremiah: Exile and Homecoming.* Grand Rapids: Wm. B. Eerdmans, 1998.

———. *Theology of the Old Testament.* Minneapolis: Fortress Press, 1997.

Bynam, David E. "Of Sticks and Stones and Hapax Legomena Rhemata." In *Comparative Research on Oral Traditions: A Memorial for Milman Parry*, ed. J. M. Foley. Columbus, Ohio: Slavica, 1987.

Cannon, William W. "The Authorship of Lamentations." *Bibliotheca Sacra* 81 (1924): 42–58.

Carroll, Robert P. *Jeremiah, A Commentary.* Philadelphia: Westminster Press, 1986.

Caspi, Mishael Maswari and Julia Ann Blessing. *Weavers of the Songs: The Oral Poetry of Arab Women in Israel and the West Bank.* Washington, D.C.: ThreeContinents Press, 1991.

Caspi, Mishael. "'My Brother, Vein of My Heart:' Arab Laments for the Dead in Israel," *Folklore* 98 (1987): 28–40.

Cave, Eleanor, ed. *Prayers Unheard: A Collection of Poems from the Former Yugoslavia.* Huddersfield, England: E. Cave, 1996.

Chadwick, H. and N. *The Growth of Literature.* Vol. 2. Cambridge: Cambridge University Press, 1936.

Chang, Iris. *The Rape of Nanking: The Forgotten Holocaust of World War II.* Penguin Books, 1997.

Chicago Tribune. "Palestinian Funerals Trigger New Clashes with Israelies." October 29, 2000.

Cohen, A. ed. *Lamentations Rabbah.* In *Midrash Rabbah*, eds. H. Freedman and M. Simon. London: Soncino Press, 1939.

Cohen, Mark E. *Sumerian Hymnology: the Eršemma.* Hebrew Union College Annual Supplements, No. 2. Cincinnati, Ohio: Hebrew Union College, 1981.

———. *The Canonical Lamentations of Ancient Mesopotamia.* Potomac, Md.: Capital Decisions Limited, 1988.

Coote, Robert E. "The Application of the Oral Theory to Biblical Hebrew Literature." *Semeia* 5 (1976): 51–64.

Crnjac, Slavica. "Vukovar." Translated by Dalia Kuća. In *Pismo iz rasapa* (Writing from Turmoil), ed. ourpa Miklaužić. Zagreb: Multimedijski ženski centar NONA, 1995.

Cross, Frank Moore. *Canaanite Myth and Hebrew Epic.* Cambridge, Mass.: Harvard Univ. Press, 1973.

———. "Prose and Poetry in the Mythic and Epic Texts from Ugarit," *Harvard Theological Review* 67 (1974): 1–15.

———. "Studies in the Structure of Hebrew Verse: The Prosody of Lamentations 1:1–22." In *The Word of the Lord Shall Go Forth*, eds. Carol L. Meyers and M. O'Connor. Winona Lake, Ind.: Eisenbrauns, 1983.

———. "Toward a History of Hebrew Prosody." In *From Epic to Canon: History and Literature in Ancient Israel*, 135–147. Baltimore: Johns Hopkins Univ. Press, 1998.

Culley, Robert C. "An Approach to the Problem of Oral Tradition." *Vetus Testamentum* 13 (1963): 113–25.

———. *Oral Formulaic Language in the Biblical Psalms.* Toronto: University of Toronto Press, 1967.

———. "Oral Tradition and Historicity." In *Studies on the Ancient Palestinian World*, 102–16. Eds. J. Wevers and D. Redford. Toronto: Univ. of Toronto Press, 1972.

———. "Oral Tradition and the OT: Some Recent Discussion." *Semeia* 5 (1976): 1–33.

———. "Exploring New Directions." In *The Hebrew Bible and Its Modern Interpreters*, 160–200. Eds. G. Tucker and D. Knight. Chico: Scholars Press & Philadelphia: Fortress Press, 1984.

———. "Oral Tradition and Biblical Studies." *Oral Tradition* 1 (1986): 30–65.

———. "Orality and Writtenness in the Prophetic Texts." In *Writings and Speech in Israelite and Ancient Near Eastern Prophecy*, ed. Ehud Ben Floyd. Society of Biblical Literature Symposium Series 10. Atlanta: SBL, 2000.

———. "The Confessions of Jeremiah and Traditional Discourse." In *"A Wise and Discerning Mind": Essays in Honor of Burke O. Long*, eds. Saul M. Olyan and Robert C. Culley. Providence, RI: Brown Judaic Studies, 2000.

Day, Peggy L. "The Personification of Cities as Female in the Hebrew Bible: The Thesis of Aloysius Fitzgerald, F.S.C." In *Reading from This Place: Social Location and Biblical Interpretation in Global Perspective*, 283–302. Ed. F. Segovia and M. Tolbert. Minneapolis: Fortress, 1995.

Dictionnaire catholicisme hier, aujourd'hui, demain, 1967 ed. S.v. "Lamentations," by E. Cothenet. 6:1725–32.

Dobbs-Allsopp, F. W. *Weep, O Daughter of Zion: A Study of the City-Lament Genre in the Hebrew Bible.* Rome: Editrice Pontificio Istituto Biblico, 1993.

———. "The Syntagma of *bat* Followed by a Geographical Name in the Hebrew Bible: A Reconsideration of Its Meaning and Grammar." *Catholic Biblical Quarterly* 57 (1995): 451–70.

Duraković, Ferida. "Morning Glory, Sarajevo." *Contemporary Poetry of Bosnia and Herzegovina*, ed. and transl., Mario Suško. Sarajevo: International Peace Center, 1993), 173.

Emmendörffer, Michael. *Der ferne Gott: Eine Untersuchung der alttestamentlichen Volksklagelieder vor dem Hintergrund der mesopotamischen Literatur.* Thbingen: Mohr Siebeck, 1998.

Encyclopaedia Judaica. 1972 ed. S.v. "Mourning," by Aaron Rothkoff. 485–94.

Euripides. *Suppliant Women.* Transl., Rosanna Warren and Stephen Scully. New York: Oxford University Press, 1995.

Ferris, Paul Wayne, Jr. *The Genre of Communal Lament in the Bible and the Ancient Near East.* Atlanta: Scholars Press, 1992.

Feuer, Avrohom Chaim and Avie Gold. *The Complete Tishah B'Av Service.* 2nd ed. ArtScroll Menorah Series. Brooklyn, N.Y.: Mesorah Publications, Ltd., 1992.

First-Medić, Kruna. "For the Girl Ivana Vujić (To Those Who Killed Her from the Barracks [called] 'Milan Stanivuković')." Translated by Višnja Pavičić. In *Na Grani od Oblaka.* Osijek: Tehnokamen, 1992.

Finnegan, Ruth. *Oral Literature in Africa.* Oxford: Clarendon Press, 1970.

———. "Tradition, but What Tradition, and For Whom?" *Oral Tradition* 6/1 (1991): 104–24.

———. *Oral Poetry.* Bloomington & Indianapolis: Indiana University Press, 1992.

Foley, John Miles, ed. *Teaching Oral Traditions.* New York: Modern Language Association, 1998.

———. *Comparative Research on Oral Traditions: A Memorial for Milman Parry.* Columbus, Ohio: Slavica, 1987.

Foley, John Miles. *Oral-Formulaic Theory and Research: An Introduction and Annotated Bibliography*. New York: Garland, 1985.

———. *The Theory of Oral Composition: History and Methodology*. Bloomington: Indiana Univ. Press, 1988.

———. *Traditional Oral Epic: The Odyssey, Beowulf, and the Serbo-Croatian Return Song*. Berkeley: University of California, 1990.

———. *Immanent Art: From Structure to Meaning in Traditional Oral Epic*. Bloomington: Indiana University Press, 1991.

———. *The Singer of Tales in Performance*. Bloomington & Indianapolis: Indiana University Press, 1995.

Follis, Elaine R. "The Holy City as Daughter." In *Directions in Biblical Hebrew Poetry*, ed. E. Follis, 173–184. Sheffield: JSOT Press, 1987.

Freedman, David Noel. "Acrostics and Metrics in Hebrew Poetry." *Harvard Theological Review* 65 (1972): 367–92.

———. *Pottery, Poetry, and Prophecy: Studies in Early Hebrew Poetry*. Winona Lake: Eisenbrauns, 1980.

———. *Divine Commitment and Human Obligation: Selected Writings of David Noel Freedman*. Ed. J. Huddlestun. Grand Rapids: Wm. B. Eerdmans, 1997.

Fuerst, W. J. *The Books of Ruth, Esther, Ecclesiastes, the Song of Songs, Lamentations*. Cambridge: Cambridge University Press, 1975.

Galambush, Julie. *Jerusalem in the Book of Ezekiel: The City as Yahweh's Wife*. Society of Biblical Literature Dissertation Series 130. Atlanta: Scholars Press, 1992.

Gerstenberger, Erhard. "The Woe-Oracles of the Prophets." *Journal of Biblical Literature* 81 (1962): 249–63.

Gevirtz, Stanley. *Patterns in the Early Poetry of Israel*. Studies in Ancient Oriental Civilization 32. Chicago, 1963.

Ginsberg, H. L. "The Rebellion and Death of Baölu." *Orientalia* 5 (1936), 172.

Gordis, Robert. *The Song of Songs and Lamentations*. New York: KTAV Publishing House, 1954.

Green, Margaret. "The Eridu Lament." *Journal of Cuneiform Studies* 30 (1978): 127–67.

———. "The Uruk Lament," *JAOS* 104 (1984): 253–79.

Greenberg, Moshe. *Biblical Prose Prayer, as a Window to the Popular Religion of Ancient Israel*. Berkeley: University of California Press, 1983.

Gunkel Hermann and J. Begrich, *Einleitung in die Psalmen: Die Gattungen der religiösen Lyrik Israels*. Göttingen: Vandenhoeck & Ruprecht, 1933.

Gunkel, Hermann. "Klagelieder Jeremiae." In *Die Religion in Geschichte und Gegenwart*. Tübingen: T. C. B. Mohr, 1912.

———. "The Prophets as Writers and Poets." In *Prophecy in Israel*, ed. David L. Petersen, 22–73. Philadelphia: Fortress Press, 1987 [1923].

———. "Fundamental Problems of Hebrew Literary History." In *What Remains of the Old Testament*. Translated by A. K. Dallas. New York: MacMillan, 1928.

Handler, Richard and Jocelyn Linnekan. "Tradition, Genuine or Spurious?" *Journal of American Folklore* 97 (1984): 273–90.

HarperCollins Bible Dictionary, 1996 ed. S.v. "Mill," by Roger S. Boraas. 684–85.

Henderson, Josesph M. "Who Weeps in Jeremiah IX 1?" (forthcoming).

Hillers, Delbert. *Lamentations*. Anchor Bible. Rev. ed. New York: Doubleday, 1992.

Holladay, William. "Style, Irony, and Authenticity in Jeremiah." *JBL* 81 (1962): 44–54.

———. *Jeremiah*. Two volumes. Hermeneia. Philadelphia: Fortress, 1986, 1989.

Holst-Warhaft, Gail. *The Cue for Passion: Grief and Its Political Uses*. Cambridge: Harvard University Press, 2000.

Holton, Milton and Vasa D. Mihailovich. *Serbian Poetry from the Beginnings to the Present*. New Haven: Yale Center for International and Area Studies, 1988.

Hurston, Zora Neale. *The Sanctified Church.* Berkeley: Turtle Island, 1983.
Jahnow, Hedwig. *Das hebräische Leichenlied im Rahmen der Völkerdichtung* (The Hebrew Funeral Song in the Context of Folk Poetry). BZAW 36. Giessen: Alfred Töpelmann, 1923.
———. u.a. *Feministische Hermeneutik und Erstes Testament.* Bonn: VG Bild-Kunst, 1994.
Joyce, Paul. "Lamentations and the Grief Process: A Psychological Reading." In *Biblical Interpretation* 1, 3 (1993): 304–20.
Kadič, Ante. "Postwar Croatian Lyric Poetry." *American Slavic and East European Review* 17 (1958): 509–29.
Kaiser, Barbara Bakke. "Poet as 'Female Impersonator': The Image of Daughter Zion as Speaker in Biblical Poems of Suffering." *Journal of Religion* (1987): 164–82.
Karadžić, Vuk. *Srpske narodne pjesme* (Serbian Folk Songs/Poems). Ed. Vladan Nedić. Belgrade: Prosveta, 1969.
———. *Srpske narodne pjesme iz neobjavljenih rukopisa Vuka Stef. Karadžića* [Serbian Folk Songs/Poems from Karadžić's Unpublished Manuscripts]. Ed. Ž. Mladenović and V. Nedić. 5 vols. Belgrade: Srpska akademija nauka i umetnosti, 1973–74.
———. *Songs of the Serbian People: From the Collections of Vuk Karadžić.* Ed. and Transl. Milne Holton and Vasa Mihailovich. Pittsburgh: University of Pittsburgh Press, 1997.
Karahasan, Dzevad. *Sarajevo, Exodus of a City.* Translated by Slavenka Drakulić. New York: Kodansha International, 1994.
Kaštelan, Jure. *Pjetao na krovu* (Cock on the Roof; 1950). In Ante Kadić, "Postwar Croatian Lyric Poetry," *American Slavic and East European Review* 17 (1958): 523.
———. "Jadikovka kamena" (Lament of a Stone, 1950). In Ante Kadič, "Postwar Croatian Lyric Poetry," *American Slavic and East European Review* 17 (1958): 528.
Kelber, Werner. *The Oral and Written Gospel.* Philadelphia: Fortress, 1983. Rev. ed. Bloomington: Indiana University Press, 1997.
Kerewsky-Halpern, Barbara. "Text and Context in Serbian Ritual Lament." *Canadian-American Slavic Studies* 15 (1981): 54.
Kirkpatrick, Patricia. *The Old Testament and Folklore Study*, JSOTS. Sheffield: Sheffield Academic Press, 1988.
Knight, Douglas H. *Rediscovering the Traditions of Israel*, SBL Dissertation 9. Missoula, 1973.
Koljević, Svetozar. "Folk Traditions in Serbo-Croatian Literary Culture." *Oral Tradition* 6/1 (1991): 3–18.
Koprivnjak, Marija, ed. *Ratni Blagoslovi* (War Blessings). Osijek, Croatia: Izvori, 1996.
———. "Jeremijine tužaljke nad Bosnom i Hercegovinom." In *Ratni Blagoslovi.* Edited, Marija Koprivnjak, 135. Osijek: Izvori, 1996.
———. "Mostar (Hercegovački Vukovar)." In *Ratni Blagoslovi*, ed. Marija Koprivnjak, 138–9. Osijek: Izvori, 1996.
Koskoff, Ellen, ed. *Women and Music in Cross-Cultural Perspective.* Urbana, IL: University of Illinois, 1989.
Kramer, Samuel N. *Lamentation over the Destruction of Ur.* Assyriological Studies No. 12. Chicago: University of Chicago, 1940.
———. *Two Elegies on a Pushkin Museum Tablet: A New Sumerian Literary Genre.* Moscow: Oriental Literary Publ., 1969.
———. "Lamentation over the Destruction of Nippur." *Acta Sumerologica* 13 (1991): 1–26.
Kuhač, Franjo Š., Editor. *Južno-Slovjenske Narodne Popijevke* [National Songs of the South Slavs]. Vol. 5. Zagreb: C. Albrechta, 1941.
Lanahan, William. "The Speaking Voice in the Book of Lamentations." *Journal of Biblical Literature* 93 (1974): 41–9.

Lee, Nancy C. "Vratimo se biblijskom naslijexu: slavopojima . . . i tužaljkama" ["Returning to the Biblical Heritage: Songs of Praise . . . and Lament"]. *Izvori* (Jan./Feb. 1998).

———. "Genocide's Lament: Moses, Pharaoh's Daughter, and the Former Yugoslavia." In *God in the Fray: A Tribute to Walter Brueggemann*, eds. Tod Linafelt and Timothy K. Beal, 67–82. Minneapolis: Fortress Press, 1998.

———. "Exposing a Buried Subtext in Jeremiah and Lamentations: Going After Baal . . . and Abel." In *Troubling Jeremiah*, eds., A. R. Pete Diamond, Kathleen M. O'Connor, Louis Stulman, 87–122. Journal for the Study of the Old Testament Supplement 260. Sheffield: Sheffield Academic Press, 1999.

Lee, Nancy C. and Borislav Arapović. "The Bible in Political Context: New Republics from Old Yugoslavia and former Soviet Union," *Interpretation* (Oct. 2001): 378–88.

Linafelt, Tod. *Surviving Lamentations: Catastrophe, Lament, and Protest in the Afterlife of a Biblical Book*. Chicago: University of Chicago, 2000.

Löhr, Max. "Der Sprachgebrauch des Buches der Klagelieder." *Zeitschrift für die alttestamentliche Wissenschaft* 14 (1894): 31–50.

Lord, Albert B. *The Singer of Tales*. New York: Atheneum, 1968.

———. "The Effect of the Turkish Conquest on Balkan Epic Tradition." In *Aspects of the Balkans: Continuity and Change*. Ed. H. Birnbaum and S. Vryonis, Jr., 298–318. The Hague: Mouton, 1972.

———. "The Nineteenth Century Revival of National Literatures: Karadžić, Njegoš, Radičević, the Illyrians, and Prešeren." In *Multinational Literature of Yugoslavia*. Ed., A. B. Lord, 101–11. New York: St. John's University, 1974.

———. "Formula and Non-Narrative Theme in South Slavic Oral Epic and the OT." In *Oral Tradition and Old Testament Studies*. Ed. Robert C. Culley. *Semeia* 5 (1976): 93–105.

———. "The Gospels as Oral Traditional Literature." In *The Relationships Among the Gospels: An Interdisciplinary Dialogue*. Ed. W. O. Walker, Jr., 33–91. San Antonio, Tex.: Trinity University Press, 1978.

———. "Memory, Fixity, and Genre in Oral Traditional Poetries." In *Oral Traditional Literature: A Festschrift for Albert Lord Bates*, 451–61. Ed. J. M. Foley. Columbus, Oh.: Slavica, 1981.

———. "The Battle of Kosovo in Albanian and Serbocroatian Oral Epic Songs." In *Studies on Kosovo*. Eds. A. Pipa and S. Repishti, 65–83. New York: Columbia University Press, 1984.

———. "The Nature of Oral Poetry." In *Comparative Research on Oral Traditions*, 313–49. Ed. J. M. Foley. Columbus, Oh.: Slavica, 1987.

———. *Epic Singers and Oral Tradition*. Ithaca, N.Y.: Cornell University Press, 1991.

Lowth, Robert. *Lectures on the Sacred Poetry of the Hebrews*. Vol. 2. Translated by G. Gregory. London: J. Johnson, 1787.

Lundblom, Jack. *Jeremiah: A Study in Ancient Hebrew Rhetoric*. Missoula, Mont.: SBL and Scholars Press, 1975.

Maier, Christl. "Die Klage der Tochter Zion: Ein Beitrag zur Weiblichkeitsmetaphorik im Jeremiabuch." *Berliner Theologische Zeitschrift* 15 (1998): 176–89.

Mandelkern, Solomon. *Veteris Testamenti Concordantiae*. Jerusalem: Sumptibus Schocken, 1955.

Mandolfo, Carleen. "YHWH is Tzaddiq?: The Dialogic Theology of Lament Psalms" (forthcoming).

McKane, William. *Jeremiah*. The International Critical Commentary. Edinburgh: T & T Clark, 1986.

Meek, Theophile J. *Jeremiah*. Interpreters Bible. New York: Abingdon, 1956.

Mertus, Julie, Jasmina Tesanovic, Habiba Metikos, and Rada Boric, eds. *The Suitcase: Refugee Voices from Bosnia and Croatia*. Berkeley: University of California Press, 1997.

Michalowski, Piotr. *The Lamentation over the Destruction of Sumer and Ur.* Winona Lake, Ind.: Eisenbrauns, 1989.
Mihailovich, Vasa S., ed. *Contemporary Yugoslav Poetry.* Iowa City: University of Iowa, 1977.
Miklaužić, ourpa. *Pismo iz rasapa* (Writing from Turmoil). Zagreb: Multimedijski ženski centar NONA, 1995.
Milgrom, Jacob. *Leviticus 1–16.* Anchor Bible. New York: Doubleday, 1991.
Mintz, Alan. *Hurban: Responses to Catastrophe in Hebrew Literature.* New York: Columbia University Press, 1984.
Mojzes, Paul. *The Yugoslavian Inferno: Ethnoreligious Warfare in the Balkans.* New York: Continuum, 1994.
———, ed. *Religion and the War in Bosnia.* Atlanta: Scholars Press, 1998.
Muilenburg, James. "Form Criticism and Beyond." *Journal of Biblical Literature* 88 (1969): 1–18.
Murko, Matija. *La Poésie populaire épique en Yougoslavie au début du XXe siècle.* Paris: Librairie Honoré Champion, 1929.
Musa, Simun and Gojko Susa, eds. *Nisam mrtav samo sam zemlju zagrlio* (I am not Dead, I only Embraced the Earth), Mostar, Bosnia-Herzegovina: HKD "Napredak," 1995.
Nagler, Michael N. "On Almost Killing Your Friends: Some Thoughts on Violence in Early Cultures." In *Comparative Research on Oral Traditions: A Memorial for Milman Parry*, ed. J. M. Foley. Columbus, Ohio: Slavica, 1987.
Neusner, Jacob. *Lamentations Rabbah.* Atlanta: Scholars Press, 1997.
New Princeton Encyclopedia of Poetry and Poetics. 1993 ed. S.v. "Dirge" by R. Hornsby and T. Brogan. 296–97.
———. S.v. "Elegy" by T. Brogan, P. Sacks, and S. Fogle. 322–25.
———. S.v. "Lament" by W. Race. 675.
———. S.v. "Yugoslav Poetry" by V. Javarek and V. Mihailovich. 1379–82.
Niditch, Susan. "Composition of Isaiah 1." *Biblica* 61 (1980): 509–29.
———. *Folklore and the Hebrew Bible.* Minneapolis: Fortress Press, 1993.
———. *Oral World and Written Word: Ancient Israelite Literature.* Louisville: Westminster/John Knox Press, 1996.
Nielsen, Eduard. *Oral Tradition.* London: SCM Press, 1954.
Notopoulos, James A. "Homer, Hesiod and the Achaean Heritage of Oral Poetry." *Hespera* 29 (1960): 177–97.
Obradović, Biljana D. *Frozen Embraces* [Zamrznuti zagrljaji: pesme]. 2nd ed. Belgrade & Merrick, N.Y.: Center for Emigrants from Serbia & Cross-Cultural Communications, 2000.
O'Connor, Kathleen M. *The Confessions of Jeremiah: Their Interpretation and Role in Chapters 1–25.* SBLDS 94. Atlanta: Scholars Press, 1988.
———. "Lamentations" *The Woman's Bible Commentary*, eds. C. Newsom and S. Ringe. Louisville: Westminster/John Knox, 1992.
———. "The Tears of God and Divine Character in Jeremiah 2–9." In *God in the Fray: A Tribute to Walter Brueggemann*, eds. T. Linafelt and T. Beal, 172–85. Minneapolis: Fortress Press, 1998.
———. "Lamentations." In *New Interpreters Bible Commentary.* Forthcoming.
———. *Lamentations and the Tears of the World* (forthcoming, Orbis).
Ostojić, Ljubica. "Record of the City in Blank Verse." Translated by Zulejha Ripanović. In *Sahat kula.* Sarajevo: Mepunarodni centar za mir, 1995.
Owens, Pamela Jean. "Charts of Semantic Fields in Lam 2." 1998 SBL National Meeting presentation.
Parun, Vesna. "Mati čovjeka" (Mother of Man; 1947). In Ante Kadić, "Postwar Croatian Lyric Poetry." *American Slavic and East European Review* 17 (1958): 518–19.

Parry, Adam. *The Making of Homeric Verse: The Collected Papers of Milman Parry*. Oxford: Clarendon Press, 1971.

Paul, Shalom M. "Polysensuous Polyvalency in Poetic Parallelism" in *"Sha'arei Talmon": Studies in the Bible, Qumran, and the Ancient Near East Presented to Shemaryahu Talmon*, eds. M. Fishbane and E. Tov. Winona Lake, Ind.: Eisenbrauns, 1992.

Perič-Polonijo, Tanja. "Oral Poems in the Context of Customs and Rituals." (Usmene pjesme u kontekstu običaja i obreda). *Croatian Journal of Ethnology and Folklore Research* 33/2 (1996): 381–99.

Pham, Xuan Huong Thi. *Mourning in the Ancient Near East and the Hebrew Bible*. Sheffield: Sheffield Academic Press, 1999.

Porteous, Norman W. "Jerusalem-Zion: The Growth of a Symbol." In *Verbannung und Heimkehr*, 235–52. Tübingen: J. C. B. Mohr, 1961.

Provan, Iain. *Lamentations*. New Century Bible. Grand Rapids: HarperCollins, 1991.

Rad, Gerhard von. *Genesis*. Translated by J. Marks. Old Testament Library. Philadelphia: Westminster Press, 1961.

Rečnik književnih termina. 1985 ed. S.v. "tužbalica," by Radmila Pešić. 838–39.

Re'emi, S. Paul. *Amos and Lamentations: God's People in Crisis*. International Theological Commentary. Edinburgh: Handsel Press, 1984.

Renkema, Johan. *Lamentations*. Historical Commentary on the Old Testament. Leuven: Peeters, 1998.

Rinklin, Helena. "Slakovci." In *Pjesme*, 1994.

Rudolf, Wilhelm. *Die Klagelieder*. Kommentar zum alten Testament. Gütersloher Verlagshaus Gerd Mohn, 1962.

Sakenfeld, Katharine. *The Meaning of Hesed in the Hebrew Bible*. Atlanta: Scholars Press, 1978.

Salters, R. B. "Lamentations 1:3: Light from the History of Exegesis." In *A Word in Season: Festschrift for William McKane*. JSOTS 42, 1986.

———. "Searching for Pattern in Lamentations." *Old Testament Essays* 11/1 (1998): 93–104.

———. "Using Rashi, Ibn Ezra and Joseph Kara on Lamentations." *Journal of Northwest Semitic Languages* 25/1 (1999): 201–13.

———. "Structure and Implication in Lamentations 1?" *SJOT* 14 (2000): 293–300.

Sanader, Ivo and Ante Stamać. *U ovom strašnom času: mala antologija suvremene hrvatske ratne lirike*. Split: Laus, 1992.

Sasson, Jack. "Time . . . to Begin." In *"Sha'arei Talmon": Studies in the Bible, Qumran, and the Ancient Near East Presented to Shemaryahu Talmon*, eds. M. Fishbane and E. Tov. Winona Lake, Ind.: Eisenbrauns, 1992.

Saulić, J. "The Oral Women Poets of the Serbs." *Slavonic and East European Review* 42 (1963): 161–83.

Schmitt, John J. "The Motherhood of God and Zion as Mother." *Revue Biblique* 92 (1985): 557–69.

———. "The Virgin of Israel: Referent and Use of the Phrase in Amos and Jeremiah." *Catholic Biblical Quarterly* 53 (1991): 365–87.

———. "The City as Woman in Isaiah 1–39." In *Writing and Reading the Scroll of Isaiah: Studies of an Interpretive Tradition*, 95–119. SVT 70. New York: E. J. Brill, 1997.

Segovia, Fernando F. and Mary Ann Tolbert, eds. *Reading from This Place: Social Location and Biblical Interpretation in Global Perspective*. Minneapolis: Fortress Press, 1995.

Sells, Michael A. *The Bridge Betrayed: Religion and Genocide in Bosnia*. Berkeley: University of California Press, 1996.

Seow, C. L. "A Textual Note on Lamentations 1:20." *Catholic Biblical Quarterly* 47 (1985): 418.

Sidran, Abdulah. *The Blindman Sings to his City* [including "Seven Poems under the Siege, 1992–1996"]. Sarajevo: Mexunarodni centar za mir: 1997.

Silber, Laura and Allan Little, eds. *Yugoslavia: Death of a Nation*. Rev. ed. New York: Penguin Books, 1997.

Sivan, Daniel. *A Grammar of the Ugaritic Language*. Leiden: E. J. Brill, 1997.

Soljić, Kata. "I Forgive the Enemy, but I Cannot Forget the Pain!" *Izvori* 3/4 (1996), 32.

Streane, A. W. *The Book of the Prophet Jeremiah together with the Lamentations*. Cambridge: Cambridge University Press, 1913.

Suško, Mario, ed. *Contemporary Poetry of Bosnia and Herzegovinia*. Sarajevo: International Peace Center, The Writers' Association of Bosnia and Herzegovinia, 1993.

Tov, Emmanuel. *Textual Criticism of the Hebrew Bible*. Minneapolis: Fortress Press, 1992.

Trible, Phyllis. *Rhetorical Criticism: Context, Method, and the Book of Jonah*. Minneapolis: Fortress Press, 1994.

Tull, Patricia. *Remember the Former Things: The Recollection of Previous Texts in Second Isaiah*. Society of Biblical Literature Dissertation Series 161. Atlanta: Scholars Press, 1997.

Vinaver, Semjo. "Mashpil Geim" (1956), on the compact disc *Tanja Mira* (Mystery of Peace) by the Pontanima Choir. Sarajevo: the Franciscan Seminary, 1999.

Volf, Miroslav. *Exclusion and Embrace: A Theological Exploration of Identity, Otherness, and Reconciliation*. Nashville: Abingdon Press, 1996.

———. Review, *The Bridge Betrayed* by Michael Sells. In *Journal of the American Academy of Religion* 67 (1999): 250–53.

Volz, D. Paul. *Der Prophet Jeremia: gbersetzt und Erklärt*. Leipzig: A. Deichertsche Verlagsbuchhandlung, 1922.

Weigle, Marta. "Women's Expressive Form." In *Teaching Oral Traditions*, ed. J. M. Foley, 298–307. New York, N.Y.: Modern Language Association of America, 1998.

Weinfeld, Moshe. *Deuteronomy and the Deuteronomic School*. Winona Lake, Ind.: Eisenbrauns, 1992.

Westermann, Claus. *Praise and Lament in the Psalms*. Translated by Keith R. Crim and Richard N. Soulen. Atlanta: John Knox Press, 1981.

———. *Lamentations*. Minneapolis: Fortress Press, 1994.

Whallon, William. *Formula, Character, and Context: Studies in Homeric, Old English, and Old Testament Poetry*. Washington, D.C.: Center for Hellenic Studies, 1969.

Ziegler, Joseph, ed. *Threni*. Septuagint. Göttingen: Vandenhoeck & Ruprecht, 1957.

INDEX OF TOPICS AND AUTHORS

INDEX OF TEXT REFERENCES

Deuterocanonical

New Testament

BIBLICAL INTERPRETATION SERIES

ISSN 0928-0731

The *Biblical Interpretation Series* accommodates monographs, collections of essays and works of reference that are concerned with the discussion or application of new methods of interpreting the Bible. Works published in the series ordinarily either give a practical demonstration of how a particular approach may be instructively applied to a Biblical text or texts, or make a productive contribution to the discussion of method. The series thus provides a vehicle for the exercise and development of a whole range of newer techniques of interpretation, including feminist readings, semiotic, post-structuralist, reader-response and other types of literary readings, liberation-theological readings, ecological readings, and psychological readings, among many others.

48. Peterson, Dwight N. *The Origins of Mark.* The Markan Community in Current Debate. 2000. ISBN 90 04 11755 5
49. Chan, Mark L.Y. *Christology from within and ahead.* Hermeneutics, Contingency and the Quest for Transcontextual Criteria in Christology. 2001. ISBN 90 04 11844 6
50. Polaski, Donald C. *Authorizing an End.* The Isaiah Apocalypse and Intertextuality. 2000. ISBN 90 04 11607 9
51. Reese, Ruth Anne. *Writing Jude.* The Reader, the Text, and the Author in Constructs of Power and Desire. 2000. ISBN 90 04 11659 1
52. Schroeder, Christoph O. *History, Justice and the Agency of God.* A Hermeneutical and Exegetical Investigation on Isaiah and Psalms. 2001. ISBN 90 04 11991 4
53. Pilch, John J. (ed.). *Social Scientific Models for Interpreting the Bible.* Essays by the Context Group in Honor of Bruce J. Malina. 2001. ISBN 90 04 12056 4
54. Ellis, E. Earle *History and Interpretation in New Testament Perspective.* 2001. ISBN 90 04 12026 2
55. Holmén, T. *Jesus and Jewish Covenant Thinking.* 2001. ISBN 90 04 11935 3
56. Resseguie, J.L. *The Strange Gospel.* Narrative Design and Point of View in John. 2001. ISBN 90 04 12206 0
57. Burnett, G.W. *Paul and the Salvation of the Individual.* 2001. ISBN 90 04 12297 4
58. Pearson, B.W.R. *Corresponding Sence.* Paul, Dialectic, and Gadamer. 2001. ISBN 90 04 12254 0
59. Räisänen, H. *Challenges to Biblical Interpretation.* Collected Essays 1991-2001. 2001. ISBN 90 04 12052 1
60. Lee, N.C. *The Singers of Lamentations.* Cities under Siege, from Ur to Jerusalem to Sarajevo... 2002. ISBN 90 04 12312 1